Law and Medical Ethics

'It would not be correct to say that every moral obligation involves a legal duty; but every legal duty is founded on a moral obligation'

LORD CHIEF JUSTICE COLERIDGE
in *R v Instan* [1893] 1 QB at 453

Law and Medical Ethics

J K Mason CBE MD FRCPath DMJ
Regius Professor of Forensic Medicine
at the University of Edinburgh

R A McCall Smith LLB PhD
Lecturer in Civil Law
at the University of Edinburgh

London
Butterworths
1983

ENGLAND   Butterworth & Co (Publishers) Ltd
           88 Kingsway, **London** WC2B 6AB

AUSTRALIA   Butterworths Pty Ltd, **Sydney, Melbourne, Brisbane,
             Adelaide** and **Perth**

CANADA   Butterworth & Co (Canada) Ltd, **Toronto**
          Butterworth & Co (Western Canada) Ltd, **Vancouver**

NEW ZEALAND   Butterworths of New Zealand, **Wellington**

SINGAPORE   Butterworth & Co (Asia) Pte Ltd, **Singapore**

SOUTH AFRICA   Butterworth Publishers (Pty) Ltd, **Durban**

USA   Butterworth Legal Publishers, Mason Division, **St Paul,** Minnesota
       Butterworth Legal Publishers, **Seattle,** Washington
       Boston, Massachusetts; and Austin, Texas
       D and S Publishers, **Clearwater,** Florida

© Butterworth & Co (Publishers) Ltd 1983

Reprinted 1984

ISBN Hardcover 0 406 40015 6
Softcover 0 406 40016 4

Typeset in 'Monophoto' Times New Roman by Cotswold Typesetting Ltd, Gloucester and Printed in Great Britain by Billings Bookplan, Worcester.

ᒡ4558/3

*This book is dedicated to
two Elizabeths*

Preface

Medical jurisprudence is something of a growth industry. The ethical issues raised by new medical techniques, fanned by rapidly changing public values, are matched in interest by the intense legal problems they provoke. The whole basis of medicine and medical practice is being questioned, patients' rights are increasingly being regarded as paramount and the scope of litigation is widening. At the same time, philosophers, doctors and lawyers have become deeply concerned as to the morality of medical progress; Departments of Bioethics have sprung up in the United States and there are few British Universities with medical schools which do not also have flourishing 'Medical Groups' concerned with medical ethics.

Not surprisingly, there is a growing body of literature on the subject, particularly in the United States. Much of this is, however, concerned with what *ought* to happen rather than with what *does* happen if a certain course of action is followed. We have tried in this book to avoid excessive involvement in philosophical debate, although we hope that the ethical implications of the subject are adequately explored. We have concentrated on what the law is in these matters; the ultimate test of a set of values is, for practical purposes, whether they will or will not be acceptable when subjected to legal scrutiny – for the law effectively represents the public conscience.

The book is designed primarily for lawyers but we hope it will be of equal interest to philosophers, doctors, politicians and, indeed, all those concerned with the provision of health care. We have concentrated on English law but we have taken account of Scots law and of legal decisions from other parts of the Commonwealth, notably from Australia and Canada where the medical profession and the courts have been active in this field. We do not attempt to discuss in detail the complexities of United States case law, although we do refer to American decisions when they are useful in illustrating a particular legal option. The United States experience in medico-legal matters has been different in many respects from that in Britain yet there can be no doubt that important lessons can be learned from what has happened there. Moreover, there is a strong American influence on public attitudes in Britain.

A major problem is, however, that there *is* no definitive law in many of the areas covered and, where this is so, it is possible only to appraise the present situation and to predict the future. Our own views in controversial areas will be apparent from the text and no doubt they have been influenced by our religious backgrounds – one in the Roman Catholic and the other in the Protestant tradition. We hope, though, that this has not affected an objective presentation of the core subject which is the interaction of the law and medical ethics.

We have received great help and encouragement from members of the Faculties of Law and of Medicine in the University of Edinburgh and we thank them all – anonymously because to do otherwise would be invidious to some and might also imply agreement with views which, we hasten to add, are our responsibility alone. The United Kingdom law is, we believe, correct as of September 1982. Our very special thanks go to Mrs E A MacDonald who has never flinched at an awesome secretarial task and we would like to acknowledge the unfailing courtesy and helpfulness of our publishers. Finally, it would be appropriate to thank our students in the Honours Class in Medical Jurisprudence who have kept us up to scratch in a way peculiar to groups of interested and involved young lawyers-to-be.

JKM
RAMcS
Edinburgh 1982

Contents

Table of statutes

References in this Table to Statutes are to Halsbury's Statutes of England (Third Edition) showing the volume and page at which the annotated text of the Act will be found.

List of cases

Introduction

1 Evolution of medical ethics

There can be few, if any, professions other than that of medicine about which it is possible to fashion a television series entitled 'Your Life in Their Hands'. But this succinctly describes the power of the doctor. Whether he is undertaking open heart surgery or simply saying 'there is nothing wrong with you', he is making decisions which, if not of life and death significance, at least represent the difference between fitness and ill-health. The doctor's involvement with his patient is thus very special but the two sides of the relationship are not always equally balanced; just as the lawyer knows more about the law than does his client, the doctor knows more about medicine than does his patient. The patient's attitude is, therefore, poised between trust in the learning of another and the general distrust of one who finds himself in a state of uncertainty. Such ambivalence leads naturally to a sense of inferiority; it is the function of medical ethics to ensure that the potential superiority of the doctor is not abused.

The progress of medicine

While we have no intention of attempting a history of medicine, a limited review is needed if the development of the doctor/patient relationship is to be understood.

Very early medicine was, of course, a matter of mystery; there being no apparent natural reason why disease struck one person rather than another, the answer had to be found in the supernatural and, supernatural powers being sparingly distributed, healing became a prerogative of a few whose power depended largely on the ignorance of others. At its inception, therefore, the medical profession was elitist and it is easy to imagine the transference of healing powers from the isolated tribal witch doctor to the priests of organised religion.

Priestly medicine extended the principle of supernatural power. Since the Gods were the arbiters of life and death, those in association with them could reasonably be expected to intervene successfully on behalf of the outsider. Disease was caused by evil spirits at war with the Gods who were, themselves, protectors of the person. Religion

3

and medicine therefore had the same objectives – a defence against evil which expressed itself in spiritual (disease of the mind) or material (disease of the body) form. But the priests had other advantages apart from their power and aloofness. They were a relatively closed community who could learn from each other and who could appreciate the advantages of organisation and codification. They could also teach and, by virtue of their privileged position, they could attract students from the higher reaches of society. Medicine thus developed both priestly and secular practitioners while still preserving the image of superiority.

Medicine in the Middle East
The first effective example of organised medicine is to be found in Egypt where the father figure of medicine practised – Imhotep, who was the archetypal combination of physician, priest and court official.[1] The Papyri discovered in the nineteenth century indicate that Egyptian medicine was comparatively advanced as early as the second millenium BC.[2] Several features of that organisation are outstanding in their relation to modern practice. In the first place, the concept of a national health service seems to have been well developed – patients were not charged for visits to the healers who, themselves, were supported by the community. Secondly, rather rigid rules were laid down as to experimental treatment – there was no culpability in failure to cure so long as the standard textbooks were followed. Severe penalities were, however, threatened for those who ignored the instructions, the reason being that very few men would be expected to know better than the best specialists who had gone before – an interesting attitude towards negligence which was still being adopted by the courts at the turn of this century (see chapter 15, below). More importantly, the notion of specialisation was deeply instilled. Medicine, however, remained very much the practice of the priest caste – indeed, the aura of mystique surrounding the physician in comparison with the overt technical expertise of his surgical colleagues has persisted until recent times.

The extension of, particularly, surgical practice into lay hands was steady and was demonstrated in the parallel practice of Babylonian

---

1 A W Beasley believes that Imhotep made a special study of trauma arising in the workers employed in building the Sakkara pyramid under his direction. If true, it would seem to be a very early example of an unethical research project ('The origins of orthopaedics' (1982) 75 J Roy Soc Med 648).
2 Our major source is A Castiglioni *A History of Medicine*, trans and ed E B Krunbhaar (2nd edn, 1947).

medicine. It is from here that the first known legal code originated – the Code of Hammurabi (c. 1900 BC). This contained an element of medical ethics and laid down, inter alia, a system of payment – based on results and, to some extent, on the ability to pay and on the status of the patient; it also tabled penalties for negligent failure, some of which were draconian to an extent which must have deterred many from entering the profession.

Greek medicine

For the origin of our modern ethics, however, one must look to Greece where early medicine must be have been derived from both Egypt and Babylon. By 500 BC, the originally strong influence of the priests had waned and had been taken over by the philosophers who, through the processes of logical thought, observation and deduction, transformed the practice of medicine. Inevitably, this led to the formation of schools involving close association, paternalism and the elements of the 'closed shop'; a code of intraprofessional conduct evolved – the dawn of what has become known as medical etiquette. In addition, the new concepts of practice dictated that the physician went to the patient rather than the patient to the temple. A standard of practice relevant to the new ideals was required and has survived as the Hippocratic Oath (appendix A).

Hippocrates remains as the most famous figure in Greek philosophical medicine but he was not alone and, indeed, it is probable that the Oath predates the school of Hippocrates himself. It therefore indicates a prevailing ethos rather than a professorial edict and it is still regarded as the fundamental governance of the medical profession. We are not, here, concerned with medical etiquette. As to medical ethics, the Oath lays down certain guidelines. Firstly, it implies the need for co-ordinated instruction and registration of doctors – the public is to be protected, so far as is possible, from the dabbler or the charlatan. Secondly, it is clearly stated that a doctor is there for the benefit of his patients – to the best of his ability he must do them good and he must do nothing which he knows will cause harm. Thirdly, euthanasia and abortion are proscribed; the reference to lithotomy probably prohibits mutilating operations (castration) but has been taken by many to indicate a proper limitation of practice to that in which one has expertise. Fourthly, the nature of the doctor/patient relationship is outlined and, in particular, to take advantage of that relationship is disapproved. Finally, the Oath expresses the doctrine of medical confidentiality.

In fact, the Hippocratic Oath did not become an integral part of ethical teaching until well into the Christian era; it lapsed with the decline of Greek civilisation and was restored with the evolution of University Medical Schools. It is doubtful if any British medical school now requires a reiteration of the Oath at gradua- tion – although Edinburgh, for one, requires assent by students to a modified version – but, avowed or not, all doctors would admit to its persuasive influence. The language of the Oath is, however, archaic and a modernised version was introduced by the World Medical Association as the Declaration of Geneva. This was amended at Sydney in 1968 (appendix B) and provides the basis of an International Code of Medical Ethics (appendix C).

The Judaeo-Christian influence
Before leaving this early evolutionary phase, one must return to a brief consideration of the Jewish influence on medical ethics. There were two main sources. Firstly, medicine was governed by the law and the law was administered by the priests – religious and medical practices were, therefore, inseparable and religious hygiene was of general benefit to the community. Secondly, the Jewish people were fighting for survival as a nation and the principle was accepted that the rights of the individual must be sacrificed for the good of the community – there was strong emphasis for example, on the isolation of cases, including those of venereal disease, the regulation of sewage disposal and the like. Much of this attitude passed to the Christians who again were forced into the group life-style, fortified by the concepts of equality, charity and devotion to the less fortunate – con- cepts which still underlie the ethical practice of medicine in Christian countries. It is small wonder that, during the Dark Ages, medicine was virtually kept alive in the monasteries which provided the template for the voluntary hospitals of later years.

From the Renaissance onward, medicine became increasingly scientifically based and the age of research had begun. This was primarily due to secularisation and concentration of teaching in the Universities. A new dilemma was being introduced. On the one hand, it is patently obvious that the science of medicine cannot improve without extensive research while, on the other, the process tends to turn the practice of medicine into a series of problem solving exercises – a diversion which, even today, stimulates some of medicine's severest critics.[3]

3 For example, I Kennedy *The Unmasking of Medicine* (1981).

The organisation of modern medicine

The cumulative effect of the scientific approach was to convince doctors that they had an expertise worth preserving and, as early as the sixteenth century, we find the establishment of the Royal College of Physicians of London together with a general tightening of the rules governing the practice of surgery. The early Royal Colleges had considerable powers of examination and registration. The latter function has now gone and the major purpose of the Colleges – which now represent some seven specialities with additional Faculties – is to maintain a standard of excellence among specialised practitioners.

As organisation proceeded, fortune began increasingly to depend upon fame, and fame in its turn upon academic superiority over one's colleagues. From all accounts, British medicine in the eighteenth and early nineteenth centuries was not the happiest of professions, power being secured by practitioners not so much through the scientific merit of their writings but rather on their content of deprecatory comment. Even so, it was not so much medical ethics, as they are understood today, that were found wanting but, rather, medical etiquette. Clearly, something had to be done to ensure the status of the profession and this need was first met by the formation of the British Medical Association in 1832. The BMA has always been deeply concerned with the way medicine is practiced but it has as a main function the protection of the doctor's interests – today it is a non-affiliated registered Trade Union.[4] Clearly, an interested party could not represent the public need for control of a profession with such power and it was largely due to the lobby of the BMA itself that the General Medical Council was established by the Medical Act (1858).[5]

The control of medical practice
It is emphasised that, while the GMC is the governing body of the medical profession, its essential function is to regulate the standards of the profession rather than professional standards; negligence is of no concern to the Council unless it brings the profession of medicine

4 Trade Union and Labour Relations Act 1974.
5 The current composition of the General Medical Council is up to 95 members. Fifty of these are elected; 34 are appointed by the Universities having Medical Schools and by the Royal Colleges and Faculties; up to 11 members are nominated by the Queen in Council and the majority of these must be laymen. The 'life and death' significance of the medical profession is indicated by the fact that a parallel General Dental Council was not established until the passing of the Dentists Act 1956.

into disrepute.[6] Currently, the main functions of the Council are to maintain the official list of medical practitioners, to supervise standards of education, to lay down standards of fitness to practise and to exercise discipline over the medical profession. The Professional Conduct Committee is the ultimate tribunal in respect of the last function, subject only to appeal to the Privy Council. A doctor appearing before the PCC may be found guilty or not guilty of 'serious professional misconduct'. This has been defined as conduct such as 'would reasonably be regarded as disgraceful or dishonourable by his professional brethren of good repute and standing'.

Until recently, the Council has refused to comment on the propriety of specific intended or past actions; guidelines have been issued but detailed advice has been a matter for the doctors' protection or defence societies. Since the passing of the Medical Act 1978, however, the Council itself has undertaken to advise when so requested by registered practitioners. It has been suggested that such a form of 'peer review', limited to professional conduct, is inadequate protection for the public but this attitude is probably mistaken. The doctor is as much subject to the criminal law as is any other citizen, remedies are available at civil law for the aggrieved patient and the doctor who breaks the terms of his contract can be disciplined through the Health Service. The GMC fills the gap in constraining such actions as are not actionable yet which would not be expected of the ethical practitioner. Thus, the law on medical confidentiality is in many ways unclear but few doctors would wish to tangle with the GMC on the issue of professional secrecy. There is nothing criminal in adultery and willing adultery is unlikely to be deleterious to the patient's health; yet the public cannot expect family relationships to be destroyed as a result of the doctor's privilege to enter the bedroom and, accordingly, adulterous conduct with a patient is dealt with exceptionally severely by the Professional Conduct Committee. As is suggested in chapter 8, many patients' rights may be better safeguarded through this type of self-audit than by legislation.

Public relations
But discipline is not all; what matters is the overall relationship between the profession and the public and it is this that has undergone such a profound change in the last century. An Edinburgh writer on ethical matters in 1772 described medicine as: 'A liberal profession . . . to be exercised by gentlemen of honour and ingenuous

6 In addition to actions for negligence as a tort (ch 10, below) professional standards may be regulated through the National Health Service legislation (National Health Service (Service Committees and Tribunal) Regulations 1974, SI 1974/45).

manners'[7]; therein lies the ratio of paternalism. In the nineteenth century, the profession of medicine, being tied to higher education, became very much the prerogative of the upper middle class; as a result, doctors tended to assume superiority to most patients – a situation which persisted into the first half of the twentieth century. The fact that Scotland's contribution to medicine around that time was disproportionately large in relation to its population may have been due to the wider availability of high quality education in that country.

There were then two major social upheavals. The doors of tertiary education were greatly widened admitting a transfusion of scientific minds and technical skills to the somewhat dilettante ranks of medicine and the National Health Service was inaugurated in 1948, effectively transforming the doctor from being a dispenser of charity to being an employee of the people. Parallel with these structural changes within the profession ran the advance of individualism in the public. The cult of autonomy and self expression spread rapidly gaining political muscle through the increased spending powers of young people and the determination of groups such as those proposing women's liberation. Existing values were severely questioned – including values in medicine – and many were rejected, including some which are closely related to medical practice such as sexual and reproductive activity.

Modern medical technology and the law

The twentieth century picture is, therefore, one of rapidly advancing medical technology effected in a strongly research oriented environment and existing within an increasingly hedonistic and materialistic society whose demands for more and more esoteric medicine and personal involvement in medicine are encouraged by intimate news and entertainment media coverage. The law, however, has moved more slowly than both medicine and the public mores. We are told that by 1963 – four years before the passing of the Abortion Act – 2 per cent of Aberdeen women had an induced abortion each year;[8] very many ventilators were turned off before the criminal courts forced the law into accepting such action as being good medical practice; artificial insemination is widely practised but we have done nothing to alleviate the effects of laws which long pre-dated the practice; to many people's surprise, recent publicity has demonstrated that it is accepted practice to allow handicapped neonates

7 J Gregory *Lectures on the Duties and Qualifications of a Physician* (1772).
8 D Baird 'Induced Abortion: Epidemiological Aspects' (1975) 1 J Med Ethics 122.

to die[9] but the intervention by the law has, thus far, been inconsistent. Philosophers, many of whom fear the advancing interference with the natural order, may welcome this seeming inertia. But, at the same time, it does leave doctors operating in an atmosphere of legal uncertainty and, furthermore, it leads to polarisation and somewhat emotive expressions of view. Thus, we find such titles as 'Doctors as Murderers' in legal journals;[10] the medical literature retaliates with 'The Legal Threat to Medicine'.[11] Indeed, the author of the latter article crystallised the problem when he wrote:

> It is a crushing indictment of our legal system that men such as Aleck Bourne [who was found not guilty of illegal termination of pregnancy] and Leonard Arthur [who was acquitted of attempted murder] should be subjected to criminal prosecution for carrying out with great devotion and skill procedures which are accepted by the profession as in the best interests of patients.[12]

Whether or not one agrees with this view, it cannot be denied that it reveals an unsatisfactory state of affairs.

Legal intervention in medicine
The crucial question, then, is that of determining the extent to which medical decisions should be the object of legal scrutiny and control. At one extreme there are those who hold that the medical profession should be left to regulate itself and that it alone should decide what is acceptable conduct. According to this view, intervention by the law is too blunt a way of tackling the delicate ethical dilemmas which doctors have to face: the individual conscience, guided by personal experience and the ethical code of the profession, must confront and resolve the day-to-day ethical issues of medical practice.

The contrary view, frequently expressed just as firmly, denies that there is any reason why doctors alone should regulate their relationship with their patients. In this view, reserving to the medical profession the right to decide on issues of life and death is an improper derogation from an area of legitimate public concern. The cloistered professionalism which it reveals will, it is argued, lead only to the denial to the individual of his right to decide for himself and

---

9 As early as 1973, it was reported that 14 per cent of infants dying in a special unit did so as a result of discontinuance or withdrawal of treatment (R S Duffy and A G M Campbell 'Moral and Ethical Dilemmas in a Special-Care Nursery' (1973) 289 New Engl J Med 890).
10 H Beynon [1982] Crim LR 17.
11 J D J Havard (1982) 284 Brit Med J 612.
12 J D J Havard 'Legal Regulation of Medical Practice – Decisions of Life and Death: A discussion paper' (1982) 75 J Roy Soc Med 351.

will conceal from the public view a wide range of matters which should be more democratically decided. According to the proponents of this opinion, the law, even if it is an imperfect and often inaccessible weapon, is at least one means of controlling the medical profession in the interest of the community as a whole. The law is designed to vindicate individual rights and to ensure that certain basic rules of social conduct are observed: why should the medical profession, alone of professions, be immune to the law's attentions?

Such an argument can be supported by concrete examples of the benign effect of legal involvement in medical issues. It is through litigation, for example, that certain rights of the mentally ill have been established. It is through litigation that the right of the patient to be informed of the nature of his treatment has been defined and clarified. And it is through litigation that the medical profession has been obliged to ensure that its procedures meet a certain standard of safety.

None of this can be denied, yet it would be unwise to dismiss the 'hands off' approach as naïve and elitist. The problem in introducing legal rules into human affairs stems from the comparative vagueness with which legal rules must inevitably be expressed. Once rules acquire a more specific meaning, usually through judicial pronouncements, they allow very much less room for manoeuvre and can be more restrictive than was originally intended by the framer of the rule. The effect of this can be to distort people's behaviour through the fear of litigation or prosecution. One may then be concerned not with doing what one feels to be right but with what one feels to be the legally safest thing to do. This explains the development of defensive medicine, where the fear of actions for negligence can lead to an unduly cautious attitude and to unnecessary waste and suffering. The bizarre spectacle of doctors struggling to keep alive a suffering patient who has no real hope of long-term survival is hardly edifying.

But when there are no alternative methods of resolving disputes between doctor and patients, other than complaints procedures which have no financial implications for the patient, the courts are bound to find themselves drawn in to act as mediators in complex and frequently distressing matters. There seems, however, to be little enthusiasm for the task and judicial hostility to medical negligence claims in this country have occasionally been overt. In *Whitehouse v Jordan*,[13] for example, Lord Denning MR took the somewhat controversial step of considering an individual claim for damages in general terms. It was clear that in making his decision he had one eye on the picture of medical litigation in the United States:

13 [1980] 1 All ER 650 at 658, CA.

There, the damages are colossal . . . Experienced practitioners are known
to have refused to treat patients for fear of being accused of negligence.
Young men are even deterred from entering the profession because of the
risks involved . . . .

Similar remarks were made in the same case by Lawton LJ[14] who
expressed the view that the system of fault-based litigation was
compelling judges to make decisions 'which they prefer not to make'.
The legal system then is faced with the classic problem of doing justice
to both parties. The fears of the medical profession must be taken into
account while the legitimate claims of the patient cannot be ignored.
It is not an easy task for any court.

The doctor's position
There is no doubt, too, that the defining of a relationship, such as that
of doctor and patient, in legalistic terms leads to a subtle but
important change in the nature of the relationship. What the law
expects of the doctor may mirror closely what codes of medical ethics
expect, but the basis of compliance in each case is essentially different.
It is more demeaning to be required to act because one fears that
litigation will result if one does not do so than to do something
because it is a moral duty or because it is in accord with the dictates of
personal conscience. Trust and respect are more likely to flourish in a
relationship governed by morality rather than by legal rules and, no
matter how appropriate the law may be for the regulation of many of
the other ordinary transactions of life, it is frequently an unfortunate
intruder into medical practice. Who, other than those with a
professional interest in the 'legalising' of medicine, could think it
anything but a tragedy if doctors became obliged to consider virtually
their every step in the light of its legal implications?

   Where, then, does the doctor stand today in relation to society? To
some extent, he is a servant of the public, a public which is, moreover,
widely – though not always well – informed on medical matters.
Society is conditioned to distrust paternalism and the modern
medical practitioner has little wish to be paternalistic. Concepts such
as consumerism in medicine have been put forward[15] on the grounds
that 'he who pays the piper calls the tune'. The competent patient's
inalienable rights to understand his treatment and to accept or refuse
it are now well established.

   Against this attitude, the profession will say that medicine in the
format of a doctor/patient relationship is an art rather than a science
and the physician must be able to practise his own brand of art. You

14 At 661–2.
15 See fn. 3, above.

cannot stand behind the portrait painter and dictate how he should interpret your features; if the result is disgracefully bad, you do not pay and, if it is not to your liking, you change your artist. The profession must experiment and must research if it is to improve that art and many would hold that a slight loss of autonomy on the part of patients is a small price to pay for a useful advance in therapeutic skills. And the profession must teach or there will be no doctors to serve future generations; some loss of confidentiality can be looked upon as a return for the best treatment and the best investigative facilities. Clearly these opposing attitudes cannot be reconciled so long as they are polarised. A middle way, based on respect and trust, must be found and this is the function of medical jurisprudence.

Even so, the world is changing and, occasionally, society itself demands practices of doctors which are questionable. The ultimate ethical problem of the late twentieth century relates to what is described as cruel, inhuman or degrading treatments or punishments. Political violence is all around us and the doctor cannot wholly dissociate himself from this; an international attempt to define his position is to be found in the Declaration of Tokyo (appendix D) which shows well the difficulties of drafting ethical codes of an academic nature – definitions of principle can only be interpreted in the mind of the individual. Who is to define a degrading procedure? Whether or not a caning is ethically preferable to deprivation of liberty is a matter of personal opinion. Is it self-evident that the well-being of an indiscriminate terrorist bomber is as valuable as is that of his potential victim? Granted that unethical biological measures are to be used in interrogation, could it not be that a doctor's presence, although disapproving, might be to the benefit of the victim? And one might ask by what right can the doctor command complete clinical independence when, in some circumstances, he may be ignorant of the widespread effect his decision may have on others? The motivation of the Declaration of Tokyo is impeccable in condemning the excesses of politically motivated punishment and torture but it fails in its general purpose because it was drafted with that rather narrow end in view. Clause (8) states that the doctor 'shall in all circumstances be bound to alleviate the distress of his fellow men and no motive . . . shall prevail against this higher purpose'. Carried to its logical conclusion, this would ostracise all those who assist in bringing criminals to justice and punishment yet forensic medicine surely provides an ethical service to the community. All codes of medical ethics are, therefore, subject to interpretation and adaptation but that is not to say that they should not be carefully guarded.

Indeed, organisations such as the prison medical service magnify and bring into focus many of the problems associated with codified ethics.

14   *Evolution of medical ethics*

Given an abnormal population, is it possible to apply to it normal methods? One would have hoped that this would be so and heavy damages have been awarded in the past to prison medical officers who were publicly accused of unethical treatment of those in their care.[16] It is, therefore, disturbing to find that all may not be as is supposed – the Government has admitted that sedative medication is sometimes given to prisoners without their consent.[17] This may, of course, be justifiable on occasions but we suggest that any fault to be found with such practices lies not so much in their doing, which is a matter of clinical judgement, but, rather, in their secrecy – a criticism which can be applied to the introduction and use of many modern medical techniques. The public as a whole probably distrusts, say, genetic manipulation but the greater part of that distrust is founded in ignorance. There is a need for publicity in these matters but, in its provision, the medical and legal professions need to shed some of their essentially paternalistic seclusion and take the lead themselves – the alternatives are subjective television and radio presentations which often do little more than pile confusion on misunderstanding. The eventual resolution of these questions should be the product of open medico-legal debate.

16 Anonymous 'Apology to Prison Medical Service Doctors' (1978) 2 Brit Med J 509.
17 *The Guardian*, 24 August 1982, p. 3.

Reproductive Medicine

2 A reform of sex law?

Sexuality is so integral a part of human nature that its influence pervades the doctor's surgery and its importance as a factor in emotional tension is increasing. At the same time, public attitudes to sex are changing rapidly. Full expression of one's sexuality is now advocated – not as a feature of minority rebellion but by responsible educational authorities. Medical knowledge and expertise are moving to serve the changing needs of young people and it is arguable that medicine is, if anything, ahead of its time. But can the same be said of the law? It is in fact doubtful if our present sex laws do accurately reflect current public mores and, even if the legal principles are agreed, doubts are raised as to the effectiveness of traditional methods in dealing with the issues at the present time.

Probably the most frequently quoted reference in jurisprudence is to Mill[1] who said:

> The only purpose for which power can rightfully be exercised over any member of a civilised community against his will is to prevent harm to others. His own good, either physical or moral, is not a sufficient warrant. He cannot rightfully be compelled to do or forebear because it would be better for him to do so, because it would make him happy or because, in the opinion of others, to do so would be wise, or even right.

Applying these criteria to sex law, it is clear that they distinguish those sexual acts which are consensual from those in which one of the parties is non-consenting. In the latter, the aggrieved party obviously needs the protection of the criminal law – the only problem to be decided is how best can that protection be given with justice to all. In the former case, the law should only intervene if it is believed that autonomous consent cannot or, as a matter of public policy, should not be given. The ability to consent depends to some extent on age but the effect of age is greatly influenced by the social environment and by education; whether the time has come for re-appraisal of the legal age for consent to sexual intercourse deserves to be considered. The reasons for regarding other sexual activities – such as incest or

1 J S Mill *On Liberty and Representative Government* Blackwell's Political Texts (1948) p. 8.

homosexuality – as being anti-social or criminal may be questioned either because there have been changes in public standards or as a result of advances in medical knowledge. Homosexuality has been the subject of enlightened legislation;[2] incest is still governed by statutes which either date from the middle ages[3] or are based on mediaeval ecclesiastical legislation.[4]

Consent to sexual intercourse

The law makes a very evident distinction between, on the one hand, the wide spectrum of sexually motivated behaviour and, on the other, sexual intercourse which is carefully defined as penile pentration of the vulva. Regulation of the former is relatively unbiased as between men and women – at least in England and Wales. Thus, indecent assaults can be perpetrated by both men and women in either a homosexual or heterosexual configuration[5] – and neither a boy nor a girl below the age of 16 can consent to such action. The Indecency with Children Act 1960, covering indecent practices short of indecent assault, refers to both boys and girls under the age of 14. In Scots law, the use of 'lewd, indecent or libidinous practices' against all children is an offence when they are below the age of puberty (12 for a girl and 14 for a boy); above the age of puberty, however, the offence can only be committed against girls and then only if they are aged less than 16 years.[6] Other sexual acts involving young persons could be prosecuted under the umbrella of shameless indecency[7] or as acts of gross indecency. The principle is clear – everyone has a right to be protected against unsolicited sexual advances. And when public opinion is outraged – as it is when children are abused – the factors of consent or error as to age should be, at most, marginally mitigating. The present approval of such policy towards the very young of both sexes was shown by the rapid passage of the Protection of Children Act 1978.

By contrast, the control of sexual intercourse is highly discriminatory. Only the general law of assault protects the male from non-consenting sexual intercourse, whereas protection of the female is one of the most emotive aspects of the criminal law. Although one might

2 Sexual Offences Act 1967, s. 1; Criminal Justice (Scotland) Act 1980, s. 80.
3 Incest Act 1567 (applicable in Scotland only).
4 Sexual Offences Act 1956, ss. 10, 11.
5 *R v Hare* [1934] 1 KB 354 CCA.
6 Sexual Offences (Scotland) Act 1976, s. 5.
7 *M'Laughlan v Boyd* 1934 JC 19.

think of this as reflecting a chivalrous protection of women, it is essentially a matter of physiology – the circumstances in which a man can be forced to have sexual intercourse must be very unusual. Further, the consenting young male suffers no recognisable anatomical damage following intercourse; the consenting girl is deflowered. At the same time, there is not much to inhibit a precocious boy from satisfying his urges although the other party might be criminally liable.[8]

Intercourse with a girl between the ages of 13 and 16 years
The very severe attitude adopted towards both rape and intercourse with girls below the age of puberty is, in fact, probably associated with the importance attached throughout history to virginity, virginity being essential to marriage and, thus, to the economic fulfilment of womanhood. While it is true that the Criminal Law Amendment Act 1885, in introducing the offence of having intercourse with a woman between the ages of 13 and 16 years, was largely inspired by a revulsion to child prostitution, the concept of lawful sexual intercourse was, nevertheless, still closely allied to the idea of marriageable age and, thus, to virginity. The importance of defloration was emphasised when it was established that emission was not essential to sexual intercourse[9] and, while it has long been agreed that sexual intercourse can be achieved without full penetration,[10] the importance attached to the integrity of the female genitalia remains and marks the difference between imprisonment for life or for two years. The problem arises as to whether this emphasis is valid or, indeed, desirable in the late twentieth century.

Like it or not, it is a fact of life that an ever increasing number of adolescent women below the age of 16 indulge in sexual intercourse at least occasionally. One out of every 240 Scottish girls aged 14–15 became pregnant between 1973–5; there were 230 abortions on girls under 16 years of age in 1973.[11] In 1974, half the women of teen age in the United States had had sexual intercourse at one time or another. The ethical conscience of the medical profession is torn apart wondering whether to prescribe contraceptive pills in secret to school-age patients. Against this tide, the number of prosecutions under section 6 of the Sexual Offences Act 1956 or section 4 of the Sexual Offences (Scotland) Act 1976 is miniscule. The experience of

8 *Faulkner v Talbot* [1981] 3 All ER 468, [1981] 1 WLR 1528.
9 *R v Marsden* [1891] 2 QB 149, now incorporated in the Sexual Offences Act 1956, s. 44.
10 *R v Nicholls* (1847) 2 Cox CC 182.
11 S Teper 'The pattern of pregnancy amongst adolescents and teenagers in Scotland' (1978) 2 Scott J Sociol 229.

many doctors in examining the 'victims' of the offence is that they are usually candid, unrepentent and unaffected by the intervention of the law. To find that a statute is widely ignored or ridiculed is not to show that it should be repealed – the acceptance of such an argument would, for example, result in an immediate change in the regulations relating to drinking and driving. But it is a different matter if, at the same time, it can be shown that such disrespect results in no public harm or, even more so, is positively approved by responsible society. That such might be the case in respect of the age of consent to sexual intercourse was shown by judicial attitudes in 1976 when prosecutions under section 6 of the 1956 Act were trivialised by the judiciary on the grounds that attitudes had changed in the previous decade; girls below the age of 16 were considered capable of organising their own sexual mores.[12]

There are, however, some cogent reasons for, at least, discouraging sexual intercourse below the age of 16 years. The facts that this age coincides with that for lawful marriage or that it is the age of consent adopted by most EEC countries are of lesser importance than that it is the same as the current school-leaving age; the law alleviates one major problem for the headteacher.

Yet we all know that school-age sex is practised and the difficulty then becomes that of distinguishing the love play of adolescence from anti-social criminal activity. There is, therefore, much to be said for adopting the concept of differential age which has been championed, among others, by the National Council for Civil Liberties.[13] Their specific proposal was that the age of consent should, in general, be 14 but that an overlap of two years on each side of that age should be allowed; the effect would be that there would be no offence in a consenting sexual act when the partners were over the age of 12 but under the age of 16. This seems a reasonable formula and the record of prosecutions indicates that, in practice, it just about represents the state of the law; it seems unfortunate that what is *de facto* cannot also be *de jure*.

Rape

Sexual intercourse without consent is, however, a different area in which it is beyond dispute that women deserve the full protection of society. What is at issue is whether they are, in fact, receiving that protection. At one side of the barrier, women's activist movements cry for vengeance on any erring male; on the other, there are those who

---

12 Referred to and explained, with little approbation, by Lawton LJ in *R v Taylor, R v Simons, R v Roberts* [1977] 3 All ER 527 at 529, [1977] 1 WLR 612 at 616, CA.
13 'Sexual Offences' (1976) NCCL Report no 13.

are fully aware that false representations can be and are made by women for varying reasons. Society is torn between rightful anger at the thought of women being abused and horror of condemning an innocent man to jail for many years. Society's compromise is, like all compromises, unsatisfactory.

In England and Wales, a man commits rape if he has unlawful sexual intercourse with a woman who, at the time of the intercourse, does not consent to it and, at that time, he knows that she does not consent or he is reckless as to whether she consents to it.[14] Unlawful sexual intercourse clearly does not refer to what is unlawful by reason of statute law; were it to do so, it would not be possible to commit rape on a mentally normal woman over the age of 16. Since this is an absurdity, the value of the phrase 'unlawful sexual intercourse' can only be to exclude 'lawful sexual intercourse' from the definition – a conclusion which puts one group of women beyond the protection of the law, i e married women who may at one time or another not consent to sexual intercourse with their husbands. The presumption of an implied consent to intercourse at a husband's whim is surely untenable in this era. The law must acknowledge prevailing public opinion and has recently done so in Scotland.[15] English law, however, is less positive in so far as it seems a husband may only be charged with rape if cohabitation has ceased or has been suspended.[16] The situation calls for reform yet opposition from male-dominated legislatures is strong. At the same time, it must be admitted that there is a serious difficulty in proving lack of consent in cases occurring within marriage and a clause revoking any absolute rights vested in the husband was deleted from the Sexual Offences (Amendment) Bill in 1976; typical amending legislation enacted in South Australia resulted in a compromise of doubtful effect – intra-marital rape being possible only when accompanied by, inter alia, assault occasioning actual bodily harm, gross indecency or humiliation.[17]

The recognition of consent outside marriage is currently unsatisfactory from the point of view of both the man and the woman. Some concern for the position of the woman was raised in *Morgan v*

14 Sexual Offences (Amendment) Act 1976, s. 1(1).
15 *HM Advocate v D* 1982 SCCR 182. The libel of rape by a husband on his wife, with whom he was not living at the time, was held to be competent. The accused was, however, found not guilty and the case did not go to appeal.
16 *R v Clarke* [1949] 2 All ER 448 where a separation order was in force; *R v Steele* (1976) 65 Crim App R 22, CA where a man had given an undertaking not to assault or molest his wife and it was held he could be charged with rape. The 'marital dispensation' is discussed at length in M D A Freeman 'But if you can't Rape your Wife who[m] can you Rape?' (1981) 15 Family LQ 1.
17 Criminal Law Consolidation Act Amendment Act 1976, cl 12(5).

DPP.[18] This bizarre case involved a husband who convinced his friends that any resistance his wife might put up to sexual intercourse was simulated. It was subsequently established that, if a man accused of rape honestly believed the woman to have consented, the reasonableness of the accused's mistake was irrelevant as a matter of law unless he was reckless – a decision which was approved by the National Council for Civil Liberties.[13] The definition of recklessness, however, has subsequently been extended by the courts with the result that the decision in *Morgan* has been rendered largely ineffective.[19] At the same time, the limits of consent seem to be narrowing and a state of what might be regarded as resigned acquiescence now qualifies as lack of consent;[20] casual sexual intercourse is becoming more hazardous for men and the law is now far removed from requiring 'resistance to the utmost' from a reluctant woman.

Nevertheless, a prosecution for rape is less likely to succeed in the absence of evidence corroborating lack of consent; clearly, the best of such evidence is the presence of injury resulting from force. Rape is defined in Scotland as the carnal knowledge of a female by a male person obtained by overcoming her will. This leads to some interesting paradoxes as regards English and Scottish practice. It is not rape in Scotland, for example, to have intercourse with a woman who is in a voluntary drunken stupor because she has no will to overcome; it would clearly be rape in England because she had not consented. The more practical point is, however, that while some evidence of a struggle is desirable in an English prosecution, it is a near necessity for a successful Scottish case.[1]

The fact of intercourse itself may be difficult to establish. Defloration during rape is relatively uncommon these days; the victim may be married, virginity is scarcely a lasting asset and the use of tampons is widespread – the torn and bleeding hymen is seen comparatively seldom. The only evidence of intercourse may be the finding of spermatazoa. Not only is emission not essential to rape but, the event having occurred, it may be difficult to demonstrate sperm after the several hours which may have elapsed since the offence. There may, thus, be no evidence of resistance and no evidence of

18 [1975] 2 All ER 347, HL.
19 *R v Pigg* [1982] 2 All ER 591, [1982] 1 WLR 762, CA. See D T Cowley 'The retreat from Morgan' [1982] Crim LR 198 for a full discussion.
20 *R v Olugboja* [1982] QB 320, [1981] 3 All ER 443, CA.
 1 But this may also be changing. In *Barbour v HM Advocate* 1982 SCCR 195 the jury were advised that the important matter was not so much the amount of resistance put up but, rather, whether the complainer was an unwilling party throughout the act.

intercourse yet the woman has been subjected to a harrowing experience. She may, indeed, have been degraded in one of many deviant ways yet there is no rape, for rape requires intercourse per vulvam.

The result is that rape is very difficult to prove and it is arguable that women are not adequately protected against the man who acts unreasonably as opposed to recklessly. There seems to be a good case, therefore, for abandoning the mediaeval concept of rape in favour of one of assault with sexual intent.[2] The Heilbron Committee looked briefly at such a proposal[3] and rejected it, firstly, on the grounds that all the existing problems – for example, as to proof of consent – would emerge with any new system. This attitude, however, still emphasises the act of vulval penetration as the essential element of rape; our feeling is that 'rape' is essentially an act of violence in which sexuality plays only a secondary part. Whether or not evidential difficulties would still arise, they could not be worse than those associated with true rape. The fact of, rather than the precise degree of, assault would be easier to prove; juries who, by nature, tend to an all or nothing policy in rape trials, would, in practice, be more likely to reach a verdict of guilty of assault, the severity of which could be reflected in sentencing. The protection of women would, thereby, be improved. Secondly, the Committee found they had insufficient time to consider the law of all offences of violence which the proposal involved; the inference is that they would have done so had the opportunity presented and that they were not so hostile to the idea as might be supposed. Their third and last objection was that the concept of rape is well established in popular thought and that the law should reflect contemporary ideas and categorisations – it is here, particularly, that we take issue with the Committee. We suggest that the public as a whole, excluding those concerned in its study, do not appreciate the definitive complexities of rape. Possibly as a result of transatlantic influence, the media and many feminist organisations will cry 'rape!' when any assault on a woman occurs – the concept of the 'Rape Counselling Centre' is an obvious example of pre-judgment. The results are frustration and anger at what seems to be male-dominated lenience in prosecution, conviction and, occasionally, sentencing. The National Council for Civil Liberties suggested that 'to take the emotion out of rape trials is to ignore the very nature of the crime'.[4] But to do so might, in the end, make the streets and countryside safer for women.

2 Interestingly, it was so regarded by Lord Robertson in *HM Advocate v D* (fn. 15, above).
3 Report of the Advisory Group on the Law of Rape (Cmd 6352) para 80.
4 'Sexual Offences' (1976) NCCL Report no 13.

Homosexuality

Attitudes to homosexuality have changed very rapidly. The Sexual Offences Act 1967, permitting homosexual practices by two consenting adults in private, was passed amid considerable public concern; 15 years later, homosexuals comprise significant political pressure groups and to refuse, say, to employ a man on the grounds of his sexual mores would certainly raise questions of unfair discrimination. But the precise legal position would change according to the nature of the employment. In *Nottingham County Council v Bowly*,[5] a male schoolteacher was dismissed fairly having been convicted of gross indecency although this was unrelated to his pupils; in *Bell v Devon and Cornwall Police Authority*[6] a homosexual canteen worker was found to have been unfairly dismissed because, inter alia, there was insufficient evidence to show that customers would have been upset by knowing he was a homosexual. Scotland, despite its traditional resistance to ecclesiastically unacceptable practices, came into line with England and Wales through an obscure clause (section 80) in the otherwise unrelated Criminal Justice (Scotland) Act 1980; so little was the public impact that it is probable that many do not even know of its passing.

Nonetheless, it would be interesting to see how much further public opinion, which is now firmly favourable to the Wolfenden concept of private morality, would go.[7] There would almost certainly be considerable resistance to relaxation in the protection of young persons. In so far as sex in nature is heterosexual, homosexual intercourse must be regarded as unnatural; and, since homosexuality is frequently seen as an acquired rather than an instinctive habit, few parents would willingly accept any lowering of the age of consent to adult practices in this sphere. There are, perhaps, two exceptions. Firstly, the law concerning consenting homosexual adulthood was clearly related to the age of majority; persons who are politically mature at 18 years should, rationally, be regarded as also being sexually mature. Secondly, the law must have regard to teenage experimentation and there is much to be said for a differential age system such as has been discussed above in relation to heterosexual activity; this, while not approving the practice, would decriminalise an almost inevitable aspect of growing up.

Of the other reforms which have been suggested, that concerning the definition of privacy seems least controversial; there is little logical reason why group homosexual sex should be proscribed any

5 [1978] IRLR 252.
6 [1978] IRLR 283.
7 Report of the Committee on Homosexual Offences and Prostitution (Cmd 247).

more than are heterosexual parties – public decency is neither less nor more outraged provided the restraints of consent and age are respected and the blinds are drawn. By contrast, the call for liberation of the armed forces borders on absurdity and would probably be resisted by the troops themselves. The problem of special relation-ships, particularly in respect of a duty of care, deserves closer attention than it has received – should there, in other words, be a particular homosexual offence analogous to incest; there does seem to be much merit in such a proposition and this is discussed further below. Finally, there is the suggestion strongly argued by Honoré,[8] that the law and, particularly, its terminology should be tidied up. Archaic words such as buggery are emotive and, as has been discussed in relation to rape, may well be self-defeating. The only homosexual deserving of criminal censure is one who forces himself on those who do not or cannot in law consent to his attentions. The concept of the offence of assault with sexual intent again has its attractions.

Female homosexuality within the limits of consent has never been regarded as criminal save in respect of public indecency and, even here, attitudes are changing, many films with an 'X' certificate regularly including explicit lesbian activity. Quite why this is acceptable in circumstances where simple full frontal exposure of the male body would cause outrage is difficult to understand. It is probably a powerful example of 'male chauvinism', the dominant class of male heterosexuals being content to condone such voyeurism.

Incest

Incest – defined in the *Concise Oxford Dictionary* as 'sexual com-merce of near kindred' – is, perhaps, the most illogical of sexual offences and the law is under close scrutiny.

The primary difficulty lies in its scope – 'near kindred' must be interpreted before any law is applied. Most legislatures limit the offence to intercourse between three generations of relations in the direct line of descent or ascent and between siblings; the relationship persists in the illegitimate state and siblings of half blood are included. This is the situation in England and Wales – with a curious dispensation for grandmothers and grandsons.[9] But around this norm there are variations ranging from an absence of the offence as such in France to the very wide restrictions, including many

8 T Honoré *Sex Law* (1978) p. 109.
9 Sexual Offences Act 1956, ss. 10, 11.

relationships by affinity, which are proscribed in Scotland.[10] No-one can be happy when a relationship is legal to the South of the River Tweed but attracts a theoretical sentence of life imprisonment in the North.

In the face of such variations, it becomes pertinent to question the rationale of the offence for which there is, undoubtedly, an innate public distaste. Few of the common reasons adduced for the so-called 'incest taboo' provide good grounds for legislation in modern times. Socio-anthropological theories depend, in many ways, on the supposed advantages to the tribe or clan of 'breeding out'; a variation on this suggests that the man who preferred to 'breed in' was an idle, inferior economic unit who was despised for both faults concurrently. In any case, such imaginings have no place in modern society with its easy access to the opposite sex outside the immediate family. More often, the case against incest is based on genetic grounds; this, we suggest, is a fundamental misunderstanding. In the first place, genetics can have no place in the historic development of an incest taboo because genetic considerations would only have been apparent to those communities who regularly practised in-breeding and, therefore, suffered from no restrictive 'horror'. Secondly, genetics are related to procreation while incest is a matter of sexual intercourse; genetic considerations are accordingly, and rightly, directed at the marriage laws. Thirdly, there is no certainty that an isolated incestuous pregnancy will result in congenital abnormality. In the worst conceivable case – that of father/daughter incest with both carrying a deleterious recessive gene – the chances of a manifestly abnormal offspring are 1:4 and this, taken with the indeterminate possibility of multi-factorial disease (chapter 6, below) would, in any case, be sufficient to render an incestuous pregnancy legally terminable under section 1(1)(b) of the Abortion Act 1967 – in addition to the obvious indications under section 1(1)(a). Far more cogently in relation to the present era, it is said that incest disrupts the family and this must certainly be so despite the suggestion, particularly from the National Council for Civil Liberties,[11] that incest is the *result* of family disharmony. Nevertheless, the same can be said about adultery yet we do not judge it as a criminal offence. A high proportion of wives to husbands indulging in incest will say that they are quite prepared to resume normal family relationships 'if only he will stop it'. Here, the argument is edging towards what must be the family's and society's basic revulsion to incest – that it exemplifies the exploitation of those in the care of or under the authority of the·

10 Incest Act 1567.
11 'Sexual Offences' (1976) NCCL Report no 13.

perpetrators. Not even apparent consent can be truly autonomous in such circumstances; effectively, incest is an insidious form of rape.

Once that is accepted, the way to modernising the law becomes very much clearer. Age becomes a significant factor – adults, who are beyond family dependence, *should* be able to give consent while increasing disparity in age increases the degree of subordination and, thus, the severity of the offence. But this is not the only feature bearing on authority. A father, in effect, has absolute authority which persists through life; a ban on father/daughter intercourse should, therefore, be absolute. Similar authority, albeit only until approximately school-leaving age, rests in the stepfather or the mother's common law husband and the same can be said of the foster father; the authority of the adoptive father, indeed, corresponds closely to that of the genetic father. None of these are related in blood to the child and none, save the Scottish stepfather, can be guilty of incest. Yet intercourse is, in every case, within the family and the effect on the child is the same – she is being sexually abused by someone she trusts.

The Scottish Law Commission[12] has given an example of how some of these principles might be put into effect. The Commission propose retaining the present definition of incest – that is intercourse involving vulval penetration – and applying the offence to intercourse between parents and children, grand- and great-grandparents and grand- and great-grandchildren, brothers and sisters, uncles and nieces and aunts and nephews, illegitimate children being placed in the same position as legitimate; they thus hope to bring the law into line with that of England save for including the great-grandparent relationship – which cannot be frequent – and, more controversially, sexual intercourse between uncle and niece and aunt and nephew. It is proposed that intercourse between adoptive parents and their adopted children should be characterised as incest but relationships by affinity are to be excluded. It is recommended that new offences be created of having intercourse with a step-child who is under the age of 16 years and having intercourse with a child under 16 years of age when one is in a position of trust or authority to that child who, at the time, is a member of the same household.

These draft proposals are a compromise between strict logic and current public opinion. Thus, the potential right of adult brothers and sisters to behave themselves in private as they please is not yet recognised while uncles and aunts could equally well be caught in the 'trust and authority' net. More importantly, the legal obsession with defloration is perpetuated. One cannot help feeling that to force

12 The Law of Incest in Scotland (Cmd 8422).

deviant sex on a young girl or homosexual acts upon a young boy are as offensive as it is to enforce natural sex; they all become of the same nature once the overall importance of trust and authority is recognised and they should, accordingly, be treated as a group. The use of the word incest to cover a wide spectrum of relationships may also be considered unwise; it should, if retained, be limited to that act which is objectionable on any rationale – a sexual relationship between parent and child. Rape, buggery, incest – all are restrictive definitions which probably fail in their objectives; we would continue to argue in favour of an all-embracing concept of assault with sexual intent.

Transsexualism

Although the civil law currently takes little note of sex, the problems of transsexualism are likely to be raised with increasing frequency and to bring serious issues in medical jurisprudence in their wake. The transsexual does not necessarily demonstrate any anatomical or physiological abnormality but, nevertheless, suffers from an intense wish to be of and be accepted as being of the opposite sex. Thus, while a proportion of transsexuals pass through a phase of homosexuality, the two states differ in that homosexuals are content with their own sexuality but prefer to express it in their own way; the former are convinced that nature has made a mistake in their case and are intent on rectifying it.

The fully developed syndrome must lead to almost unbearable distress. Nevertheless, living with a problem is a personal matter and, in the absence of identification cards, National Service and the like, society is scarcely concerned to regulate the outward trappings of transsexualism such as transvestism. But the sufferer may be unable to adapt to society or find a sympathetic environment. Rectification becomes essential and the public morality is concerned at three heads – the treatment of the condition, the recognition of treatment and, perhaps most particularly, the marital status of the transsexual.

Psychiatric treatment, as opposed to simple support, of the fully fledged syndrome is generally ineffective; the patients need to change their sex organs and this goal can really be achieved only by radical surgery. This includes castration in both males and females; an artificial vagina can be fashioned in the male but the alternative in the female is clearly not practical. In 1970, Meyers[13] questioned the legality of such operations on the grounds that consent to such physical invasion was legally impossible; certainly, castration as such

13 D W Meyers *'The Human Body and the Law'* (1970) p. 66.

would be a common law maim in England. Some countries have legislated for this. Swedish law specifically devoted to transsexualism puts the age of consent at 18; in Germany it is 25. Elsewhere, legal consent is generally based on a tacit understanding between medicine and the law. Although such an operation is still, strictly speaking, criminal in some places – e g in Argentina, where a doctor was imprisoned for mutilation in 1969 – 'sex change' operations are nearly everywhere justified under the doctrine of 'necessity' or of 'genuine medical treatment'; the ethical problem then becomes that of case selection. A recent review of the subject[14] has emphasised what a small number of applicants should, in fact, be recommended for operation. Something of the order of 1 per cent of requests were accepted for treatment in the large Johns Hopkins Hospital programme which has now been abandoned; about 2,000 total cases, including 360 females, have been operated upon within the British National Health Service; some foreign national centres, however, have a higher turnover – of anything up to 800 cases per year.

It is obvious that the success of treatment of a condition such as this must depend to some extent on society's reaction. Outside Scandinavia, and, particularly, Sweden, this has not been all that helpful – particularly as it is exemplified by the law. Basically, one can hope to determine a person's sex from their genital organs, from their gonads or from their chromosomal make-up; their gender, or role, can be determined from their secondary sex characteristics and their psyche. It is a matter of common observation that these vary from person to person – the genitalia may be congenitally malformed in the male or they may be grossly masculinised in the female (the adrenogenital syndrome); at one extreme, rudimentary female genitalia together with well-developed secondary characteristics may be present in a chromosomal male with non-functioning testes (the testicular feminisation syndrome); rarely, one sees a true hermaphrodite with gonads of both sexes present in the one person. Faced with a conflict of evidence, the medical solution is to 'assign' a person to the sex which they are most likely to be able to support in society, the function of the chromosomal sex being then regulated to that of an indicator of the direction in which to steer an infant's upbringing. In later life, the one characteristic of sex or gender which is apparent to no-one, including the principal, is the state of a person's chromosomes. Unfortunately, that is the feature which appeals most to the lawyer, a recent example being from Australia[15] when it was used as proof of mistaken identification.

14 M Roth, 'Transsexualism and the Sex Change Operation: A Contemporary Medico-legal and Social Problem' (1981) 49 Med-leg J 5.
15 *Re C and D* (1979) 53 ALJ 659.

The most appealing attribute of chromosomal sex lies in its immutability. The law has resolutely turned its face against 'sex change' and only a genuine mistake at birth can justify an alteration in one's birth certificate.[16] In practice, this matters surprisingly little. Ormrod himself has pointed out the relative unconcern of the law with sex[17] and several 'corrected' transsexuals have been officially re-registered for National Insurance and employment purposes. The ultimate test, however, lies in marriage which is the union between a man and a woman. The leading British case in this context is *Corbett v Corbett*[18] in which it was held that, irrespective of reconstructive surgery, the so-called wife was not a woman for the purposes of marriage and had at all times been a biological male. It was further held that, not withstanding the validity of the marriage or of the sex of the 'wife', she was physically incapable of consummating a marriage by the use of an artificial cavity. The case was thus distinguished from *SY v SY*[19] in which a decree of nullity had been refused on the grounds that a vestigial vagina could have been corrected by forming an artificial passage; Wilmer LJ commented:

> if a woman with an artificial vagina is incapable of true sexual intercourse she cannot be raped or commit adultery. I would regard such a result as bordering on the fantastic;[20]

the irony of the distinction between the two cases is that it would seem to have been made on the basis that SY was an imperfect woman – today it is likely that she would have been diagnosed as a case of testicular feminisation and, accordingly, as a chromosomal male. Medical science, and the basis it provides for the law, moves relatively swiftly.

The decision in *Corbett* which, at the time, was fully approved by no less a body than the House of Commons, has since been criticised on the general grounds that it is unfeeling and fails to take into account the total sexual ambience of an individual. In a discussion of *Corbett* in association with *C and D*,[1] it has been proposed that a transsexual marriage should be valid if the transsexual is found to be capable of fulfilling the essential role of the sex he or she has assumed and that this should include the ability of the two partners to love and

---

16 *X Petitioner* 1957 SLT (Sh Ct) 61.
17 R Ormrod 'The Medico-legal Aspects of Sex Determination'(1972) 40 Med-leg J 78.
18 [1971] P 83, [1970] 2 All ER 33.
19 [1963] P 37, CA.
20 Ibid at 60.
 1 H A Finlay 'Sexual Identity and the Law of Nullity' (1980) 54 ALJ 115.

understand one another. Bailey,[2] concerned only with *C and D*, concluded that the medical profession might feel, with justification, that its efforts in the complex field of sexual medicine had been frustrated by the law.

There are, however, dangers in moving too fast. Kennedy,[3] in putting the case for legalising converted transsexual marriage, went on to extrapolate this to the authorisation of homosexual marriages – 'I have no doubt it will occur', he said 'later if not sooner'. Such a conclusion, albeit logical, must be generally unacceptable. It would be a pity if arguments involving a massive change in moral values were to inhibit progress towards what could be welcomed as humane assistance to a small minority who are existing in most distressing conditions.

2 R J Bailey 'Family Law – Decree of Nullity of Marriage of True Hermaphrodite who has undergone Sex Change Surgery' (1979) 53 ALJ 659.
3 I M Kennedy 'Transsexualism and Single Sex Marriage' (1973) 2 Anglo-Amer L Rev 112.

3 Modern reproductive technology

Some 10 per cent of marriages are said to be infertile and the couple desire children in, at least, a high proportion of these. In addition, there are couples who should not have children for genetic reasons either because one may carry a dominant deleterious gene or because both are known to bear recessive characteristics (see chapter 6, below). Again, children may be wanted but facilities for adoption are now meagre; the substitution of one or other partner may ensure a normal infant which is related genetically to at least one of its social parents. In either case – of infertility or of genetic incompatibility – methods are now available for by-passing the natural process. Almost inevitably, these sometimes conflict with laws which were mainly fashioned before such techniques were considered.

Artificial insemination

Artificial insemination by donor (AID) may provide a solution where there is male infertility, a condition which accounts for roughly 50 per cent of cases of involuntary failure to conceive. In this procedure, semen obtained from a donor is injected into the woman and this results in conception in a high proportion of cases. The husband's semen may similarly be introduced into the uterus by artificial means (AIH) if a couple's inability to conceive is due to causes other than male infertility. Many couples who have recourse to artificial insemination are, nevertheless, loathe to abandon all hope of husband/wife offspring. In such circumstances, the semen of the apparently infertile husband is mixed with that of the donor in order to allow the couple belief that the ovum may actually have been fertilised by the husband's sperm. This form of artificial insemination is known as AIHD.

Artificial insemination by the husband
AIH gives rise to no major legal or ethical problems. All that is entailed is that the woman conceives by a method other than that of normal sexual intercourse and the procedure will only be regarded as

questionable if there is objection to *any* interference with nature in this area.

Only two legal issues arise. The first concerns the possibility of 'sperm banking' for use by a wife after her husband's death. In our opinion, the problems related to disposal of estates and succession are such that there is a need to categorise children so born as resulting from AID of a single woman (see below). A second is possible nullity of the marriage. A decree of nullity could still be obtained if a woman conceives in this way and the marriage has not been consummated; approbation might, however, exclude such a decree.[1] Any children would still be regarded as legitimate on the grounds that the parents were married at the time of conception.

Artificial insemination by donor
By contrast, AID attracts many legal and ethical complexities. These revolve around the choice of circumstances in which AID is performed, the status of the child conceived in this way and the rights of parties over the child. The issues have been widely discussed but have, so far, escaped both legal and ethical resolution.

There are those who object strongly to the entire concept of AID. These objectors take the view that the basis of the marriage bond is compromised by the wife's pregnancy through another man. It is supposed that the privity of marriage is invaded and that, in this respect, AID is little different from adultery.

AID and the marital bond
The question of whether AID constitutes adultery in legal terms was extensively debated in the Scottish case of *MacLennan v MacLennan*[2] where it was determined that adultery could not be held to have taken place because there was no sexual contact between the woman and the donor. The *MacLennan* approach to the question would probably be acceptable throughout the Commonwealth despite the obiter remarks in the Canadian case of *Orford v Orford*:[3] AID without the consent of the husband may, however, be taken as constituting cruel and unreasonable conduct for divorce purposes. Apart from these misgivings, there also tends to be an aesthetic objection and past critics of the practice have chosen to describe AID as 'disgusting' or 'abhorrent'.[4]

1 *L v L* [1949] P 211, [1949] 1 All ER 141 (see also *G v G* 1961 SLT 324).
2 1958 SC 105.
3 (1921) 58 DLR 251, in which it was suggested that AID without the husband's consent could constitute adultery.
4 See for example, H Hubbard (1956) 34 Can Bar Rev 425.

It is difficult to sympathise with these views. When AID is carried out on a married woman with the full consent of her husband, it is merely fulfilling their perfectly legitimate desire to have a child. The very fact of agreement to AID testifies to the strength of the bond between the parties, as is indicated by the comparative low incidence of divorce in couples who have chosen AID. Only in a highly metaphysical sense is the marital bond disturbed by the procedure and this disturbance is, in any event, actively sought by the couple.

This is not to recommend that AID be undertaken lightly. Clinics in Britain where the procedure is carried out normally place great emphasis on the need for counselling before the insemination is performed. Both parties have AID explained to them and are warned of any psychological or legal complications. The desire to go ahead with the procedure is carefully tested before the clinical practice is embarked upon. These safeguards will not necessarily be observed everywhere and it will be possible, through consulting unethical doctors, to have AID performed in a casual fashion with scant or little enquiry into background and motives. In the United States, where artificial insemination has been extensively used, the clinical restraints on the procedure have varied widely[5] and, indeed, some States have now been prompted to introduce controlling legislation.

Major ethical problems
The principal ethical problems do not, therefore, arise in the normal husband and wife situation. But it may be that a single woman or an unmarried couple request AID or the request may even come from a lesbian couple. Since there is no legal regulation of the matter, a doctor will have to decide on ethical grounds alone whether or not to proceed in these circumstances.

The Royal College of Obstetricians and Gynaecologists gives some answer to this in the guidelines it has laid down for its members. These recommend that AID be performed only on a married woman and, then, with the consent of her husband in writing. Some would say that this is excessively conservative; a single woman may feel precisely the same desire for a child as a married woman and has the same right to a child as her married counterpart. The same argument may be put forward on behalf of the homosexual woman whether she is living by herself or with a partner. Should the experience of giving birth and raising a child be denied in either case because of the absence of a husband? Why should society exclude the possibility of conception in this way when it allows such women to conceive by

5 M Curie-Cohen et al 'Current Practice of Artificial Insemination by Donor in the United States' (1979) 300 New Engl J Med 585.

normal means and permits them to keep their children as a normal right of parenthood?

Nevertheless, we do not feel that the use of AID is ethically acceptable in such circumstances. The right to procreate cannot be absolute in that it involves interests other than those of the progenitors. Even if the principal objective of AID is to satisfy the desire for a child, thought has to be given to the child who is the end result. In participating in the process of procreation, the doctor is performing an act which is not morally colourless; he must question whether he should play a part in the creation of a person who may be denied the chance of a *reasonably* stable upbringing. Such an upbringing should include a normal family life if possible. A fatherless child is at a disadvantage as to his peers with fathers, just as any single parent child is likely to have a more difficult childhood than is one with a full complement of parents.

The Feversham Committee, which reported in 1960 on all aspects of artificial insemination,[6] considered the question of AID for single women and decided against allowing it. The Committee considered the argument that there is no valid reason why a single woman should not be allowed to have a child through AID when she is allowed to adopt. The Committee thought, however, that there was a distinction to be made between the two cases in that the adopted child was already in existence and that only occasionally would it be found that the best place for such a child would be with a single woman. But that was in 1960 and the Committee was conservative; attitudes have changed. Even so, the proponents of AID for single women will still have to deal with the objection that the parental selection procedure is rigorous in adoption and the motives and circumstances of the single parent are thoroughly scrutinised. At present, the screening of prospective AID candidates is nowhere near as thorough and demanding as is that carried out by adoption authorities.

These antipathetic arguments are even more applicable when the prospective mother is a lesbian. The sexual and social development of children is a fragile matter at the best of times, and a child with a homosexual parent is more likely to encounter emotional and social difficulties than is one reared in the customary family circle. No matter how loving such a parent may be, the psycho-sexual development of a child in such a position would be at risk and we doubt if an ethical doctor should involve himself in the introduction

6 Report of the Departmental Committee on Human Artificial Insemination (Cmnd 1105). In British Columbia, the Royal Commission on Family and Children's Law reached a different conclusion, recommending that AID be made available to unmarried women: see B Dickens *Medico-legal Aspects of Family Law* (1979) ch 1, fn. 5.

of a child to such an environment. If a lesbian woman wishes to have a child, there is nothing, apart from sexual disinclination, to stop her from securing the help of a male friend. The decision as to whether or not to have a child is then hers alone and no medical decision is entailed.

Legal considerations
The child conceived by AID which is born to a married couple is in a different legal position from that of the naturally conceived child born during wedlock. Since the AID child is not the child of the wife's husband, he is illegitimate and must face the disadvantages which illegitimacy carries. These are certainly not as draconian as they used to be and are now limited, in English law, to an inability to succeed on intestacy to collateral relations and ascendants other than his parents.[7] Citizens' rights are, however, affected. An illegitimate child born to a British citizen outside the United Kingdom is not entitled to United Kingdom citizenship. Social disadvantages, of course, persist since illegitimacy still carries a considerable stigma despite the development of more enlightened legal attitudes.

There is no good sociological reason why the child conceived through AID should be in any different position to that of a child which the same couple might have had by natural means. The whole purpose of AID is, after all, to enable the couple to have a family and their intention is to treat the child as their own. For this reason, the AID child should occupy and enjoy the same rights as a naturally conceived child. This implies that some legal means should be devised of legitimating such children and of ensuring that all legal links with the donor are ended, thus bringing the law into line with social reality.

At present, AID children are not often recorded as such when their births are registered. The husband, who normally registers the birth, usually declares himself as the father of the child, either in ignorance of the fact that he is committing an offence under the Perjury Act 1911 or in the belief – when his own semen has been mixed with the donor's – that there is at least a possibility that this is true. There is,

---

7 The consequences of illegitimacy were mitigated in English law by the Family Law Reform Act 1969 and, in Scots Law, by the Law Reform (Miscellaneous Provisions) (Scotland) Act 1968. Succession to titles of honour still depends on legitimacy; the Feversham Committee voiced very strong objections to AID children succeeding to such titles: 'Succession through blood descent is an important element of family life and as such is the basis of our society. On it depends the peerage and other titles of honour, and the Monarchy itself' (para 163). This would seem to be the right approach if one approves of hereditary titles but, in other respects, the significance of blood ties in the family unit is now less important than it was when the Committee reported.

therefore, nothing on the birth certificate to reveal the child's origins and, in practice, the child will be considered legitimate. Although this expedient is perfectly understandable, it can hardly be legally condoned.

There is more than one choice for the reform of the law in this field. In some jurisdictions in the United States, legislation has provided for attribution of legitimacy in respect of the AID child when both partners in a marriage have consented to the procedure.[8] Another option is that of adoption. The child, once born, can be adopted by the couple and thereby enjoy a status which is free of the disadvantages of illegitimacy. The agreement of the father – in this case, the donor – would not be required as the child is illegitimate. However, under existing laws, adoption can only take place when a child has reached a certain age and something simpler is preferable to the somewhat cumbrous process of adoption.

The solution currently favoured by the Law Commission would involve legislation providing for the AID child to be declared to be the child of the couple, thus relieving it of any consequences of illegitimacy.[9] A feature of such a deeming provision would be to terminate any legal connection between the donor and the child, a connection which has always been the cause of speculation in academic comments on the current law. The thought of the donor finding himself liable for maintenance of an AID child (or, even worse, a whole gaggle of children) has discomfited all concerned. In practice, this is a highly unlikely situation, as the secrecy which surrounds the donor's identity is not easily penetrated although, in theory, it might be if the matter were to come to court proceedings.[10] The reality of the situation is that AID children are normally not informed of the fact that they were conceived in this way. This, in contrast to the position in cases of adoption, is probably for the best. If they were informed, they might logically argue that they were entitled to find out the identity of their real fathers just as adopted children are. One may accept the intensity of the desire but it is submitted that the AID child at least knows who is one of his parents, which is better than being totally in the dark – the ethical basis for secrecy can be justified on the grounds of necessity. But, perhaps the major reason for non-disclosure is that the donor enters into the arrangement on the understanding that he will not be identified. If his

8 See J M Shaman 'Legal aspects of Artificial Insemination' (1979) 18 J Fam Law 331.
9 Family Law: Illegitimacy (Law Com Working Paper no 74).
10 But it has been suggested that, even then, the court might adopt a public policy line and permit non-disclosure (D Whelan 'The Law and Artifical Insemination with Donor Semen (AID)' (1978) 1 Med J Austral 56).

identity is later made known, his legitimate interest in anonymity is compromised and, in practice, the possibility of disclosure would discourage the great majority of potential donors. Balancing the two interests – the child's in knowing the facts of its paternity and the donor's in remaining anonymous – it is the donor's which would seem the weightier.

It is sometimes suggested that anonymity must be broken lest the practice of AID leads to later incestuous matings – for example, more than 25 successful donations by an individual might raise the possibility in Scotland. Certainly, consanguinity is of more importance in the context of AID than has been suggested in chapter 2 in relation to the criminal law. But the control of in-breeding is a matter of limiting the number of insertions from an individual donor or from a single specimen preserved in a 'sperm-bank'; there may, indeed, be a case for legislation in this respect. Thus, the identity of the donor must be known to the doctor or the clinic but this is irrelevant to the question of disclosure to the resultant child. The impediment of potential incest does not alter our view that the right of the donor to anonymity outside the clinic should be firmly protected.

The infertile wife

Artificial insemination is essentially a means of circumventing incapacity or sterility on the part of the husband. The wife may similarly be beset by anatomical problems – of which the most important is blockage of the Fallopian tubes – or by primary infertility, either of which will prevent her having children by natural means. Despite the fact that ova are far more scarce and are more difficult to handle than are spermatozoa, modern medical techniques have evolved by which the female's disability may be circuited and these opportunities have been supplemented by increasingly open or permissive attitudes to sexual behaviour. It would still be repulsive to most people to develop full term fetuses in a laboratory environment and this cannot, in fact, be done; embryo culture can be maintained for only a few days. Providing an ovum is, therefore, pointless without, at the same time, providing a womb. Both may be contributed by the same woman or they may be available independently. These are the bases of the legal and moral problems complicating the treatment of the infertile wife.

In vitro fertilisation (IVF)
It is now possible to collect ova from a wife's abdomen, fertilise them with her husband's sperm in the laboratory and transfer the resultant

embryo to her uterus. Blocked tubes are, thereby, by-passed and a normal pregnancy ensues. The problems of technique are formidable but, in the best hands, a continuing pregnancy rate approaching 20 per cent of abdominal operations is obtainable; IVF therefore offers a good, and perhaps optimal, treatment for one of the commonest types of female infertility.

The rationale of the process corresponds closely to that of AIH and, as such, presents no legal problems. The genetic and natural parentage of the resulting infant are not disputed. All that has occurred is that a technique has been substituted for a natural process; if any would protest that this is in some way immoral, they would, at the same time, have to contend that the surgical treatment of any disease is similarly immoral.

There is, of course, no technical reason why the sperm must be those of the husband and, in the unlikely event of combined male infertility and an impassable female genital tract, donor semen could be used in the same way. In such circumstances, the legal problems would be those of AID which have been discussed above.

Ovum donation

An alternative situation is that the ovum is donated by another woman. The need might arise as being the only way in which a woman with, say, abdominal adhesions could have children and it might be highly desirable in the event of a potential mother carrying a sex linked genetic disease (see chapter 6). The practicality is not so remote as might be supposed – an excess of ova are removed from women undergoing treatment and it may be possible soon to cryopreserve these in liquid nitrogen; moreover, a large number of women would be prepared to donate ova while being sterilised.

The scenario is now that the donated egg is fertilised by the husband's semen and the embryo then transferred to the wife's womb. In such circumstances, which broadly correspond to the female equivalent of AID, the genetic or biological parentage of the child will be confused but natural parentage will be acceptably clear; we submit that the act of carrying a fetus from implantation to full term confers true motherhood on a woman who has been actively seeking that state. It is difficult to see any circumstances in which parenthood would be challenged and, in a patrilineal society, there are fewer objections to an admixture of ovum-derived genes in the family than to those which arise as a result of AID.

But what of the similar wife with an infertile husband? Such cases would be regarded as too rare to merit mention were it not for the fact that they have been treated by a combination of donated ova

fertilised by donated sperm.[11] The legal complications then lie
somewhere between those of in vitro fertilisation and those
surrounding surrogate motherhood and are best discussed, later,
under that heading. Even so, it is emotionally, morally and legally
important to distinguish unrelated embryo transfer from surrogate
motherhood – the intense relationship between mother and fetus
occurs in both but, despite the absence of genetic affiliation, it is only
in the former that this progresses naturally to the bond between
mother and child.

The legal position of the doctor
The theoretical hazard which is common to all procedures involving
in vitro embryo transfer is that the embryo will be damaged during
manipulation and that an abnormal fetus will result. Animal
experiments indicate that there is no higher incidence of abnormalities in reimplanted live born neonates than in those which are
conceived normally and, so far as is known, no excess of human cases
beyond the probability of chance has occurred. The legal position
would be interesting were they to do so. Causation would, inevitably,
be difficult to prove but, having done so, the terms of the Congenital
Disabilities (Civil Liability) Act 1976, would be difficult to apply.
Section 1(4) refers to accidents preceding the time of conception
and, presumably, conception has taken place once the ovum has been
fertilised; otherwise, the section precludes any action when the
parents knew of a risk of their child being born disabled. Section 1(5)
covers professional negligence but refers only to treating or advising
parents; this might conceivably be stretched to include manipulation
of the embryo but one would hope that a remedy would be found in
common law – 'Justice requires that the principle be recognised that a
child has a legal right to begin life with a sound mind and body'.[12]
Whatever the true status of the pre-implant embryo may be, it seems
wrong that doctors and patients should have to operate in a state of
legal uncertainty. There has been much official activity intended to
clarify the issues of modern reproductive technology in the United
States. There, the newly formed Ethics Advisory Board was given as
its priority task an assessment of in vitro fertilisation and allied
techniques;[13] the Board is advisory only to the Secretary of Health,
Education and Welfare but its deliberations must be very persuasive
in the Courts. At the time of writing, a similar study group has been

11 I Craft and J Yovich 'Implications of Embryo Transfer' (1979) 2 Lancet 642.
12 *Smith v Brennan* 31 NJ 353, 157 A 2d 497 (1960) at 503, per Proctor J.
13 B J Culliton and W K Waterfall 'Flowering of American Bioethics' (1978) 2 Brit
    Med J 1270.

established in the United Kingdom – the Warnock Committee – and it is to be hoped that its deliberations will provide adequate guidance for doctors involved in the field.

The surplus embryo

It is inevitable that surplus ova and surplus embryos will be produced whether IVF or embryo transfer is being attempted. The status and disposal of such embryos have significance which is independent of the problems of successful implantation.

The destruction of embryos conceived in vitro is an act of abortion in so far as the process of cell division and organisation is 'aborted' but this is not the definition of abortion intended in the criminal law. The Offences against the Person Act 1861 (section 58) defines abortion as procuring a miscarriage while the Abortion Act 1967 refers to terminating pregnancy. The process of disposal is, thus, clearly not abortion and, equally clearly, it is not murder since the embryo can in no way be considered to have achieved a separate existence in a legal sense. Should the 'Brave New World' come upon us and it be possible to develop laboratory embryos to term, it may be necessary to invent an offence of feticide but, until then, it is difficult to see that any criminal offence is committed by the simple disposal of embryos.

That being so, the problem is purely ethical and devolves on the nature of the embryo. Dr Walters, of the Kennedy Institute of Ethics, is quoted as defining the moral status of the human embryo conceived in vitro as being 'more than a mouse embryo but less than that of a full human fetus'.[14] Such subtle demarcation seems to be neither helpful nor necessary; in the end, the decision must be clear cut and one is left with two alternatives – either the embryo is a full human being within the rigid theological, perhaps mainly Roman Catholic, doctrine or it is a laboratory artefact.

The former view seems scarcely tenable. Ensoulment and humanity are inseparable; humanity, in its turn, depends upon a natural human environment. It seems reasonable to regard the embryo as deriving its humanity only after having established normal unity with its human mother; prior to such an 'infusion of humanity', it appears both kinder and more practical to look upon the embryo as a laboratory artefact.

In accepting this premise, one simultaneously solves one's moral problems as to embryonic experimentation which, when well done, must be valuable to the community as a whole. Such research can then be likened to the culture of fibroblasts – which, when all is said

14 See fn. 13, above.

and done, have 46 chromosomes in their nuclei. The concept of acquired humanity also serves to differentiate research on embryos from research on fetuses which is discussed as a separate issue in chapter 16, below.

The fact that such a differentiation can be made depends, firstly, on the integrity of the researchers and, secondly, on the state of technology. Currently, it is doubtful if the most dedicated research worker in the field would wish to maintain an embryonic culture for longer than a few days and, equally, it is technically impossible to do so. Legal intervention might become necessary were these conditions to change.

Surrogate motherhood

Surrogate motherhood requires the active co-operation of an otherwise uninvolved woman in the process of pregnancy and birth. It thus introduces a completely new element – that of the commercial world of buying and selling services – into what has been, up to now, essentially a doctor/patient relationship. It is, therefore, fundamentally foreign to the principles of British medicine and, so far as is known, is very rarely practised.[15] Commercialism is, however, accepted in American medical practice – for example, blood is bought and resold – and there does seem to be considerable activity in this field in the United States where the occasional court decision has already been provoked.

At its simplest, the infertile woman and her husband arrange with another woman that she will carry a child conceived by artificial insemination with the husband's semen and will surrender it to its genetic father after birth. The process is, therefore, akin to a pre-emptive adoption with the advantage that the 'adopted' baby shares at least half its genes with its 'adopting' parents. Since the practical possibility of following the normal process of adoption is decreasing steadily, there is much to be said, theoretically, in favour of surrogate motherhood as a treatment for the wholly infertile wife. Yet one instinctively shys away from accepting it as a means of satisfying an urge to parenthood – why? The reason has been put succinctly by Winslade:[16] 'The practice has a potential for economic exploitation, moral confusion and psychological harm to the surrogate mothers, the prospective adoptive parents and the children'. These views

15 One case has been reported in the Press where the parties acted without medical advice. The reasons for the publicity given may have been that the surrogate refused to part with the baby having decided that the adoptive mother was unsuitable.

16 W J Winslade 'Surrogate Mothers: Private Right or Public Wrong?' (1981) 7 J Med Ethics 153.

deserve immediate consideration despite the fact that surrogate motherhood is a problem related more to the future than to the present.

The legal issues
The possibility of exploitation is exemplified in the analogy between surrogate motherhood and adoption. The purchase of babies is expressly forbidden by the Adoption Act 1976, section 57, and all American States have laws prohibiting 'baby selling' or private placement of infants. There is, therefore, a real possibility that surrogate motherhood, which involves some sort of commercial transaction, is already illegal and such has been decided at least once in the United States.[17] But there is much to be said for the view that the two processes are distinct.[18] In the first place, the surrogate mother is not pregnant at the time the proposition is put to her. She is under no economic pressure to support a child who is already causing her financial embarrassment and a main reason for prohibiting a trade in babies is, therefore, absent. Against this, it has been pointed out[19] that 40 per cent of volunteer surrogate mothers in the United States are unemployed or are in receipt of welfare; the economic incentive is present but the element of urgency is still lacking. The nature of the payment is certainly different in the two cases. In one it is a simple matter of purchase of a commodity for sale; in the other it is a matter of expenses coupled with payment for services rendered – not totally unlike a man paying for the support of the mother of his illegitimate child and supplementing this with a generous present on her bringing it to term. The legality of surrogate motherhood seems, ultimately, to depend on the acceptance or rejection of this principle because it will be hard to legitimate the child unless its birth is linked with subsequent legal adoption. There are many reasons for this – the surrogate *is* the mother, she is registrable as such and she cannot simply surrender her parental duties;[20] the courts on both sides of the Atlantic would certainly uphold her status in the event of any dispute and there would be a paradoxical presumption of legitimacy were the surrogate married. Two legal possibilities are open to the father. He may attempt custody where his rights are, at best, tenuous and, in practice, virtually non-existent.[1]

17 *Doe v Kelley* (1980) 6 Fam L Rep (BNA) 3011, affd. No 50380 (Ct App May 5, 1981).
18 T M Mady 'Surrogate Mothers: The Legal Issues' (1981) 7 Amer J Law Med 323.
19 See fn. 16, above.
20 Children Act 1975, s. 85(2).
 1 An access order granted to a man in this situation was reversed in the Court of Appeal (*A v C* (1978) 8 Fam Law 170).

Alternatively, he may try, with his wife, to adopt; were the passage of money to have negatived any potential rights or advantages to them, the whole concept of surrogate motherhood would fail on legalistic grounds – but one wonders whether it is right that it should do so if the relevant moral objections can be overcome.

Here, the critical factor is the validity of any contract – does a contract to bear a child for someone else accord with or is it against the public policy? In the United States a Michigan court[2] has indicated a compelling interest in forbidding financial arrangements from creating family relationships. In Britain, one would have to look to fairly old case material. In *Humphrys*,[3] a contract by a mother to give up her illegitimate child was declared invalid by reason of the fact that she could not, in law, divest herself of maternal responsibilities; there was, however, no question of paternity involved and the contract was arranged only after the birth of the child – in any event, the concept of illegitimacy and the laws relating to adoption have changed since the turn of the century. In a Scottish case at about the same time, it was considered very dangerous to allow proof of an agreement to let another keep a child permanently against the wishes of its mother;[4] but, again there was no question of paternity and the 'contract' was dissimilar from that under consideration. There is, however, one recent case[5] in which the judge condemned as being pernicious and void an agreement between a couple and a girl that she should have the man's child by AID for them to keep.[6] It was suggested in *Kerrigan* that there might be liability for financial loss, an idea which leads to a consideration of whether a surrogate motherhood contract, even if acceptable on public policy grounds, could even be binding.

There is no doubt that an abortion under the terms of the Abortion Act 1967 would be an inviolate right of the surrogate; since the reason for the abortion would be medical and beyond the control of the mother, the adoptive parents would probably have no claim for restitution of benefits already paid – they might, as well, be liable for the expenses of the abortion but a great deal would depend upon the specific terms of the contract. Then, what action could be taken in the present state of the law should the sponsoring couple refuse to accept the child or the surrogate refuse to surrender it? The courts would be unlikely to order the specific implementation of the contract. What if

2 See fn. 17, above.
3 *Humphrys v Polak* [1901] 2 KB 385, CA.
4 *Kerrigan v Hall* (1901) 4 F Ct of Sess 10 at 13, per Lord President Balfour.
5 *A v C* (1978) 8 Fam Law 170.
6 Quoted in D C Parker 'Legal Aspects of Artificial Insemination and Embryo Transfer' (1982) 12 Fam Law 103.

the reason for non-acceptance – for example, a deformed infant – was possibly attributable to negligence on the part of the surrogate? It is problems such as these that have led to the suggestion that a legal prohibition of surrogate contracts is unnecessary in view of the impossibility of enforcement of those entered into, given the current state of the law.

A possible policy
The main concern in any of these newer reproductive techniques must, however, be for the resultant child and, while there cannot be any evidence on which to base an opinion, we suggest that there are two major relevant issues. Firstly, any extension of the practice of surrogate motherhood beyond the treatment of the infertile woman – e g to satisfy the needs of employment or simply of convenience – must surely be against the interests of the resultant child and, therefore, against public policy. And, although it is more acceptable genetically, we would extend this prohibition to the rather bizarre possibility of transferring a fertilised ovum of one's own to another woman's uterus – 'womb-leasing'; such a course can be justified on medical grounds, e g heart disease in the wife, but the genetic, emotional and moral complexities are such that an absolute ban is preferable. Secondly, there is the dilemma surrounding disclosure of motherhood. Here it seems possible only to be pragmatic and accept the fact that it is impossible to maintain anonymity of the surrogate mother. Moreover, if the process culminates in adoption, the child has a right to know his or her parentage. It is not established whether it is any more or less traumatic to a child to know he or she is genetically related to his or her father alone rather than knowing there is no more than an environmental association with either parent; but, since both situations are catered for in the Adoption Act, they must both be acceptable to our legislature.

In summary, it would seem that there are circumstances in which surrogate motherhood could be an advantageous procedure but that, at the same time, the practice is open to abuse; there is a strong case for enabling legislation which is, simultaneously, restrictive. We would, therefore, suggest that the practice be legalised subject to several conditions.

Firstly, it should be legal only if tied to authorised adoption; but the fact that an agreement had been made should entitle the intending parents to a preferential right to adoption vis à vis any other potential adopters – this right should be subject only to the now statutory six weeks' post-partum delay for the necessary maternal consent.

Secondly, it should be legal only if it is medically certified as being the appropriate treatment for infertility or other contra-indications to pregnancy. It should be supervised medically by a qualified consultant – this to enforce adequate genetic screening of the surrogate etc. – and it should be accomplished by artificial insemination only; we regard this as essential to avoid the possibility of subsequent divorce proceedings founded on adultery which would have an adverse effect on the child. Thirdly, a contract which allowed for the surrogate's expenses and medical supervision and for the payment of an honorarium on completion of the adoption proceedings would be valid subject to the surrogate's natural right to retain her infant; should she so decide, the only remedy for the genetic father would be to apply for custody on the grounds of the child's best interests – a petition which would be unlikely to succeed if the selection of the mother had been properly supervised.

The overriding interests of the child lead, finally, to a consideration of the problems of legitimacy in both embryo transfer and surrogate motherhood. The conditions, taken together, can give rise to a bewildering array of genetic permutations and, consequently, of legalistic interpretations which are complicated by the *'pater est quem nuptiae demonstrant'* doctrine. There is no need for us to specify these – the reader is equally able to do so – but the wide range of possibilities strongly indicates the need for some form of unifying legislation. We have already indicated our belief that, in the interests of the child, the child born by means of consensual AID should be regarded as, and be registrable as, the legitimate offspring of husband and wife; the same should apply when sperm donation is combined with ovum donation. The potentials for alleviating female infertility argue strongly for some additional concept of *'mater est quam gestatio demonstrat'*; we believe that it should be an irrebuttable presumption that a woman who has carried a child and given birth to it is its mother – no genetic niceties should obscure the fact that these are the essential features of motherhood.

4 The control of fertility

Sterilisation

The aim of sterilisation is to end the patient's ability to reproduce. A number of surgical procedures may be used to achieve this. In males, the most common method is vasectomy, in which the vas deferens is cut or tied. Sterilisation in females is usually achieved by division of the Fallopian tubes which carry the ova between the ovary and the womb. An important feature of the operation from the legal and ethical standpoint is that it is generally considered to be irreversible; although it may, in some circumstances, be possible to repair the operation, attempts to allow for reversibility are likely to result in procedures which fail in their primary purpose. Sterilisation, therefore, constitutes what is, to all intents and purposes, the permanent bringing to an end of an important human function.

Ethical objections to sterilisation usually focus on this aspect of irreversible interference with the ability to reproduce. Those who object on these grounds would argue that such interference is not justified in that the individual may later undergo a change of mind and may wish to return to a position which is now irrevocably closed. This argument would stress that it is often the case that the decision to sterilise is one in which subtle, social and personal pressures are involved; the likelihood of the decision being entirely free is, thereby, diminished. While the sting may be later taken out of other decisions which are not entirely free, this is not the case with sterilisation. The objection of the Catholic Church is more direct. In Catholic teaching, sterilisation is a mutilation of the body which leads to the deprivation of a natural function and is, therefore, to be rejected. Sterilisation can only be accepted if it is carried out for therapeutic purposes – that is, where it is necessary for the physical health of the patient. The performance of hysterectomy in the treatment of menorrhagia, for example, is admissible according to this view although the removal has the effect of sterilising the patient. In so far as it is possible to identify a lay consensus on the matter, it is that sterilisation is an acceptable method of contraception provided that the person undergoing the operation is adequately informed of the implications.

Very strong objections may be voiced, however, when there is any question as to the reality of the patient's consent.

There has, in the past, been some doubt over the legality of sterilisation, even when the patient is an adult and in full possession of his or her mental faculties. A major source of the disquiet lay in the minority judgment of Denning LJ in *Bravery v Bravery*,[1] a divorce case in which a wife sought to establish cruelty on the part of a husband who had undergone a sterilisation operation without her consent and in the face of her frequently expressed desire for more children. In the event, the Court of Appeal rejected the wife's claims, but what is of interest for us is the remarks on the operation which were made by the judges. In Lord Denning's view, a sterilisation operation performed for a 'just cause', such as the prevention of the transmission of a hereditary disease, is quite lawful. But he continued:

> when it is done without just cause or excuse, it is unlawful, even though the man consented to it. Take a case where a sterilisation operation is done so as to enable a man to have the pleasure of sexual intercourse without shouldering the responsibilities attaching to it. The operation then is plainly injurious to the public interest. It is degrading to the man himself. It is injurious to his wife and to any woman whom he may marry . . . It is illegal, even though the man consents to it . . .'.[2]

The basis on which Lord Denning took this view is the criminal law doctrine that consent to injury does not make such injury lawful if its infliction is injurious to the public.[3] By contrast, the majority of judges in this case expressly rejected this reasoning. One of the precedents on which Lord Denning based his judgment involved consent in a prize fight, which may reasonably be held to be injurious to the public interest. The majority felt that this was an inappropriate analogy to a sterilisation operation.

In 1967, the Secretary of the Medical Defence Union wrote:

> We now have no hesitation in advising members of the medical profession in Britain that sterilisation carried out merely on the grounds of personal convenience, in other words as a convenient method of birth control, is a legitimate legal undertaking[4]

1 [1954] 3 All ER 59, CA.
2 [1954] 3 All ER at 67–8.
3 See *R v Coney* (1882) 8 QBD 534. Lord Denning also referred to the famous case of Coke's 'young, strong and lustie rogue' who had a friend cut off his left hand in order to avoid the need to work. See the further discussion of consent in the chapter devoted to transplantation.
4 P Addison 'Legal Aspects of Sterilisation and Contraception' (1967) 35 Medico-Leg J 164.

and the matter is now settled in the United Kingdom by virtue of the fact that provision for vasectomy is made in legislation.[5] The legality of the operation was not called into question by the court in *Re D (a minor)*,[6] a case which is discussed in detail below. As to the Commonwealth, the problem was addressed in the Canadian case of *Cataford v Moreau*[7] in which the Quebec Supreme Court accepted the legality of the operation.[8]

Liability for a failed sterilisation

Liability for a failed sterilisation operation will not be imposed unless it can be established that the failure of the sterilisation to achieve contraceptive results was due to medical negligence rather than to the inherent possibility that conception might occur after an attempted sterilisation. There are no reported cases on this matter in the United Kingdom, but there are useful Canadian decisions and also a considerable body of American case law on the subject.

In the Canadian case of *Doiron v Orr*[9] the plaintiff agreed to a sterilisation operation by means of a procedure which was more reversible than was the conventional tubal ligation method. The plaintiff subsequently became pregnant. The judge accepted that there was no liability on the part of the doctor performing the operation, negligence not having been established, but the question of damages was fairly fully discussed by the court. The judge stated that he would have been prepared to award damages for mental anguish caused to the plaintiff, but was adamant in his refusal to accept that in such a case there could be liability for the cost of bringing up an unwanted child:

> I find this approach to a matter of this kind which deals with human life, the happiness of the child, the effect upon its thinking, upon its mind when it realised that there has been a case of this kind, that it is an unwanted mistake and that its rearing is being paid for by someone other than its parents, is just simply grotesque.[10]

Damages for sterilisation negligently performed were awarded in *Cataford v Moreau*.[7] In this case the patient was a woman who had had 10 children already and had agreed to undergo sterilisation in

5 National Health Service (Family Planning) Amendment Act 1972.
6 [1976] Fam 185, [1976] 1 All ER 326.
7 (1978) 114 DLR (3d) 585. This case is discussed by R P Kouri in 'Comment' (1979) 57 Can Bar Rev 89.
8 See, in general, R P Kouri 'The Legality of Purely Contraceptive Sterilisation' (1976) 7 Revue de droit de l'Université de Sherbrook 1.
9 (1978) 86 DLR (3d) 719.
10 Per Garrett J at 722.

order to avoid the birth of further children. When she subsequently gave birth to her eleventh child, an action was instituted against the doctor, claiming damages in respect of loss of enjoyment of life due to interrupted sexual relations, inconvenience and anxiety in giving birth to an eleventh child, general pain and suffering and pain and suffering in respect of the subsequent operation which was necessary to ensure effective sterilisation. In addition, the plaintiff, as in *Doiron v Orr*, claimed for the cost of bringing up the unwanted child.

The Supreme Court of Quebec, unlike the High Court of Ontario in *Doiron v Orr*, did not expressly exclude the availability of damages in respect of the cost of bringing up the child. The court declined to pronounce on the competence of such a claim but remarked that in any event the cost of bringing up the child would be almost off-set by welfare allowances received in respect of it, and the balance would be compensated for by the general benefit of having the child.

American courts have not taken a uniform approach to this problem. In some cases the courts have refused to grant damages to parents who have had unwanted children as a result of negligent sterilisation, taking the view that children are a blessing and that parents cannot be considered to be damaged by having them.[11] In others, damages have been awarded not only in respect of the mental anguish involved in an unwanted pregnancy but also, in some instances, in respect of the cost of rearing the child to maturity.[12]

The English case of *Scuriaga v Powell*[13] is not concerned with the sterilisation operation but nonetheless provides some authority. Here the plaintiff consulted a doctor who agreed to perform a legal abortion on her. In the course of the operation the doctor failed to find fetal parts and, instead of referring the plaintiff to a consultant, merely washed his hands of the matter. A healthy child was subsequently born by Caesarian section. The court held that there was no public policy reason preventing a claim against the doctor in such a case and damages were awarded in respect of the diminution of the plaintiff's marriage prospects, pain and suffering, and anxiety and distress.

One of the difficulties that will always be encountered in such cases is that of determining the measure of damages. It may be relatively simple to quantify a loss of earnings and also to make an award under such heads as pain and suffering; what is much more problematical is

11 *Terrell v Garcia* 496 SW 2d 124 (1973).
12 *Troppi v Scarf* 186 NW 2d 511 (1971). For an analysis of these cases, see E G Sarno 'Tort Liability for Wrongfully Causing One to be Born' 83 ALR 3d 15; H H Clark 'Wrongful Conception: a New Kind of Medical Malpractice' (1979) 12 Fam L Q 259.
13 (1979) 123 Sol Jo 406.

the task of deciding to what degree the plaintiff has suffered by being 'burdened' with a child whose birth it was sought to avoid. Against a claim that such a child would be an unmitigated burden, it can be argued that the plaintiff is bound, nonetheless, to be enriched to some extent by the child's presence in the home. But how does the court assess the financial value of the joy and companionship which a child may bring? The problem here is essentially the same one the courts face in respect of assessing the negative value of pain or anxiety but the fact that such assessments are made regularly in these fields does not seem to encourage the courts in their task of assessing the value of an unwanted child.

The court may have considerable misgivings in burdening the medical defendant with the cost of the child's upkeep for the period of its minority. This sort of expense is different in an important sense from such expenses as those of the hospital treatment of an injured plaintiff which, clearly, are a justifiable burden on the person who negligently caused the injuries. In the case of a failed sterilisation, however, it may be felt that the plaintiff is attempting to pass on to the defendant the full costs of a child for whose existence he, the plaintiff, may be said, at the very least, to share responsibility with the negligent doctor.

Non-consensual sterilisation

If consensual sterilisation raises certain ethical misgivings, then non-consensual sterilisation is a minefield of powerful objection. This form of sterilisation has been carried out in some countries as an official or unofficial part of programmes of eugenic improvement or birth control. In the United States, for example, the enthusiasm for eugenics which was the feature of the earlier part of this century led to legislative measures in a number of States providing for the sterilisation of mental defectives, those suffering from certain forms of genetically transmissible disease and, in some cases, criminal recidivists.[14] Such laws were declared unconstitutional in some States and, in others, the number of compulsory sterilisations carried out were small but compulsory sterilisation measures remain on the statute books in a number of jurisdictions. In those American States where no legislative authorisation exists, the courts would be prepared to allow sterilisation provided they were satisfied of the justification for the procedure.[15]

14 D W Meyers *The Human Body and the Law* (1970) pp. 28ff.
15 For example, in *Re Grady* 405 A 2d 851 (1979) the court authorised the sterilisation of an 18 year old girl suffering from Down's syndrome. In this case, consent was sought by the parents.

In England, the decision of Heilbron J in *Re D (a minor)*[16] demonstrates that the courts will be extremely cautious in respect of any attempt at the sterilisation of a minor or of a person who, through mental handicap, is incapable of looking after his or her own interests. The minor in this case was an 11 year old girl who suffered from a rare condition known as Sotos' syndrome. This condition involved, among other symptoms, epileptic seizures, clumsiness, dull intelligence, precocious growth and a variety of personality problems. The girl's IQ was roughly 80, a rating which need not necessarily make it impossible for the person in question to cope reasonably well in everyday life and even to marry and raise a child. There was medical evidence to the effect that these conditions showed some signs of improvement and that this improvement could continue.

Approached by the mother, D's doctor agreed that sterilisation was appropriate, the basis for this decision including both medical and social grounds. The medical grounds were that there was a risk that D might give birth to an abnormal baby, that her epilepsy might cause her to harm the baby and that the only satisfactory method of birth control was sterilisation. Socially, it was felt that she would be unable to cope with a family and could only survive in a sheltered environment.

In her judgment in this case, Heilbron J was strongly swayed by the medical evidence given to the court to the effect that sterilisation was not always appropriate in such cases and that such a decision was not within the scope of the clinical judgment of a single doctor dealing with the case. Also to be taken into account was the irreversibility of the operation and the significance of carrying it out on so young a person:

> A review of the whole of the evidence leads me to the conclusion that in a case of a child of 11 years of age, where the evidence shows that her mental and physical condition and attainments have already improved, and where her future prospects are as yet unpredictable, where the evidence also shows that she is unable as yet to understand and appreciate the implications of this operation and could not give a valid or informed consent, that the likelihood is that in later years she will be able to make her own choice, where, I believe, the frustration and resentment of realising (as she would one day) what had happened could be devastating, an operation of this nature is, in my view contra-indicated.[17]

The child in *Re D* obviously fell into the category of those mentally handicapped persons who should not be subjected to non-consensual sterilisation. Where there is a more substantial handicap, however,

16 [1976] Fam 185, [1976] 1 All ER 326.
17 [1976] Fam at 196.

the position may well be less clear-cut. If a mentally handicapped person is quite incapable of raising a family and where the prognosis definitely excludes any improvement, it is possible to put forward a much more convincing case for sterilisation if that is shown to be the only realistic method of birth control in the circumstances. The alternative is to allow a person manifestly ill-suited for the bearing of children to saddle the community with the cost of raising children who will themselves, unless adopted, be deprived of the opportunity of a normal upbringing. This argument, of course, leads one into the extremely difficult area of determining the precise ambit of the right to reproduce. If this right exists, then is it an absolute one, to be exercised by whomsoever pleases to exercise it? Or is it a socially defined right, one which may legitimately be limited by the community in certain cases? A consequence of regarding the right as absolute must be to accept the possibility of the exercise of the right by those who are not fully aware of the implications of their actions and who are incapable of assuming even the minimal responsibility of parenthood.

There seems to be no set public policy on this issue but at least 14 children under the age of 16 together with a further 22 aged between 16 and 18 years were sterilised in England during 1973–4.[18] It can be assumed that the great majority were mentally subnormal but it is to be noted that these figures pre-date the decision in *Re D*. The argument that society is greatly disadvantaged by abnormal – and not necessarily mentally abnormal – children being born to unsatisfactory mothers is forceful but is balanced by the alternative view that certain human rights – amongst them, the right to have children – are part of the natural law and apply equally to the normal and the abnormal. Moreover, one wonders whether doctors should be able to take what is essentially a social decision independently and the rights of parents to consent to non-therapeutic measures on behalf of their children is disputed. It may well be that the problem is not so widespread as is often supposed and that it can be contained by the Abortion Act 1967 which is one expression of society's view on eugenic or social birth control. We would, therefore, suggest that irrevocable sterilisation should not be carried out on children under the age of 16 without the approval of the court and that a similar attitude should be adopted in respect of adults who, by reason of subnormality, are unable to give an autonomous informed consent.[19]

18 G Porter in 'Child Sterilisation' (1975) 1 J Med Ethics 163.
19 The question of whether a parent could give consent to the sterilisation of a mentally retarded adult was considered in the Canadian case *Re Eve* (1981) 115 DLR (3d) 283. The court decided that this was possible. For criticism of this decision, see B Starkman 'Sterilisation of the Mentally Retarded Adult: the Eve case' (1981) 26 McGill Law J 931.

Other forms of contraception

The legal and ethical issues thrown up by other forms of contraception are mainly limited to the question of their provision to minors. The ethical dilemma of a doctor who is consulted by a minor female patient requesting contraceptive prescription is that of deciding whether he should do anything which might facilitate her engaging in sexual activity. If his patient is, say, 14 or 15, he may well be of the view, which would be shared by the vast majority of adults, that 14 or 15 is too young an age for sexual intercourse. This need not be on the grounds of disapproval of sexual intercourse outside marriage; the disapproval is more likely to be based on the view that sexual activity at such an age may lead to emotional trauma which is best avoided. On the other hand, a refusal to prescribe contraceptives may ultimately be more damaging to the patient in that sexual activity, once embarked upon, is likely to be continued and may result in pregnancy. While emotional upset is not uncommonly recovered from fairly quickly, giving birth to a child at such an age is likely to be severely disruptive of the patient's life. If pregnancy were to be legally terminated then, although the disruption would be less, the major psychological risk entailed in abortion would have to be taken into account.

The ethical dilemma by no means disappears once the decision is taken to provide contraception; the doctor then has to make the difficult decision whether or not to inform the patient's parents. This is really an issue of medical confidentiality which is discussed in detail in chapter 8, below. The decision in each case would, however, depend on the circumstances. A doctor who informs parents of the fact that their 13 year old daughter has taken to prostitution could surely claim that it was in the best interests of the child to do so; this may not be the case when a 15 year old girl is doing no more than engaging in sexual activity with one partner.

Two distinct legal issues are raised in this connection. The first is the question as to whether the doctor can properly treat a minor without the consent of the parents. We believe that parental consent is required for the treatment of a child below the age of 16 unless the treatment can be justified on the grounds of necessity or unless it can be demonstrated that the minor was capable of giving an informed consent.[20] In practice, there would be few cases where the minor seeking contraception would be held to be incapable of giving a perfectly valid consent to the treatment involved.

The second issue – the question of the potential criminal liability of

---

20 See further discussion of consent and minors in chapter 9, below.

the doctor in these circumstances – continues to feature in debate. Can a doctor who provides contraceptive advice to a girl under the age of consent be said to be party to the offence committed by the man who has sexual intercourse with her? There is no British case in point, but the matter was dealt with by the Supreme Court of Australia in *Casey v Grossman*.[1] The charge in this case was that the selling of contraceptives to a child was an act likely to lead the child to follow a career of vice. The court, however, took the view that no cause or connection has been established between the selling of the contraceptives and the actual pursuit of a career of vice. It is probable that the same view would be taken in the unlikely event of the matter ever coming before the British courts and the doctor's act would be held to be causally irrelevant so far as the act of illegal intercourse was concerned.[2] Nevertheless, the doctor has an obvious ethical duty to encourage the girl to discuss the matter with her parents, to warn her of the dangers of both oral contraception and of pregnancy and to tell her what she may well not know – that, if sexual intercourse did occur, her male friend would be committing a criminal offence.

Post coital contraception
Certain types of contraception are designed to or, in practice, do work after the embryo has formed. These are referred to as interceptive methods – of which the intra-uterine device is the prime example – or displanting methods which include the so called 'morning after' pills. Menstrual extraction, which is performed as soon as a period has been missed, also comes into this category. The legal difficulty is that, strictly speaking, such methods are abortifacient rather than contraceptive and are, therefore, illegal in so far as they are not protected by the Abortion Act 1967. Possibly excepting the deliberate act of menstrual extraction, which is referred to in slightly greater detail in chapter 5, below, such a conclusion is absurd; the use of an IUD is, both physically and morally, infinitely preferable to the legal destruction of a recognisable human fetus. The neglect of the law in this field has been described as 'disgraceful' and a plea has been made, with which we would agree wholeheartedly, that these valuable methods of contraception should be put beyond prosecution.[3]

1 (1949) 51 WALR 77.
2 Nor is it likely that the doctor could be accused of counselling and procuring. See the review article in (1980) 281 Brit Med J 318.
3 V Tunkel 'Abortion: How Early, How Late, and How Legal?' (1979) 2 Brit Med J 253.

5 Abortion

The essential interest in legal abortion is not whether it should be allowed; the practice has been with us since the passing of the Abortion Act 1967 and it is here to stay. Rather, the current significance of abortion lies in the effect it has had on medical thinking. The moment the Act was accepted by doctors was the moment the profession abrogated a main tenet of its Hippocratic conscience – as late as 1968, the Declaration of Geneva, as amended in Sydney, was reiterating 'I will maintain the utmost respect for human life from the time of conception' (appendix B). By 1970, the Declaration of Oslo, while retaining this moral principle, had changed the tune: 'Diversity of response to this situation [the conflict of vital interests of the mother with vital interests of the child] results from the diversity of attitudes towards the life of the unborn child. This is a matter of individual conviction and conscience' (appendix E). This ethical watershed has spilled over to influence the attitude of doctors and to doctors in relation to all aspects of life and death – while we pay homage to Vishnu, we give due regard to Shiva. For the first time, modern medicine is flirting with the concept of the wanted and the unwanted. The ethos underlying legal abortion is, if only historically, still an important issue; future developments in the field are of immediate concern.

The evolution of the law on abortion

The evolution of legislation to decriminalise abortion is so well known as to merit only brief description. The fundamental law in England and Wales lies in the Offences Against the Person Act 1861, sections 58 and 59. The Act proscribes abortion of a woman by a third party, self-induced abortion, attempted abortion and supplying the means of abortion. It makes no distinction between criminal and therapeutic activity and has not been repealed. The proscription was so strong that, in addition to being punished by the courts, a doctor involved in an abortion was extremely likely to have his name erased from the Medical Register. As a result, and because of the attitudes adopted to extra-marital pregnancy, a large number of abortions were performed by persons of varying skill and in varying conditions; many women died, were mutilated or were poisoned by potent drugs which had little value in their intended purpose. The extent of this type of abortion has never been established; suffice it to say that, 40 years ago, it provided an appreciable contribution to forensic pathology.

The first statutory break in this melancholy chain of events is to be found in the Infant Life (Preservation) Act 1929 which introduced the offence of child destruction or causing the death of a child capable of being born alive before it has an existence independent of its mother. The offence was not committed, however, if the act was done in good faith for the purpose only of preserving the mother's life. This slight concession to the needs of therapy was, on the face of it, still highly restrictive both as to reason and as to time. It was left to the case of *R v Bourne*[1] to temper the legal influence on medical practice in the field. Mr Bourne performed an abortion, with no attempt at secrecy, on a 15 year old girl who was pregnant following a particularly unpleasant rape. Although he was indicted under the Offences Against the Person Act 1861, he was clearly challenging the Infant Life (Preservation) Act 1929 – a point which McNaughten J effectively accepted when he linked the two statutes and ruled that, in a case brought under the 1861 Act, the burden rested on the Crown to satisfy the jury that the defendant did not procure the miscarriage of the girl in good faith for the purpose only of preserving her life; the word 'unlawful' in the 1861 Act 'imports the meaning expressed by the proviso in section 1(1) of the Infant Life (Preservation) Act 1929'.[2] Mr Bourne was acquitted, the summing-up essentially recognising that a woman's life depended upon her physical and mental health and that an abortion was not illegal if it was performed because these were in jeopardy.[3] The law and the medical profession then lived in harmony for many years; the *Bourne* decision was undoubtedly stretched to the limits of interpretation by many doctors but the law turned a sympathetic eye.

But it is never a good thing for any section of the public, no matter how well intentioned, to flirt with illegality; moreover, there was still no authority for abortion in the event of probable deformation or other handicap of the fetus when born – a proposition which many would regard as being of the first importance. The situation was resolved when the Abortion Act, which started life as a private

1 [1939] 1 KB 687, [1938] 3 All ER 615. There are several interesting differences of emphasis in the two reports.
2 [1939] 1 KB at 691.
3 [1938] 3 All ER at 619.

member's Bill, was put into law in 1967; it has remained unchanged despite repeated attacks.

It is interesting to compare the historic attitudes in England and in Scotland where abortion, either self or otherwise induced, has been a common law offence without the benefit of statute. The subject, including a review of the 1967 Act, occupies less than three pages in *Gordon*[4] and the difference in concern lies in the Scots emphasis on the evilness of intent in crimes at common law; by and large, doctors are assumed to be acting in good faith and there is no doubt that Mr Bourne would have been unable to provoke a test case in Scotland. The 1967 Act, which applies throughout the United Kingdom except for Northern Ireland, states at section 5(1): 'nothing in this Act shall affect the provisions of the Infant Life (Preservation) Act 1929' – the purpose being to limit the circumstances in which abortion may be carried out legally beyond the 28th week of pregnancy. Since the 1929 Act does not run to Scotland, it follows that, even now, the Scots law on abortion is more liberal than is the English.

The Abortion Act 1967
In summary, the 1967 Act states that a person shall not be guilty of an offence under the law of abortion when termination is performed by a registered medical practitioner and two registered medical practitioners have formed the opinion in good faith that the continuance of the pregnancy would either involve risk to the life of the pregnant woman – the life-saving ground, or risk of injury to the physical or mental health of the pregnant woman – the therapeutic ground, or risk of injury to the physical or mental health of any existing children of her family – the social clause; all these conditions are subject to the risk being greater than if the pregnancy were terminated. The pregnancy may also be legally terminated if it is considered that there is a substantial risk that if the child is born it will suffer from such physical or mental abnormalities as to be severely handicapped – the eugenic clause. Termination under the Act may be carried out in National Health Service Hospitals or in places approved for the purpose by the Minister or the Secretary of State (section 1(3)). It is this clause which legalises abortions performed privately and for a fee.

The great majority of legal abortions are performed for therapeutic reasons (94.4 per cent of Scottish cases in 1979) and it is clearly a complex problem to decide whether the risk of injury from

4 G H Gordon *The Criminal Law of Scotland* (2nd edn, 1978) ch 28.

continuance is greater than if the pregnancy were terminated.[5] The ethical basis of the Abortion Act thus depends to a large extent on the words 'in good faith'. There is an interesting distinction between Scotland and England as to where abortions are performed. In Scotland in 1979, 2.5 per cent of abortions were carried out in approved places where the absence of good faith, if there is any such lack, is most likely to express itself; the comparative figure in England was 63 per cent or 54 per cent if foreign women are excluded. There has always been a feeling that the concentration of approved places within easy reach of major airports and the like has indicated something less than strict adherence to the Act but the 1974 Lane Committee[6] recommended very few changes. Moreover, the medical profession as a whole has resisted the various Amendment Bills on the grounds that the Act is working adequately and that, where it is failing, it is doing so because of inadequate facilities.[7] From the legal aspect, we have been able to find only one conviction under the Act[8] and this appears to have arisen mainly because of the way the operation was performed.

The comparative position

Usage has, undoubtedly, extended the scope of the Abortion Act; many would say that its present application, which effectively extends to abortion on demand for those who can pay for it, goes far beyond that envisaged by its originators. Gardner,[9] referring in somewhat emotional terms to the erosion of its principles, wrote 'the Abortion Act has got cancer'. It is tempting to attribute this to the growth of private practice in the field, but experience in America shows that the same path can be plotted through legal influence. Abortion laws in the mid-twentieth century differed in the various States of the USA. Some, as in New York, were wholly liberal; some, as in Texas, corresponded roughly to the English Infant Life (Preservation) Act; but the majority followed variations of the UK Abortion Act. Then, in 1973, the Supreme Court, with what might be regarded as a left and

5 The risks of pregnancy and childbirth are not constant. Overall, the mortality rates following child birth and abortion are about equal but the risk of pregnancy increases with age. Conversely, the risks of abortion in young nulliparae are relatively greater than of pregnancy unless the procedure is completed in the first eight weeks of pregnancy (P R Myerscough (1975) 1 J Med Ethics 130).
6 Report of the Committee on the Working of the Abortion Act (Cmnd 5579).
7 T Smith 'Abortion (Amendment) Bill' (1979) 5 J Med Ethics 209.
8 *R v Smith (John)* [1974] 1 All ER 376, [1973] 1 WLR 1510, CA.
9 R F R Gardner 'A New Ethical Approach to Abortion and its Implications for the Euthanasia Dispute' (1975) 1 J Med Ethics 127.

a right hook – *Roe v Wade*[10] and *Doe v Bolton*[11] – silenced the traditionalist cause. The effect of these decisions has been detailed by Shapiro[12] but can be summarised: it is an invasion of a woman's constitutional right to privacy to limit her access to abortion by statute – and this applies also to schoolchildren although their parents may still be informed of the circumstances;[13] the expression 'to preserve the life' of a woman is unconstitutionally vague although 'to preserve the life or health' is acceptable – which raises an intriguing conflict. It has been suggested[14] that health is inclusive of convenience which effectively allows for abortion on demand – this despite the fact that the Supreme Court specifically stated that such was not an absolute constitutional right. To confirm the principles involved, the Court also ruled that an appeal on the grounds that wholly liberal laws were invalid because they deprived unborn children of the right to life was not available to an individual. Nevertheless, the Court did give some regard to the rights of the developing fetus. In the first trimester, the question of abortion was to be decided solely between the woman and her physician; during the second trimester, the State could intervene by reason of its interest in the health of the mother, no such interest being vested in the fetus – interference of this type could include stating where and by whom an abortion could be done. After 'viability', which the Court assessed as somewhere between the 24th and 28th week of pregnancy, it was agreed that the State had a compelling interest in the health of the fetus and could, therefore, constitutionally intervene on its behalf excepting when the conditions threaten the life or health of the mother. All this would, however, seem to be subject to the laws of economics; it has subsequently been determined that federal funding in the form of 'Medicaid' is available for abortions only in limited circumstances – such as preserving the life of the mother or terminating pregnancies resulting from rape or incest – and that, accordingly, the individual State health systems need not contribute towards expenses incurred on other grounds.[15]

The rights of the fetus

Roe v Wade highlights the fundamental ethical issue in abortion – at

10 93 S Ct 705 (1973).
11 35 L Ed 2d 201 (1973).
12 S R Shapiro 'Validity under Federal Constitution of Abortion Laws' (1973) 35 L Ed 2d 735.
13 *HL v Matheson* 101 S Ct 1164 (1981).
14 J H Ely 'The Wages of Crying Wolf: A Comment on *Roe v Wade*' (1973) 82 Yale Law J 920.
15 *Harris v McRae* 100 S Ct 2671 (1980).

what point does a fetus become a person and at what point does that person have rights to an existence? At one extreme lies the strict legal principle – slightly eroded by the Congenital Disabilities (Civil Liability) Act 1976 – that no rights are vested in a human being until it has achieved a separate existence from its mother; at the other, there is the conservative religious view, as exemplified by Roman Catholicism, that the fetus has, and should be regarded as having, a life of its own from the time of conception. Without wishing to prolong the debate, we suggest that few other than academic theologians would accept the practicability of the latter tenet. Equally, there cannot be many who would seriously uphold the view that the fetus is no more than a complex cellular appendage to its mother – the 'wart on the face' philosophy falls down if only on genetic principles. Some middle view has to be reached if we are not to drift into accepting the principle that the unwanted should be destroyed simply because they are unwanted – Ely[16] remarked, in relation to the right to privacy, that there is not a wide difference between being inconvenienced by a fetus and being inconvenienced by an unwanted infant. Philosophically, there is much to commend Gardner's concept of the maternal-fetal unity, if for no other reason than that it forces consideration of the individual pregnant woman rather than simply of a woman or of a fetus – a dichotomy which must provoke polarised opinion.

Although such a concept cannot now obtain legally, the precise status of the fetus does have purely legal connotations particularly at the beginning and towards the end of pregnancy.[17] The 1967 Act deals with the termination of pregnancy but certain procedures, in particular menstrual extraction, are performed partly because a pregnancy might exist and before any definite diagnosis can be made. The Lane Committee[18] made recommendations to cover such operations but, in the absence of any amendment to the Act, the state of the law is uncertain – whether or not there is attempted compliance with the conditions laid down in the Act. 'Post-coital contraception' is that form of 'after the fact' action to prevent the birth of an unwanted baby which is least likely to offend the public conscience and it is ridiculous that it may be uniquely liable to censure under the Offences against the Person Act, section 58. It is difficult to conceive of anyone bringing a prosecution in these circumstances but it remains another point of contact between good faith and criminality.

16 See fn. 14, above.
17 V Tunkel 'Abortion: How Early, How Late, and How Legal?' (1979) 2 Brit Med J 253.
18 Report of the Committee on the Working of the Abortion Act (Cmnd 5579).

The problem is far more real at the other end of pregnancy when both legal and ethical considerations are concerned with 'viability'. 'Viability' is something of a legal fiction designed to define some point at which the fetus can be presumed to be capable of an existence separate from its mother. As has been seen, the US Supreme Court puts this point at between the 24th and 28th week of pregnancy while English law sets it at 28 weeks. These must be construed as being in the nature of safety, or maximum, limits. Philosophically, many would equate the point of 'viability' with 'quickening' – a concept which clearly invokes some form of 'ensoulment'. But any such definition is a generalisation which ignores the ultimate test of viability which is the capacity of the fetus to live – and this, itself, is a compound of the state of the fetus and of its environment, including the efforts of its attendants. Inevitably, therefore, late abortions may result in births which could survive in a sophisticated environment or, indeed, would survive unless deprived of attention. What, then, is to be done about an aborted infant who 'breathed or showed other signs of life' after delivery? On the one hand, the gynaecologist has effectively contracted to relieve a woman of her fetus. On the other, he is confronted by an infant who, on any interpretation, is entitled to a birth certificate and, if necessary, a certificate as to the cause of death;[19] the Infant Life (Preservation) Act is presumptive only – in no way does it infer that a fetus of less than 28 weeks gestation is *not* capable of a separate existence. As Tunkel has carefully argued,[20] failure to attempt to sustain the living infant could result in charges of, either, attempted child destruction or of actual homicide. Legal precedents are lacking in Great Britain and, what few there are, are inconsistent. In one case, an Area Health Authority inquiry concluded that allowing an aborted fetus to die was an action which was fully within the law. In another, where an infant lived for 36 hours after having been aborted at 23 weeks, the Coroner found that death was due to prematurity and that there was no culpability on the part of the medical staff. In America, Dr Waddill, who ordered 'oxygen only' for a 26 week delivered fetus, was not so fortunate.[1] He was brought to trial for murder and two juries failed to agree, whereupon all criminal charges were dismissed.

It seems unfortunate that resolution of the question of legality should rest on a 'hung' jury but the practical dilemma is acute and difficult to solve. One can only suggest that such abortions as can and

---

19 See Lord Wells-Pestell, 355 HL Official Report (5th series) col 776 (12 December 1974).
20 See fn. 17, above.
 1 B Towers 'The Trials of Dr Waddill' (1979) 5 J Med Ethics 205.

do live should be regarded as parentless infants and be offered for adoption on that basis – it is hardly likely that there would be any shortage of potential adoptive parents provided the process was simplified to accord with the unusual circumstances. In theory, it is difficult to see how a 'let it die' attitude could easily avoid a Coroner's finding of 'death due to want of attention at birth' and subsequent action in criminal law. But the protection of doctors is not the real issue – this lies in the near impossibility of distinguishing medically the mature abortion from the premature birth when both are crying for the incubator. If the distinction is made on a 'will and pleasure' basis it is a very small step to ignoring the unwanted full-term infant who is crying for food. The frontier between abortion and neonaticide has then been crossed without difficulty and is discussed in chapter 7, below.

Other people's rights

The great majority of what is written on the subject of abortion is directed to a discussion of the rights of the mother and the fetus – comparatively little attention is given to those who participate as third parties.

Conscientious objection

This unconcern may well spring from the fact that the Abortion Act (at section 4) excuses the conscientious objector from participating in treatment by abortion unless that treatment is directed towards the saving of life or of preventing grave permanent injury to the health of the mother. But, while this would seem to be perfectly clear, the doctor's situation is not uncomplicated.

The curious provision which stipulates that the English doctor must prove his conscience while his Scottish counterpart's sworn word will, quite properly, be accepted at face value is illogical but is of minor significance. Of greater importance is the undeniable and unfortunate result of the 1967 Act that the profession of gynaecologist is now virtually closed to those who feel unable to accept its wide terms, whether this be on religious or on Hippocratic grounds. Even so, while a doctor may, in general, refuse to take part in the abortion procedure, he remains under an obligation to advise. Such advice is subject to the normal rules of medical negligence and the conscientious objector's only recourse is, therefore, to refer his patient to another practitioner, a practice which is only marginally compatible with a strong conscience and which must damage the essential bond of trust between doctor and patient. There is, of course, no right to conscience in treating the *results* of a legal abortion and these considerations apply equally to the nursing staff.

The nursing staff

The role of the nurse in therapy of all sorts is becoming more significant; this is exemplified in the sphere of abortion by the increasing use of prostaglandin infusions for induction of premature labour. Nurses have so great a part to play in this process that some doubt was raised as to whether they were, in fact, thus guilty of performing illegal abortions in the sense that they were not 'registered medical practitioners' as required by the Act; the Royal College of Nursing accordingly sought a declaration to the effect that the advice in a departmental circular[2] to the effect that, irrespective of the precise action taken, an abortion was legal provided that it was initiated by and was the responsibility of a registered medical practitioner, was wrong in law. The complexities were such that the Royal College lost its case in the High Court, won it in the Court of Appeal and, finally, lost it in the House of Lords.[3] Effectively, therefore, abortion, no matter how it is performed, is a team effort and is no different in this respect, from any other form of treatment. It is, nevertheless, interesting that, in total, five out of nine judges involved took the view of the nurses.

The father

The anomalous position of the father in the right to life debate also falls to be considered. In fact, it is clear from both British and American decisions that, in so far as abortion is concerned, he has *no* rights.[4] It seems incongruous that this should be so irrespective of the reason for the abortion and that it should apply even in cases which do not relate to the health of the mother; a father could not, for example, save the existence of a *potentially* haemophiliac son.

The nature of duty

Yet the issues are not completely solved. Stephenson LJ has asked, in

---

2 (CMO(80)(2)).

3 *Royal College of Nursing of the United Kingdom v Department of Health and Social Security* [1981] AC 800, [1981] 1 All ER 545, HL.

4 *Paton v British Pregnancy Advisory Service Trustees* [1979] QB 276, [1978] 2 All ER 987; *Planned Parenthood of Missouri v Danforth* 428 US 52 69 (1976). The decision in *Paton* was upheld by the European Commission of Human Rights (*Paton v United Kingdom* [1980] 3 EHRR 408). The Commission was, however, clearly worried – but, nevertheless, indecisive – as to the rights of the fetus in later life (cf *Roe v Wade*, above).

a different context (see chapter 6, below), how there could be imposed upon a doctor a duty toward the child to take away life by means of abortion:

> to impose such a duty towards the child would be to make a further inroad – in addition to that created by the Abortion Act 1967 – into the sanctity of human life which would be contrary to public policy.[5]

This view is not easy to accept as, apart from the saving of the mother's life, the 'eugenic' clause of the Abortion Act is probably that part which offends the Hippocratic conscience least.

However, the observations were directed at the rights of the fetus and Stephenson LJ also stated that there might be a duty to the mother to give her an opportunity to have the life of the fetus terminated – the possibility of a negligence action against the doctor who failed in that duty would, therefore, remain, and in the final analysis, the precise legal determinants of an action are of little personal concern to the defendant.[6]

---

5 In *McKay v The Essex Area Health Authority* [1982] 2 WLR 890 at 902, CA.
6 At the time of writing, *McKay* is proceeding to trial on this point.

6 Prenatal screening and wrongful life

The importance of genetically dependent diseases is rising as there is increasing control of those due to infection. Currently, the proportion of childhood deaths attributable wholly or partly to genetic factors runs at about 50 per cent.

Types of genetic disease

Genetic diseases are of three main types. Some are chromosomal – the structure or the number of chromosomes is altered and typical disease states arise, many of these being associated with mental illness. The classic example is Down's syndrome or mongolism. Some chromosomal abnormalities increase markedly with maternal age. Approximately 2 per cent of women aged 40 will produce a chromosomally defective child, half of these suffering from Down's syndrome; by the age of 45, the risk of a mongol child rises to about 4 per cent. There is some evidence that advanced paternal age may also be a risk factor.

The second group of inherited diseases includes those conditions described as unifactorial in origin. Genes are positioned on chromosomes which exist in the cells in pairs, one member of each pair being derived from each parent. Unifactorial disease results from the presence of a specific abnormal gene and, since either of a pair of genes can be donated at random by either parent to their offspring, it is a simple calculation to determine the statistical probability of an infant being so endowed (see Fig. 1, p. 73, below). The genes may be 'autosomal dominants' in which case they will express themselves, in this case as a disease, when the pair of genes contains only one which is abnormal. Normal natural selection should lead to the eradication of dangerous dominant genes. They may arise by mutation, or spontaneous change, a process which is greatly augmented by, say, ionising radiation, or the gene may possess some special attribute – Huntingdon's chorea, for example, persists because the symptoms associated with the responsible gene often do not appear until after marriage and procreation. Alternatively, the gene may be

66

an 'autosomal recessive' in which case its expression is repressed by its normal dominant partner. Those persons possessing a single abnormal recessive gene will be 'carriers' of the disease with which it is associated. Frank disease will result only if an individual inherits the same two recessive genes – which means that both parents must have been carriers or one was a carrier and the other diseased; this, incidentally, provides the genetic basis for discouraging in-breeding.

Finally, unifactorial disease may be 'sex-linked' – or, better, 'X-linked'. Simplistically, this implies that the abnormal gene is present on part of the X chromosome which has no counterpart on the Y chromosome, the possession of which determines maleness. An abnormal recessive X-linked gene will be suppressed in the female by the dominant normal gene on the other X chromosome; it will, however, be free to express itself when coupled in the male XY configuration. Haemophilia is a classic example of such a disease.

Another group of disorders, referred to as multifactorial traits, are believed to be the result of both environmental factors and the effects of many genes. The environmental factors may be of several types and interactions and it is, therefore, generally impossible to predict mathematically the occurrence of this commonest type of genetic disorder. Coronary heart disease, for example, is to some extent genetically determined but the occurrence of symptoms will depend upon a number of uncertain features such as the potential patient's job, diet, recreation and smoking habits. Neural tube defects – spina bifida and anencephaly – represent the most important multifactorial diseases in the present context.

Some form of behavioural or surgical treatment is, therefore, available for those suffering from multifactorial disease and the same is true for a few unifactorial conditions. But there is no curative treatment for most of the more serious genetic disorders, the control of which then depends on prevention. This is primarily the function of the genetic counsellor.

Genetic counselling

Thus baldly put, the task seems easy; in practice, it abounds with practical, ethical and, inevitably, legal problems. Modern genetic counselling is more than merely quoting risks. The tendency is to avoid a directive approach but, rather, to concentrate on the psychological circumstances so that the couples can be led to make decisions which are right for them rather than right for the scientists. Almost inevitably, however, the counsellor's opinion will be sought and how this is reached depends particularly on whether the counselling is retrospective or prospective – are parents seeking advice because they already have an abnormal child or is the consultation based on information available from other sources?

If the latter be the reason, the extent of ethical difficulty depends on whether the couple are actually seeking advice or whether this is being offered to them. A request for guidance implies foreknowledge and understanding and poses relatively few problems. But what of the 85 per cent of high risk couples who are reported as having no knowledge of their condition? Information as to this must have come to the counsellor in ways which may well raise issues of confidentiality particularly if those being counselled require to know the source. The problem of confidentiality has been considered by those advocating genetic registers, several of which are successfully operated and which are approved by the World Health Organisation; safeguards include that no-one shall be placed on the register without their consent and that security of access is strictly controlled.[1]

Even so, while the prevention of genetic disease must be wholly admirable community medicine, there are difficulties when the principles are applied to the individual. Should one impose knowledge on someone who has not sought it and who may well, perhaps irrationally, be disturbed as a consequence? At what stage should this knowledge be used? It is arguable that premarital advice is preferable to prenatal warning but such a policy would have scarcely acceptable implications. On the other hand, has a doctor a moral duty to impose counselling? It might almost be asked if there is a legal duty in so far as an action might be brought were parents to discover after the birth of an abnormal child that relevant information had been available. For our part, we believe that, once the information is available, there is both a moral and a legal duty to use it but that this is determined to some extent by the severity of the condition and by the probability of it being passed on to children – this being in accordance with the general policy of genetic registrars to concern themselves only with 10 per cent or greater risks. Perhaps illogically, we would feel that information and guidance which have not been requested should be given only in the event of pregnancy – many who would resent gratuitous advice that they were, or might be, carriers of a disease would adopt a completely different attitude were it known that a child was involved. The force of the counter-argument is, however, appreciated. In any event, the information should be passed only to the general practitioner of the subject; he alone is able to assess the situation in the light of all the background knowledge.

1 For a review of the principles of genetic registers see A E H Emery et al, 'A Report on Genetic Registers' (1978) 15 J Med Genet 435.

But, in the great majority of cases, the genetic counsellor will be consulted retrospectively because an abnormal child has been born and his opinion is asked as to the advisability of further pregnancy. The solution of the problem is still difficult but, with one exception, the goal is reasonably clear. The exceptional difficulty arises, again, in connection with other members of the family, especially the siblings of the unfortunate parents. Given the fact that the doctor or his specialist advisor now knows that they are in the high risk category, should he so inform them? Clearly, this cannot be done without the consent of the affected couple but, even when this is given, the problems of providing unsought, and perhaps unwanted, information are revived. There are, in our opinion, unassailable reasons why the relatives should not be informed direct but there seems little doubt that their practitioners should be advised of the position. His decision must, in turn, depend upon the severity of the disease and the likelihood of its reappearing; he must also be influenced by the family circumstances as a whole.

As to the immediate problem of the couple, the counsellor can virtually never make a firm statement as to having or not having a further child. He can take extraneous circumstances – e g religious or financial status – into consideration but, in the end, he is down to speaking about probabilities. In the case of unifactorial disease, he can give accurate figures – i e if both the mother and father carry recessive deleterious genes, the chances of an overtly affected child are one in four pregnancies. But in the event of a chromosomal or multifactorial condition, the probabilities can only be derived in an empirical fashion. Even then, the prospects must be interpreted. Thus, having had a child with spina bifida, one can say there is a 10 per cent chance that the couple will have a further child with developmental abnormality; it will sound quite different when expressed as a 90 per cent chance of a normal infant. Moreover, nine to one are acceptable odds to many; others might regard anything less than 99 to 1 as an unacceptable risk. In the end, the choice rests with the couple and this choice is a product of their ability to understand and the skill of the counsellor.

One thing is certain, no woman can be forced not to have a child; to procreate is her basic right.[2] But, in advising, the counsellor has several options: he can dismiss the risks, he can advise sterilisation of either partner, he can put the options of artificial insemination by donor or of ovum donation, or he can arrange for a suitable

2 See Heilbron J in *Re D (a minor)* [1976] 1 All ER 326 at 332, [1976] 2 WLR 279 at 286.

controlled pregnancy coupled with the alternatives of live birth or abortion as conditions indicate.

Controlled pregnancy
The counsellor may have advised a pregnancy or he may be presented for the first time with a couple in whom the wife is already pregnant; in either event, should he feel that a risk exists, he now has at his disposal a considerable technical armamentarium to help in closing the gap between probability and certainty. His methods may be non-invasive or invasive.

Non-invasive techniques
X-rays of the fetus are contra-indicated save in an emergency. The alternative is visualisation by means of ultrasound. This appears to be innocuous as far as the fetus and mother are concerned but its long term effects on the live born infant, if any, cannot yet be apparent. From being, at one time, regarded as a fairly gross diagnostic tool, ultrasound is now likely to become the main method of diagnosing not only external abnormalities, such as spina bifida or anencephaly, but also congenital disease of the internal organs.[3] Its use in locating the placenta is an essential preliminary to amniocentesis (see below).

Maternal invasion
Fetuses with neural tube defects – spina bifida or anence-phaly – secrete the protein alpha-fetoprotein into the amniotic fluid and some of this is transferred to the maternal circulation. Testing the maternal serum thus offers a simple and risk-free method of diagnosing abnormality in the fetus and is very acceptable to mothers. While 80 per cent of neural tube defective fetuses can be diagnosed in this way, the test is best regarded as a major indication of the need for amniocentesis. In this role, it is slightly less significant than is maternal age but nearly seven times as many terminations of pregnancy result from alpha-fetoprotein analyses.[4]

Uterine invasion
Although the number of invasive techniques which involve the fetus

3 R Harris and A P Read 'New Uncertainties in Prenatal Screening for Neural Tube Defect' (1981) 282 Brit Med J 1416.
4 D J H Brock 'Impact of Maternal Serum Alpha-fetoprotein Screening on Antenatal Diagnosis' (1982) 285 Brit Med J 365. There is growing evidence that neural tube defects may respond to methods of primary prevention – e g dietary regulation.

or its environment is increasing, amniocentesis still provides the most important method of direct investigation.

Approximately 1 per cent of British mothers undergo amniocentesis although this may be higher where the service is well established and publicised. It consists of needling the sac surrounding the fetus and withdrawing fluid which contains excretions and metabolites of the fetus together with representative cells; the latter can be grown in culture for chromosomal studies and to detect certain metabolic diseases, the fluid can be used for biochemical testing.

Biochemical tests can be made rapidly and can directly diagnose some rare diseases of defective metabolism of the gargoylism type. The onset of 'Rhesus disease' can also be detected. But by far the most important test is for alpha-fetoprotein by means of which an efficient laboratory can now diagnose all neural tube lesions. Cell culture can indicate the presence of chromosomal disorder in some 10–20 days and, at the same time, will indicate the sex of the fetus. In expert hands, the presence of what are termed 'inborn errors of metabolism' can be detected after some six weeks culture.

On the face of things, therefore, amniocentesis provides very powerful means of preventing genetic disease but, at the same time, it presents both technical and ethical problems. Firstly, considerable expertise is required, the procedure is costly and, as a result, the number of centres practising amniocentesis is limited. A 'defensive' policy of amniocentesis for all would offer little benefit in terms of the proportion of positive results and might be self-defeating; in practice, some selection has to be imposed and it has been suggested that routine amniocentesis should be offered only to mothers with a raised serum alpha-fetoprotein, those who already have a child with neural tube defect or in whom there is such a family history, those with a family history of chromosomal abnormality and mothers over the age of 35 years.[5] Even in the best hands, fluid can only be obtained after about the 14th week of pregnancy; no fluid is obtained in some 5–10 per cent of cases and the test must be repeated; add to this the time required for effective cell culture and it will be seen that one is dangerously near producing a viable infant in the event that termination of pregnancy is indicated. Thirdly, there is a 1 per cent risk of fetal death and a small risk of induced fetal deformity. Amniocentesis cannot be used in a 'blanket' fashion – only specific diseases can be sought and discovered. And finally, irrespective of negligence, some false positive or false negative tests are inevitable and will increase with the complexity of the tests undertaken. For all

5 See fn. 4, above.

these reasons, research is now directed towards primary prevention – for example, towards identifying the underlying environmental cause in multifactorial disease; amniocentesis is, however, likely to be the only tool for the prevention of unifactorial disease for some time to come.

Limitations of technique give rise to ethical problems. By current techniques, it is impossible to distinguish normal male fetuses from those suffering from sex-linked disease; if all males at risk are aborted, at least 50 per cent will have been perfectly normal. Again, a raised alpha-fetoprotein level does not give a clear indication of the degree of neural tube defect. The routine abortion of such fetuses will, therefore, result in the destruction of some salvageable – and lovable – children; on the other hand, some 10–20 per cent of 'missed' cases will have a severe defect and will require much corrective surgery. Similarly, the presence of the typical chromosomal abnormality does not indicate the likely severity of Down's syndrome. There are other problems of interpretation: given a chromosomal abnormality, what does it mean? Certain arrangements are well known to be associated with severe disease but in others – notably the 'XYY syndrome' – the evidence is by no means clear. XYY boys are said to be prone to vicious behaviour but prone is a very relative concept. Should doctors, on the one hand, abort all such fetuses as a precaution or, on the other, inform the parents, allow the pregnancy to run normally and possibly poison the parent/child relationship for ever?

Some of the difficulties can be overcome by more modern techniques. Fetoscopy, for example, allows for direct inspection of the fetus and, thence, an assessment of the degree of abnormality; at the same time, fetoscopy carries with it a fetal mortality of about 5 per cent. Fetal blood sampling, when perfected, will, for example, settle the problem of the potential male haemophiliac and will help to distinguish the severe forms of inherited blood diseases from the carrier state.

But increasing sophistication to some extent only serves to increase the fundamental moral issue of prenatal screening which is – how far is one to go in defining abnormality? The concept of parents obtaining a termination for frivolous reasons such as the sex of a child is obviously unacceptable but one can foresee more plausible dilemmas of conscience. Cases of Down's syndrome or of spina bifida which have not been discovered through prenatal screening are already candidates for neonaticide or local authority care. Is such disposal to run parallel with an increasing prenatal diagnostic capability when, as a result, more parents reject what will be regarded as imperfect children on increasingly demanding criteria? It is for such

FIGURE 1 UNIFACTORIAL DISEASE

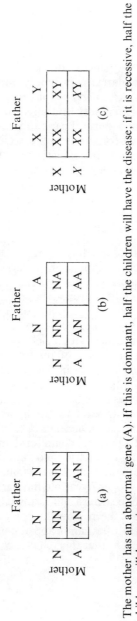

(a)

(b)

(c)

(a) The mother has an abnormal gene (A). If this is dominant, half the children will have the disease; if it is recessive, half the children will be carriers.

(b) Both the mother and the father have one deleterious recessive gene (A); half the children will be carriers and one in four will suffer from the disease.

(c) The mother is a carrier of an abnormal sex linked gene (X). Half the male children will have the disease and half the females will continue to carry the disease.

reasons that we argue later for legislation ensuring the overriding interests of the neonate in such circumstances.

On the other side of the coin, it seems clear that genetic counsellors should not over emphasise the quite proper interests of the State in reducing the incidence of genetic disease but, rather, should concentrate on the particular circumstances and interests of the parents in wanting a child. An elderly couple, for example, might see a pregnancy as their last possibility and might prefer to take their chance in the ignorant way of natural parenthood – and they should be allowed to do so. Actions for wrongful life, which are, essentially, actions for negligence brought against genetic counselling, must be viewed in the light of this complex and, sometimes, conflicting moral background.

Counselling and negligence

If a genetic counsellor or doctor fails either to advise prospective parents of the risk of genetic illness or to carry out appropriate diagnostic procedures which would disclose abnormality in the fetus, the parents of an afflicted child may choose to raise an action against him in respect of his negligence – the counsellor or doctor owes them a duty of care in which he has failed and, as a result of this failure, the parents find themselves burdened with a sick or handicapped child. Damages may be sought in respect of the distress occasioned the parents by the existence of the defect in their child and in respect of the extra costs which are entailed in bringing up the child.

Courts in the United States have been divided in their attitudes to such claims but the trend appears to be in favour of awarding damages in these circumstances. In *Becker v Schwartz*[6] the New York Court of Appeals allowed a parental claim for damages in respect of the cost of the institutional care of a child suffering from Down's syndrome. The negligence in question was the failure of the doctor to recommend amniocentesis to a 37 year old mother who, by virtue of her age, had a higher risk of bearing a child handicapped in this way.[7] The American courts have been slow to recognise damages for distress caused by the birth of a handicapped child as a legitimate claim but there are indications that this reluctance may lessen in the future.

6 386 NE 2d 807 (1978).
7 For an analysis of the American decisions, see A Capron 'Genetic Counselling and the Law' (1979) 79 Columbia LR 619.

The rights of the fetus

The basis of a parental claim may be clear enough, but what is the juristic nature of a claim brought on behalf of the child itself? The status of the child in utero is legally established – the fetus has a general right not to be injured by the wrongful act of a third party. This right was recognised at common law in Canada and in Australia in two important decisions, *Duval v Seguin*[8] and *Watt v Rama*.[9] Similar recognition is afforded to the fetus by the common law in Scotland and the matter was settled in England by the Congenital Disabilities (Civil Liability) Act 1976.

But the fetus's rights under the Act are not absolute. In the first place, they come into existence only if the child is born alive and survives for at least 48 hours; moreover, they cannot be vindicated against everybody. The Law Commission considered the question of whether a child should have a claim against its mother in respect of damage resulting from her negligence during pregnancy, but decided that such an action should not be available. It was felt that a claim of this type would compromise the parent/child relationship and might also be used as a weapon in matrimonial disputes. Accordingly, the English legislation excludes claims by a child against its mother except as to injuries sustained during traffic accidents; here, special policy grounds and the availability of insurance were held to justify the admissibility of such claims. The matter remains open in Scotland because there is no legislation on the subject and there is no reason in law to exclude a claim by a child against its mother in respect of prenatal injuries. It is possible, however, that the courts may be unsympathetic to such claims on policy grounds. It is also difficult to determine the extent to which the mother's duty of care towards her unborn child might be held to limit her freedom of action during pregnancy. Smoking and drinking during pregnancy, though strongly supposed medically to be risk factors, would hardly be viewed in law as negligence; a failed attempt at suicide, however, might form an obvious basis for a claim by a child thereby injured in utero.

Diminished or wrongful life actions

Apart from the straightforward case of an injury to the fetus in utero, a child born with an abnormality may argue that some other sort of wrong has been done it. Firstly, he or she may claim that there was negligence prior to its conception, and that this negligence has resulted in its being born with certain abnormalities. An example of such a claim is provided by the American case of *Lazevnick v General*

8 (1973) 40 DLR (3d) 666.
9 [1972] VR 353.

Hospital of Monro County Inc;[10] this concerned a child born suffering from brain damage due to haemolytic disease of the newborn which occurred because the hospital failed negligently to treat Rhesus immunisation of the mother by a previous pregnancy. Such a claim would also be competent in English law provided that, at the time of conception, the parents were not aware of the risk that their child would be born disabled. This exemption does not apply if, in an action by the child against its father, it is established that the father knew of the risk while the mother did not.[11]

The child may also bring a claim in respect of its 'wrongful life'. The basis of this claim is that, through the negligence of the defendant, the child's parents were not afforded the opportunity to abort the fetus and that the mother gave birth to a disabled child as a result. In such an action, the child is effectively stating that it should not have come into existence at all and is claiming damages in respect of the impaired existence which it is obliged to lead. The negligence in question may occur either before the child's conception – as in a case of negligent genetic counselling – or after conception – as when a doctor fails to detect an abnormality in the fetus.

A distinction may thus be drawn between actions for 'diminished life', in which a valid comparison can be made between an impaired life and a normal one, and 'wrongful life' in which the claim is against having been born, with or without impairment. The court is being asked in this type of action to contrast the value of life as it occurs against non-existence.[12] There has been a cautious acceptance of preconception torts and of the concept of diminished life whereas the courts in the United States have been distinctly cool in their approach to claims for wrongful life which have been attempted in a number of States but which have generally been unsuccessful.

In *Gleitman v Cosgrove*[13] the plaintiff was born deaf, mute and nearly blind as a result of his mother's exposure to German measles during pregnancy. The Supreme Court of New Jersey dismissed the plaintiff's claim for damages against the doctors who were alleged to have told the mother that there was no risk of German measles harming her child. The basis on which this claim was dismissed was that acceptance of it would amount to a statement that it was better not to be born at all than to be born handicapped; it was logically impossible, the Court felt, to weigh the value of a handicapped life against non-existence. As the court expressed it:

10 Civ Act 78–1259 (MD Pa Aug 13, 1980).
11 Congenital Disabilities (Civil Liability) Act 1976, s. 1(4).
12 See B R Furrow 'Diminished Lives and Malpractice: Courts Stalled in Transition' (1982) 10 Law Med Health Care 100 for discussion.
13 296 NY S (2d) 689 (1967).

It is basic to the human condition to seek life and to hold on to it however heavily burdened. If Jeffrey [the plaintiff] could have been asked as to whether his life should be snuffed out before his full term of gestation could run its course, our felt intuition of human nature tells us he would almost surely choose life with defects against no life at all. 'For the living there is hope, but for the dead there is none'. . . .

Later cases have followed this line of reasoning. In *Stewart v Long Island College Hospital*,[14] the claim of a child similarly damaged by its mother's illness was rejected on the grounds that to allow a claim based on failure to abort the plaintiff would be the antithesis of the principles of the law of tort which is directed towards the protection of the plaintiff against wrongs. The greatest wrong, it was pointed out by the court, is to cause another person's death. In other cases, the courts have chosen to reject the claims of handicapped children on the grounds that it is impossible to assess the child's damages.[15]

Although the overwhelming judicial consensus has been against the award of damages to children alleging wrongful life, there have, nevertheless, been signs that some courts are prepared to be sympathetic to such actions. In *Curlender v Bio-Science Laboratories*,[16] the California Court of Appeals awarded damages to a child born suffering from Tay-Sachs disease whose parents had been negligently informed that they were not carriers of the disease. Subsequently,[17] the Supreme Court of California allowed a child in a wrongful life claim based on inadequate genetic counselling to sue for special costs connected with the handicap but rejected a claim for such items as pain, suffering and emotional distress. The Supreme Court thus moved towards an acceptance of the principle of wrongful life claims while withdrawing from an important part of the consequences of doing so. The logical difficulty in comparing the claims of existence and non-existence proved, once again, to be an insuperable hurdle.

The matter had not been decided upon in an English Court until the Court of Appeal's decision in *McKay v Essex Area Health Authority*.[18] Previously, the Law Commission had considered the merits of the wrongful life action in its Report on Injuries to Unborn Children[19] and had come to the conclusion that it should not be allowed. The gravamen of its decision lies in the belief that to allow

14 296 NYS (2d) 41 (1968).

15 For example, *Dumer v St Michael's Hospital* 233 NW 2d 372 (1975).

16 165 Cal Reptr 47 (1980).

17 *Turpin v Sortini* 182 Cal Reptr 337 (1982). For comment, see B R Furrow (fn. 12, above).

18 [1982] 2 All ER 771, [1982] 2 WLR 890, CA.

19 Law Com no 60.

such actions would place 'an almost intolerable burden on medical advisors' who might be under 'subconscious pressures' to advise abortions in doubtful cases. As a result of these recommendations, the Congenital Disabilities (Civil Liability) Act 1976 would appear to exclude the right of a child to sue in such circumstances.[20] The infant plaintiff in *McKay* was, however, born before 22 July 1976 and, therefore, did not come within the ambit of the Act; the issue of wrongful life was, therefore, open to the Court.

In this case, the mother of the handicapped child had been in contact with the virus producing German measles and had consulted her doctor. A blood sample was taken but this was mislaid. A second sample of blood was taken and the mother was duly informed that neither she nor the infant had been infected with rubella; however, the infant girl was found to be severely handicapped when she was born. The plaintiffs alleged that there was negligence on the part of the defendant in that they either failed to carry out the necessary tests on the blood samples or failed to interpret them correctly. A number of claims were made as a result of this alleged negligence, including a claim by the child for damages in respect of entry into a life of distress and suffering.

The court discussed the major issues of legal policy to which this case gave rise in an extensive judgment. While recognising that there was no reason why a mother in such circumstances may not be able to claim in respect of the negligent failure to advise her of her right to choose abortion, the court was not prepared to recognise any claim by a child to damages for wrongful life. The grounds on which this decision was reached are similar to those which have appeared in the American cases.

The initial analysis is in terms of the duty of the doctor. The doctor clearly owes to the fetus a duty not to do anything to injure it, but what duty is owed to a fetus which has been damaged by some agency for which the doctor can bear no responsibility – in this case by the rubella virus? The only duty which the court could see would be an alleged duty to abort the fetus and the question which the court consider was whether this could ever be legal. The case has already been discussed in relation to the Abortion Act 1967 (see chapter 5, above). As to 'wrongful life', it was held that an *obligation* to abort:

Would mean regarding the life of a handicapped child as not only less

---

20 A strong argument can be made out that the Act does not exclude wrongful life actions and that it only governs actions for prenatal injuries. This argument involves taking a different view of s. 4(5) of the Act from that which was adopted by the Court in *McKay*.

valuable than the life of a normal child, but so much less valuable that it was not worth preserving, and it would even mean that a doctor would be obliged to pay damages to a child infected with rubella before birth who was in fact born with some mercifully trivial abnormality. These are the consequences of the necessary basic assumption that a child has a right to be born whole or not at all, not to be born unless it can be born perfect or 'normal', whatever that may mean.[1]

Having declined to find a duty basis of the claim, the Court also cavilled at the difficulties of assessing damages in such a case. Here the impossibility of comparison argument was seen as a strong one: how could a court compare the value of a flawed life with non-existence or, indeed, with any 'after life' which an aborted child was experiencing? – the Court declined to undertake any judgment on the conflicting views of theologians and philosophers on the latter aspect. Even faced with this conceptual difficulty, Stephenson LJ was of the opinion that it was better to be born maimed than not to be born at all except, possibly, in the most extreme cases of mental and physical disability.

The almost unanimous judicial rejection of these claims from handicapped children has not dissuaded the proponents of this form of action either from attempting to claim damages or from arguing in favour of such actions. In one recent academic contribution to the issue, strong objection has been taken to the courts' frequently expressed view that existence is always to be preferred to non-existence. Such a decision, it is argued, is not for the courts to take but for the handicapped child. There is no illogicality in the plaintiff's argument that he would rather not have been suffering as he is but that, since the defendant's wrongful conduct preserved his life, he is going to take advantage of his existence by claiming damages.[2]

It may be true that non-existence is preferable to existence in some circumstances. But, if one agrees that such a decision should be made by the individual whose existence is being assessed rather than by the court, then this surely leads one back to the conclusion which the courts have consistently reached – the child is being denied the opportunity of itself assessing the merits of existence by imposing a duty on the doctor to facilitate abortion. The possibility that life, even flawed life, may be found to have at least some attraction is precluded by abortion.

Ethically, the questionable aspect of the wrongful life action lies in the fact that it requires that the court should say to the plaintiff: 'Yes, it would be better had you not been born'. This judgment, however

1 Per Stephenson LJ, [1982] 2 WLR 890 at 902.
2 A Capron (see fn. 7, above).

sympathetic the motives behind it, would seriously compromise the value of human life which the courts are more usually called upon to endorse. The disabled should be helped and, if possible, compensated for the suffering which their lives may entail but the moral basis for such compensation should be the desire to make life more comfortable and bearable – not the notion that they should not be in existence at all. There is clear ethical justification for compensating parents for denying them the chance to opt for abortion of an abnormal fetus – and the appropriate person to bear the cost of this is the negligent defendant. There is, however, the strong general argument that any compensation for the child should come from the state, just as the state should ideally provide support for other categories of disabled persons.[3]

---

3 See, for example, Lawton LJ on medical mishaps in *Whitehouse v Jordan* [1980] 1 All ER 650 at 662, CA.

7 Neonaticide

By neonaticide, we imply the killing of the neonate – that is, the infant within its first 28 days of extra uterine life; we extend this definition to include 'letting die' because, as will be seen from the discussion, the distinction between killing and letting die is blurred at this time of life. We admit that we cannot find the word 'neonaticide' in any of the medical dictionaries we have consulted and the term is used *faute de mieux*. Infanticide is a statutorily defined offence limited to the mothers of children who are killed,[1] child destruction is a term already used to describe killing a fetus capable of being born alive[2] and the general alternative, murder, cannot be used to describe the condition we are considering; hybrids such as infantile manslaughter also prejudge a controversial issue. We prefer the non-committal 'neonaticide' which is a word not positively associated with any currently recognised offence.

We have separated neonaticide from the general subject of euthanasia for two main reasons. Firstly, we believe that neonaticide and euthanasia at the end of life's span pose completely different ethical problems for which we suggest there should be different legal rules. In the second place, it is intimately associated with the subject of abortion of which it is, in our view, little more than an extension.

Amniocentesis, which we have discussed in detail in chapter 6, is especially valuable in the diagnosis of chromosomal disease and neural tube disorders in the fetus. Both may well be detected during pregnancy particularly as high risk mothers can often be identified. The majority of people would probably support the early termination of such pregnancies but what of those which come to full term undiagnosed? Where does public opinion and the law stand between the extremes of an absolute right to life at one end and the positive policy of extermination of the imperfect at the other? There has to be a middle road but, this time, we must find it without the aid of statute.

---

1 Infanticide Act 1938.
2 Infant Life (Preservation) Act 1929.

Sanctity or quality of life?

The doctors' dilemma is self-evident – are they practising truly 'good' medicine in keeping alive a neonate who will be unable to take a place in society or will be subject to pain and suffering throughout life? In short, is one to sacrifice the Hippocratic, and theological, concept of the sanctity of life and adopt instead a standard related to the quality of life? The situation resolves itself into a catalogue of almost unanswerable questions – who is to determine the minimum quality of life? whose life should we be considering, the infant's? – or are we also taking into account that of the parents and, indeed, the well-being of society? do we, in fact, *want* a society where the right to life is dependent on achieving a norm which is largely measured in material terms? Should the abnormal infant who resolutely refuses to die be helped on its way? and, if so, is this help to be through omission or should positive steps be taken to end life? In the general discussion of euthanasia which follows in chapter 14, much stress is laid on the relationship between the quality of life and the proportionate or disproportionate treatment which is required to maintain that quality. But, at the beginning of life, the patient can express no opinion and, since the many relevant circumstances cannot be foreseen, the ordinariness or otherwise of the individual's therapeutic environment cannot be assessed. There is, thus, a movement towards inviting a parental 'life or death' decision as regards their abnormal offspring. They will be guided by the doctor whose advice is likely to be on the lines that the preservation of life is secondary to the main consideration which is the prevention of suffering – but the decision is theirs.[3] Medical leadership supports this parental right – 'in the absence of a clear code to which society adheres, there is no justification for the courts usurping the parents' rights'[4] – and it has the backing of academic legal thought – 'the criminal law should stay its hand. The decision of the parents should prevail'.[5]

The rights of the neonate
All of which may be good medical socio-economics but it is far from certain that it is good ethics. The right to ownership of one's body is a major argument in favour of a woman's right to abortion and this proposition has been widely accepted when related to an immature fetus. But, by the same argument, a newly born baby has a right to

3 E Slater 'Severely Malformed Children: Wanted – a New Basic Approach' (1973) 1 Brit Med J 285.
4 Editorial Comment 'The Right to Live and the Right to Die' (1981) 283 Brit Med J 569.
5 G Williams 'Life of a Child' (1981) Correspondence, *The Times*, 13 August 1981.

self-ownership, in which case child destruction or murder can never be morally permissible.[6] At the same time, no-one has an absolute obligation to sustain life[7] which, presumably, justifies Dr Dunn's evidence at the trial of Dr Arthur (see below):

> No paediatrician takes life but we accept that allowing babies to die is in the baby's interest at times

– and the wealth of distinguished supporting evidence showed that this is certainly acceptable paediatric practice.

It is to be noted that this expert opinion embodies a number of assumptions:

(a) that there is an essential difference between activity and passivity when the same end – death – is realised by either and, arising from this, that passivity does not conflict with the doctor's duty to 'maintain life from the time of conception';[8] moreover, passivity is clinically preferable from the patient's viewpoint;
(b) that there is a point at which death is preferable to life;
(c) that someone can decide that point in surrogate fashion and that it is right and proper for some person to act on that judgment.

The legal position

Yet there must be surely some divergence here from the law. To kill a living being deliberately is murder and, except in relation to the closely defined offence of infanticide,[9] the age of the victim has no relevance. Killing a child by omission could be prosecuted under the Children and Young Persons Act 1933, section 1; it is more likely to be charged as manslaughter although it could be murder,[10] in which regard the paramount consideration is whether or not there is a duty of care.[11] It is difficult to see how the physician in charge of the paediatric ward does not have a duty of care to his patients – even if as no more than a part of his contract with the Health Service. Some unusual hypotheses have been raised to justify a failure to treat – perhaps the most extraordinary being that murder, as the unlawful killing of any reasonable creature in being, might, therefore,

---

6 E F Paul and J Paul 'Self-ownership, Abortion and Infanticide' (1979) 5 J Med Ethics 133.
7 As argued by G Williams 'Down's Syndrome and the Doctor's Responsibility' (1981) 131 NLJ 1040.
8 Declaration of Geneva (see appendix B).
9 See fn. 1, above.
10 *R v Gibbins and Proctor* (1918) 13 Cr App Rep 134, CCA.
11 *R v Stone, R v Dobinson* [1977] QB 354, [1977] 2 All ER 341, CA.

exclude 'monstrous' or abnormal infants.[12] Such a proposition is not, as might be supposed, confined to bizarre legal reasoning – one article we have noted[13] described hydrocephalic infants, albeit with some reluctance on the part of the author, as 'these unfortunate organisms'. 'Pigeons' said the writer, 'have more personality than this unfortunate moon-calf in our midst', Obviously, there could be some substance in a rather less extreme view and Farquharson J, in his charge to the jury in *R v Arthur* (see below)[14] said:

> I imagine that you will think long and hard before concluding that eminent doctors have evolved standards that amount to committing a crime.

Which suggests there is a legal option not to apply the law if sufficient numbers of persons disregard it in good faith.

Modern case law

Such direct case law as there is provides only inferential guidance. The leading case, taken through the civil courts, is *Re B*.[15] This is an unusual illustration as the common stance of the profession, which has been indicated above, was reversed. B was a Downsian infant suffering from the well known complication of intestinal obstruction. Her parents refused permission for the necessary life saving surgical operation and the doctors applied for court wardship. On an application to perform the operation being turned down, the local authority appealed and won their case. The judgment of the Appeal Court was essentially based on the interests of the child to which the views of the parents had to take, at best, second place. The further implication arising from the judgment is that, had it been clear to the court that the child's life would have been intolerable, they would *not* have ordered the operation to be performed. Indeed, 'the child should be put into the same position as any other mongol child and must be given the chance to live an existence'.[16] Only a few weeks after the case of B, the Director of Public Prosecutions decided that no action would be taken against a doctor who had been reported to the police having allegedly refused to sustain a baby, Stephen Quinn, who was suffering from spina bifida.[17] On one reading, the two decisions are compatible, so long as it is accepted that baby Quinn would have been

---

12 Legal Correspondent 'Dr Leonard Arthur: His Trial and its Implications' (1981) 283 Brit Med J 1340.
13 J Lachs 'Humane Treatment and the Treatment of Humans' (1976) 294 New Eng J Med 838.
14 Fn. 17.
15 [1981] 1 WLR 1421, CA.
16 [1981] 1 WLR 1421 at 1425, CA, per Dunn, LJ.
17 *The Times*, 6 October 1981, p. 1.

not only physically and mentally handicapped but would also have been in considerable pain. Others would say, however, that they are contradictory in that *Re B* shows that the courts are ready to override the rights of the parents, or to 'interfere' in the traditional doctor/patient relationship, whereas the Quinn affair, by contrast, demonstrates an inherent reluctance to do so.

Then came *R v Arthur*,[18] the salient features of which are: a baby was born with apparently uncomplicated Down's syndrome and was rejected by its parents; Dr Arthur, a paediatrician of high repute and impeccable professional integrity, wrote in the notes 'Parents do not wish it to survive. Nursing care only'; the baby died 69 hours later; Dr Arthur was charged with murder and, during the course of the trial, the charge was reduced to one of attempted murder; Dr Arthur was acquitted. In the event, this apparent test case provided no precedent. The defendant, being charged with murder and subject to statutory sentencing to life imprisonment, had no latitude in which to defend his principles; the case became clouded by the medical evidence which was introduced by the defence in an unusual manner. There can be no doubt but that the verdict was correct as related to motive but there is nothing to suggest that it might not have been different in slightly different circumstances.[19]

The legal vacuum

As a result, the subject of neonaticide must still be argued in the abstract where all interested parties are, to some extent, still uncertain of their ground. The medical profession is no exception. The British Medical Journal expressed relief in a leading article that 'The LIFE campaigners have lost this round in their attack on selective treatment for handicapped neonates' and followed this with 'an infant with physical or mental handicaps that are not immediately life threatening should not, we believe, be allowed to die by default'.[20] Elsewhere, the Journal advises 'a new born baby has the right to accept or reject treatment [through its parents]';[21] we suggest that there is a world of difference between withholding treatment from a dying patient and refusing sustenance to one who shows firm evidence of a will to live. Morally, it is difficult to introduce the proportionate/disproportionate therapeutic form of argument in an uncomplicated case; no matter what the surrounding circumstances,

18 *R v Arthur*, *The Times*, 6 November 1981, pp. 1, 12.
19 G Williams (see fn. 7, above) has suggested that this case provides a further argument against the mandatory life sentence following conviction for murder.
20 Editorial Comment 'Paediatricians and the Law' (1981) 283 Brit Med J 1280.
21 Medical News (1981) 283 Brit Med J 567.

it is stretching sophistry to its limits to characterise feeding as extraordinary means of treatment. Legally, it seems impossible to reconcile the reasoning in *Re B*[1] with what must have affected the jury in *Arthur;*[2] it is difficult to see why the parents' wishes as to the death of their offspring should be overruled when major surgery is involved yet be regarded as ultimately decisive when it is not. If it be agreed that this is all part of accepted medical procedure, one could then ask what it is that particularly justifies death by omission which is, by definition, a prolonged process; might it not be held that positive action is a logical and, possibly, better alternative? It is also noticeable that few involved in this debate appear to have considered the effect on other parties – particularly the nurses, who cannot be unaffected by 'no treatment' orders. But these are aspects of the general euthanasia debate which is developed in chapter 14, below.

Neonaticide as a separate issue

There are, however, good reasons, of which two are fundamental, for isolating the issues in the perinatal period from those which are essentially perimortal. In the first place, decisions in this situation rest on prognosis which is another way of expressing an informed guess as to the future. But this may, in any event, be difficult and, while we know that we are dealing with only short term survival at the end of life, this is not the case at birth – we may be confident of what will be the state of affairs next week but we cannot say the same about the next decade. Moreover, the neonate is not passing from a settled norm into a progressively less satisfactory condition; he is developing in a milieu which *is* his norm – can one say with any certainty that the mongol, who has never known anything different, is, dissatisfied with his existence *within himself?* Thus, we would take issue with the reasoning of Professor Williams who has said: 'If a wicked fairy told me she was about to transform me into a Down's baby and would I prefer to die I should certainly answer yes'[3] because this is *not* the question being asked of the infant.

The second major distinction between life and death decisions at the extremes of life is that, while the adult sufferer is likely to be able to express an opinion or, save in a few cases, to have previously intimated his wishes, there is no way in which the neonate can consent to treatment, suffering or death. Consent must be parental and one

---

1 See fn. 18, above.
2 See fn. 17, above.
3 G Williams 'Down's Syndrome and the Duty to Preserve Life' (1981) 131 NLJ 1020.

then asks where, in fact, do lie the parents' rights that the doctors fear
will be usurped by the courts? Have they any more right to reject a
child than to abandon it? If it can be criminal to disbar an older child
from treatment,[4] why is it less culpable to fail or connive at failure to
provide the minimum of neonatal treatment – infant feeding? How
do these rights differ when exercised in the light of medical advice
rather than of simple intuition in the privacy of home? Is it likely that
a blind eye would be turned on parents who, on their own initiative,
decided to abandon their defective child? And can the parents who
are, in addition to their emotional involvement, economically and
socially concerned, make a truly objective decision on behalf of the
child?

The law itself does seem to be in confusion at this point. At least
one commentary has it that the parents' wishes should be disregarded
in the interests of the child; the law, it is suggested, is either out of step
or has evolved double standards.[5] The American position is also
complex. There, the courts' reluctance to interfere with the parents'
autonomy as to treatment or non-treatment seems to be deeply
entrenched but, again, is not absolute: 'Since the State should
normally defer to the wishes of the parents it has a serious burden of
justification before abridging parental autonomy by substituting its
judgment for that of the parents.'[6] But parents are bad decision
makers and legislative action is regarded by some as essential.[7] It is,
however, significant that the American literature does not consider
the uncomplicated Down's infant as coming within the discussion – mortal inactivity with respect to non-dying but defective
infants is illegal under United States law;[8] the severely defective
newborn is defined in America as one not likely to survive without
surgical and medical intervention, a definition which would, incidentally, include the results of severe perinatal trauma.

We believe that, in fact, much of the confusion surrounding the
subject of neonaticide stems from a failure to distinguish between, on
the one hand, the uncomplicated case of mongolism from, at the
other extreme, the severe neural tube defect. The latter will probably

4 *R v Senior* [1899] 1 QB 283, CCR.
5 D Brahams and M Brahams '*R v Arthur – is Legislation Appropriate?*' (1981) 78
   Law Soc Gaz 1342. The doubtful basis of the parental autonomy doctrine is further
   argued in D Brahams 'Acquittal of Paediatrician Charged after Death of Infant with
   Down Syndrome' (1981) 2 Lancet 1101.
6 Per Caldecott PJ in *Re Phillip B* App 156 Cal Rptr 48 (1979). The court refused to
   declare a 12 year old Down's syndrome boy a dependent child of the court for the
   purpose of repairing a congenital heart defect.
7 T S Ellis 'Letting Defective Babies Die: Who Decides?' (1982) 7 Amer J Law Med
   393.
8 R Sherlock 'Selective Non-treatment of Newborns' (1979) 5 J Med Ethics 139.

die even with repeated and painful surgery; the former, if it is not to live, must be helped and guided towards death. The two cases are practically and ethically different. There is much to be said, in considering legislation, for abandoning the quality of life test – which involves the uncertainties of prediction – and substituting a medical feasibility standard.[9]

A need for legislation?
While we do not wish to fan the emotional fires engendered by the concept of neonaticide, we believe that there are two even more uncomfortable aspects which have to be taken into account. Firstly, once the premises of the Abortion Act have been accepted, there are, like it or not, logical grounds for approving the practice. Depending on the severity of the abnormality, a positive policy of neonaticide will obviate a deal of suffering or hardship to the child or to its parents; in a number of cases, the pressures imposed on the social services or on the Health Service force one to consider the rational deployment of scarce resources as discussed in chapter 11. There are more subtle and logical arguments in its favour which stem directly from the provisions of the Abortion Act. As previously mentioned (chapter 6), it is difficult, if not impossible, to tell the degree of abnormality when spina bifida is diagnosed by amniocentesis – why not wait until birth and have a look? Currently, we do not know which of the male children will be affected by sex linked disease – is it not better to kill those found to be affected at birth than to abort them all indiscriminately? If we would have aborted a fetus if an intra-uterine chromosome analysis had been done, why should we not recover the situation when the effects of our omission become manifest at birth? Or there is the other side of the picture, suppose a pregnant woman says that her psychic health will be damaged if she has her baby – why not give her the chance to change her mind when she actually sees it? One can go on like this until it becomes clear that, in simple brutal logic, neonaticide is scientifically preferable to abortion. Yet, in practice, such a concept is abhorrent and intolerable.

Secondly, we conclude, with reluctance, that there are some infants who *ought* not to live. The incapacitated child has as much right to die in peace as has his grandfather and there are times when it is clear that that right should be exercised. In such circumstances, there is a real need for some form of relief from the basic law of homicide. Whatever else it is, neonaticide or perinatal euthanasia is not murder

9 E S MacMillan, 'Birth Defective Infants: A Standard for Non-Treatment Decisions' (1978) 30 Stanford L Rev 599.

when it is directed by responsible doctors and it may, on occasions, be the only humane form of 'treatment' available. A primary object of any proposed legislation would, therefore, be to protect doctors who are acting in good faith. There is no question of creating a new offence – what is needed is enabling legislation to lay down the conditions under which a doctor commits *no* offence. It is equally important that legislation should anticipate and forestall the 'domino effect'. It does not need much imagination, for example, to envisage parental rejection as being justified by a club foot or even unattractive features; the possibility of a change of mind in favour of rejection after a few months must be considered; if mental handicap at birth is to justify extinction, is it not a short step to concluding that a similar handicap following a fall at the age of one year merits a similar fate?

In the discussion of abortion, it has been implied – and illustrated through *Roe v Wade* – that the right of the fetus in relation to its mother increases as full term is approached. It follows that, after parturition, the right to 'self-determination' should be absolute, a principle which was followed in *Re B*. Any legislation legalising neonaticide must acknowledge the absolute rights of the infant when decisions are made. Neonaticide is far too close to feticide by abortion; thinking on the latter tends to affect the former and we would not approve draft Bills which effectively regurgitate the Abortion Act in a post-partum situation.[10] The application of the Abortion Act has escalated and the practice of neonaticide must not be allowed to do the same – whether it be by default or by unfortunate drafting.

For all these reasons, we believe there should be legislation to tidy up an untidy state of affairs and to give confidence both to the public and to the medical profession; but, to satisfy all, it must be very circumscribed. We suggest something of a single clause Bill:

> It will not be an offence if two doctors, one of whom is a consultant paediatrician, acting in good faith and with the consent of both parents if available, arrange within the first 72 hours of life for the termination of the life of an infant because further life would be intolerable by virtue of pain and suffering or because of severe cerebral incompetence; and the underlying condition is not amenable to reasonable medical or surgical treatment.

Subject to improved professional drafting, we believe that this emphasises the interests of the infant. Other considerations must not be allowed to intrude lest yet another complex medical and ethical – and legal – problem area be thrown into the political pot.

10 See fn. 5, above.

Comments such as:

> The war against abortion is well and truly on. Its political implications as
> America moves further and further to the Right, are frightening[11]

are more frightening than are the problems themselves.

A right to life?

The underlying theme of this chapter has been that the problems of
abortion, child destruction and neonaticide are of the same essential
quality. It is possible to devise an ethical argument which, even if it is
not acceptable to everyone, can be applied logically across the whole
spectrum while, at the same time, acknowledging the practicalities of
the modern world. But such a holistic view cannot be applied in
practice without consideration for those who must participate.

The most important of such considerations lies in conscientious
objection to the procedures. Subject to certain conditions (see
chapter 5, above), s. 4 of the Abortion Act 1967 excuses the
conscientious objector from participating in treatment by abortion.
It is clear that any legislation which legalises neonaticide in specified
circumstances must include a similar clause; one could only hope that
the specialism of paediatrician would not then be closed to those
expressing their opposition. We have also mentioned the role of the
nursing staff and, in particular, the recent decision which relieved
them from being in the potential position of illegal abortionists; any
statute legalising limitation of treatment must be well enough worded
so as to avoid such a very finely balanced division of judicial
interpretation. It is from the nurse, not the doctor, that the infant
expects its food; the nurse cannot be held responsible for refusing it.

The anomalous position of the father in the right to life debate
must also be considered. In so far as abortion is concerned, he has *no*
rights but, once the baby is born he would seem, in current practice,
to have a voice equal to the mother's as to the disposal of an
abnormal infant. He could, presumably, override his wife's rejection
of the baby despite the fact that he would be unlikely to undertake
much of the burden of caring but, for obvious reasons, this point has
not been openly decided. In practice, common attitudes to the
disposal of abnormal infants are based on the assumption of marital
harmony in that they relate so firmly to the wishes of the parents. The
decision in *Re B*[12] was surprisingly badly received by the professions
because of a belief in these so-called rights; the significance of

11 In B Towers 'The Trials of Dr Waddill' (1979) 5 J Med Ethics 205.
12 But, for a spirited defence of the decision, see M D A Freeman 'Using Wardship to
   Save a Baby from its Parents' (1982) 12 Fam Law 73.

possible clashes of interests would be minimised if the absolute importance of the infant's rights were defined by law.

Pope John Paul said, during his 1982 visit to Britain, that, in some instances, defective babies possess qualities and provoke qualities which are intrinsically good. It is an unfortunate fact that the opposite is also sometimes true – at least in respect of provocation. It is essential that the medical and legal professions as well as society at large should make sure of the lines they intend to draw in this area of conflict.

Medical Practice

8 Medical confidentiality

The concept of medical confidentiality is almost as old as medicine itself. One suspects that, in the era of priestly medicine, the principles of confidentiality were rather less than patient orientated – it is more likely that the maintenance of a closed profession was the overriding concern. It has been maintained by some[1] that this also applied to the Hippocratic School and that, accordingly, basing what is accepted as altruistic ethics upon the Hippocratic Oath is building upon sand. Nevertheless, the Oath, as amended in its modern counterpart, the Declaration of Geneva (or Sydney) (appendix B), is a good starting point because it represents the roots which sustain the intraprofessional code of conduct; and this is, in practice, the patient's main safeguard of what is generally considered to be his right.

The legal and moral bases of confidentiality

There is, in fact, very little legal support for the doctrine of strict confidence between patient and doctor. There being no specific law of privacy as such in the United Kingdom, any legal right to confidentiality must lie either in contract or in common law. A confidential contractual association between doctor and patient is often assumed but it is difficult to see how this can obtain outwith the wholly private sector. The doctor's contract within the National Health Service is with the Area Health Authority whether it be a contract for services or a contract of service. Contractual rights and responsibilities accordingly rest with the administration and the patient's legal right vis à vis the individual doctor must, therefore, be founded on other grounds. The status of the Hippocratic Oath then becomes of some importance. If it has the strength of a moral or ethical doctrine, the words of Lord Coleridge CJ may apply: 'A legal common law duty is nothing else than the enforcing by law of that which is a moral obligation without legal enforcement'.[2] The legal rights of the patient then depend upon the courts' view of the moral

1 E g I E Thompson 'The Nature of Confidentiality' (1981) 5 J Med Ethics 57.
2 In *R v Instan* [1893] 1 QB 450 at 453.

position of the medical profession. This is overseen in the United Kingdom by the General Medical Council which has very great authority based on statute.[3] It has, indeed, been argued[4] that, in so far as legal regulation inevitably saps the 'ethics of virtue', patients' medical confidences are safer in present circumstances than they would be if protected by law. But, if the Hippocratic principle is to be read as no more than a statement of medical etiquette, the patients' rights depend on little more than practicalities – in the absence of a code of professional secrecy, patients would not confide in their doctors, doctors would not consult with one another and professional skills would diminish on both accounts.

It would be unsatisfactory if such a situation were to arise and the Law Commission[5] have suggested that breach of confidence, which would include breach of medical confidentiality, should be defined as a tortious act by legislation. Inclusion in a general regulation might satisfy those who feel patients are not adequately protected by professional standards without, at the same time, damaging those standards and it may well be that legislation will be forced upon us. Medical confidentiality in France and Belgium is absolute and is protected in the criminal code.[6] With the unrestricted interchange of doctors between the countries of the European Economic Community it might well be that our partners will pressurise us into taking steps to limit erosion of what they regard as a fundamental principle.

Relaxation of the rule

There certainly is a degree of mainly bureaucratic erosion in the United Kingdom although it is to be noted that all the recognised Codes of Practice imply some qualification of an absolute duty of secrecy. Thus, the Hippocratic Oath has it: 'Whatever ... I see or hear ... which ought not to be spoken of abroad, I will not divulge' – which clearly indicates that there are some things which *may* be published. The Declaration of Geneva modifies this prohibition to: 'I will respect the secrets which are confided in me' and

---

3 Medical Acts 1858–1978.
4 J M Jacob 'Confidentiality: the Dangers of Anything Weaker than the Medical Ethic' (1982) 8 J Med Ethics 18.
5 Report on breach of confidence (Law Com no 110).
6 France: Penal Code, art 378; Belgium: Penal Code, art 458. Attention is also drawn to the Evidence Amendment Act 1980 in New Zealand where, subject to minor reservations, privilege is accorded to medical confidence (ss. 32 and 33); the rights of the dead are specifically covered as is, incidentally, the religious confessional (s. 31).

the word 'respect' is open to interpretation. The 1981 edition of the *Handbook of Medical Ethics*[7] contains the following advice: 'A doctor must preserve secrecy on all he knows. There are five exceptions to this general principle.' In the current absence of positive directions from the General Medical Council (see chapter 1, above), the BMA's handbook is the most authoritative alternative available. The five exceptions to the rule of professional secrecy therefore provide a sound base for discussion.

Consent to publish
The first, and most easily recognisable, exception is when the patient consents to a relaxation of secrecy. The situation is simple when viewed from the positive angle – a positive consent to release of information elides any obligation to secrecy owed by the person receiving that consent.[8]

Looked at from the negative aspect, however, the position is not so clear and may be frankly unsatisfactory. How many patients know whether the person standing with the consultant beside the hospital bedside is another doctor, a social worker or just an interested spectator? Would they have consented to their presence if they had been informed? Not all professions or trades have the same close controlling body as does the consultant who may, or may not, be responsible if, as a result, there is a breach of confidence – but this is small consolation to the patient who feels his rights have been infringed. What patient at a teaching hospital out-patient department is likely to refuse when the consultant asks 'You don't mind these young doctors being present, do you?' – the pressures are virtually irresistible and truly autonomous consent is impossible, yet the confidential doctor/patient relationship which began with his general practitioner has, effectively, been broken.

In practice, it is obvious that such technical breaches must be, and generally are, accepted – a modern hospital cannot function except as a team effort and new doctors have to be trained, the return for a technical loss of patient autonomy being access to the best diagnostic and therapeutic aids available. According to the BMA, the doctor retains responsibility for confidentiality to the patient even after he has given information to others with a 'need to know'. It is difficult to see how such a responsibility is reasonably acceptable but it is clear that he has an absolute liability for the *amount* of information transmitted verbally to para-medical groups and to students. Any

7 *Handbook of Medical Ethics* (1981).
8 *C v C* [1946] 1 All ER 562.

infringements might be the basis of a complaint to the Health Service Commissioner.[9]

The patient's interests

The second exception – that it is ethical to break confidentiality without a patient's consent when it is in his own interests to do so and when it is undesirable on medical grounds to seek such consent – is unexceptional save to those fanatically opposed to so called professional paternalism. Such instances must be rare in these days of public medical instruction through the news media. When they occur, decisions rest, by definition, on clinical judgment – a properly considered clinical decision cannot be unethical whether it proves right or wrong and, in the event of action being taken on the basis of breach of confidence, the fact that it was a justifiable breach would offer a complete defence both in the civil courts and in the Professional Conduct Committee of the General Medical Council.

The doctor in society

The doctor's overriding duty to society represents what is arguably the most controversial permissible exception in so far as it rests on subjective definitions. Society is not homogeneous but consists of groups amenable to almost infinite classification – regional, political, economic, by age and so on: it follows that what one man regards as a duty to society may be anathema to another. Individual doctors are bound to weigh the scales differently in any particular instance while, in general, all relative weighting must change from case to case – there is, for example, a great deal of difference in respect of confidentiality between a bee sting and venereal disease. While it is clear that no rules can be laid down, some aspects of this societal conflict are of sufficiently wide importance to merit individual consideration.

The most dramatic dilemma is posed by the possibility of violent crime. What is the doctor to do if he knows his patient has just committed rape – particularly if there is evidence that this is but one of a series of attacks on women? Perhaps even more disconcertingly, what if it becomes apparent that his patient is about to commit such an offence? Statute law is helpful here only in a negative sense – misprision of felony, other than as related to treason, is no longer an offence.[10] There is case law to the effect that the doctor need not even assist the police by answering their questions

9 National Health Service Act 1977, Pt V.
10 Criminal Law Act 1967, s. 5(5).

concerning his patients although he must not give false or misleading information.[11] Both medical and legal opinion on the issue is, or has been, somewhat divided although published statements are largely confined to the subject of illegal abortion. Thus, at the turn of the century, Hawkins J gave strong expression to the view that there was no duty on the part of doctors to report to the authorities 'whensoever they thought that a crime had been committed'.[12] On the other hand, Avory J, in 1914, said:

> There are cases where the desire to preserve [the confidential relation which exists between the medical man and his patient] must be subordinated to the duty which is cast on every good citizen to assist in the investigation of serious crime.[13]

In reply, the Royal College of Physicians passed and published resolutions concerning the duties of medical practitioners which included advice to the doctor to urge the patient to make a statement against the person who had performed an illegal operation but that, in the event of her refusal to do so, he was under no legal obligation to take further action.[14] It is difficult to see the ethical rationale behind protecting a potentially lethal abortionist in preference to betraying a confidence but abortion has always been an intensely emotional subject and it is by no means certain that the profession's leaders would take today a similar attitude to serious assaults. While there are many who would approve an absolutist approach, it is doubtful if disclosure of confidence which was designed to protect the public as a whole would be regarded as professional misconduct; such law of confidence as there is does not protect information indicating an 'iniquity' or 'misconduct'.[15]

Problems of employment of persons with contagious or infectious disease used to loom large under this general heading. This in particular, concerned those with venereal disease working in public places such as swimming baths or public houses. In practice, such questions are now a matter of history because modern therapy sterilises infected persons rapidly save in very exceptional circumstances. Consequently, confidentiality is strictly enforced.[16]

---

11 *Rice v Connolly* [1966] 2 QB 414, [1964] 2 All ER 649.
12 *Kitson v Playfair* (1896) Times, 28 March; 1 Brit Med J 882. But, even here, the Judge drew a distinction between abortion and murder.
13 Birmingham Assizes, 1 December 1914. Reported in (1914) 78 JP 604. The Judge referred to a possible moral duty in the event that the patient was not dying; his views as to strict moral duty were mainly concerned with the loss of evidence in failing to take a dying declaration from a moribund patient.
14 (1916) 1 Brit Med J 207.
15 See fn. 4, above.
16 National Health Service (Venereal Diseases) Regulations 1974, SI 1974/29.

Pari passu, however, the importance of disease in drivers has increased and presents one of the major dilemmas for the conscientious doctor. The urgency of decisions is maximised by the facts that driving licences are now issued for the life time up to the age of 70 and that responsibility for reporting physical deficiencies is placed firmly on the licence holder. Heart disease is always thought of as being paramount in this context but, in practice, very few car accidents resulting in personal injury are caused by cardiac conditions. Moreover, the majority of cardiac patients are mature and conscious of their responsibilities. Epilepsy is a far more apposite example. Nearly half the instances of unconsciousness at the wheel of a car are epileptic in origin and the condition is found to have been undisclosed in over three quarters of these – the public need is clear but what is the doctor to do? The standard answer is that he should either persuade the patient to report the disability or obtain the patient's consent to disclosure but this does not help when, as is likely, both courses are rejected. It has been suggested[17] that a doctor who knew that an unsafe patient of his was continuing to drive and who then failed to take any action on the point might be liable in damages for negligence to anyone harmed by his patient on the roads. Such an extrapolation seems improbable but serves to indicate the way in which opinion is shifting. It would be reasonable to conclude that not only are doctors protected against any action for breach of confidence by qualified privilege but also that they have a positive moral duty to inform the medical authorities at the vehicle licensing centre of patients who are a danger on the road by virtue of their medical condition.

Confidentiality within the family
A narrower and perhaps more controversial area of societal privilege lies within the family where the doctor may be the first to recognise the signs of violence. The police are, in general, disinclined to interfere in cases of marital violence because of the unsympathetic reception they are likely to get from both sides in so doing. But this may not always be the case and the doctor cannot be content while watching his patient suffer not only physical injury but also intense mental trauma. In the end, however, it is clear that an adult woman of sound mind is entitled to her autonomy; she has the opportunity of reporting to the police or, often more usefully, she has access to one of the many voluntary shelters which are now being established. She now has far greater protection under the law.[18] All the doctor can

17 Anonymous 'Doctors, Drivers and Confidentiality' (1974) 1 Brit Med J 399.
18 Domestic Violence and Matrimonial Proceedings Act 1976; Matrimonial Homes (Family Protection) (Scotland) Act 1981.

effectively do is to advise and, in this, he may be able to help by arranging for treatment of the offender – 'wife battering' is markedly associated with alcoholism and neurotic symptoms in the husband.

The position is different in the case of child abuse. Here, the victim is defenceless and the victim is the patient. Parental autonomy must be forfeited on the grounds of impropriety while the doctor is surely covered by the doctrine of necessity – in this case to assume consent to disclosure by one who cannot give consent – and he may properly report the matter to the appropriate authority. It has been suggested that, as a matter of law, such action probably does constitute a technical breach of the duty of confidence[19] but this seems hardly tenable. Rather, the doctor is beset by a clinical dilemma which, although less publicised, is of greater importance. The introduction of registers for infant at risk from violence and the obvious merit in nipping violence in the bud act as servo-mechanisms to one another. The possibility is increasing that truly accidental injuries are being misdiagnosed with a consequent reluctance on the part of parents to seek help for fear of being 'branded'; children may, therefore, actually suffer despite the doctors' concern for their safety. A case misdiagnosed as child abuse may lead to an action for defamation – although, as argued above, the defence of qualified privilege would probably be available; a missed case which ends in murder can bring great recrimination on the doctor. There is much help to the profession from the decision that a recognised caring authority may refuse to disclose the name of an informant.[20] But that decision was arrived at by the barest majority. In the end, it is not the fact of confidentiality which provides a right or privilege of non-disclosure – what matters is the public interest.

Parental autonomy and confidentiality are further concerned at teen age. Consent to treatment is discussed in detail in chapter 9, below; in the present context, we are concerned only with confidentiality and, particularly, with the doctor's relationship with the family. It is difficult, though not impossible, to conceive of other medical conditions which a minor might wish to conceal from his or her parents but, in practice, such conditions are likely to be limited to their sexual affairs. As has already been indicated, young persons of both sexes do have intercourse and the doctor may be confronted by requests as to contraception or abortion by young girls or for treatment of venereal disease by minors of either sex.

There can be no doubt that to perform an operation without

---

19 A Samuels 'The Duty of the Doctor to Respect the Confidence of the Patient' (1980) 20 Med Sci Law 58.
20 *D v National Society for the Prevention of Cruelty to Children* [1978] AC 171, [1977] 1 All ER 589, HL.

parental permission on a child too young to understand the issues and, hence, give a consent would constitute an assault and, logically, this applies to abortion. In practice, short of very intense religious views, it must be very rare for the parents of an unmarried girl below the age of 16 – and, therefore, of marriage – not to consent to termination of pregnancy but the issue here is that of confidentiality; *must* the parents be informed prior to a legal abortion on a minor? and will the legality of the operation be compromised by failure to do so? For apposite case law one must look at the United States where, since *Roe v Wade*[1] (see chapter 5, above) the abortion laws have been very liberal but where, equally, the concept of parental autonomy is deeply entrenched. The position there would seem to be that, while parental consent to abortion of a minor is not required,[2] the parents of an unemancipated child must be informed,[3] the reason being that the right to such information preserves the integrity of the family and the parents' views help the doctor in reaching his decision. There is certainly support for this attitude in the United Kingdom. Samuels,[4] for example, speaks of any other course 'leading to uncertainty and a weakening of proper parental rights' and others are even more positive. The Abortion Act itself makes no distinction between age groups and, therefore, the under-age pregnant woman presumably has the same rights as her elders which would, then, include the right to privacy. It is hard to believe that all of the order of 3,500 abortions performed each year on 13–15 year olds are performed with parental knowledge. Although the knowledge and agreement of the parents are clearly desirable and although the law is probably comparable to that developing in the United States, it is likely that a doctor who, faced with an adamant refusal of consent to parental disclosure, nevertheless terminates a minor's pregnancy, would be secure from action taken either in the courts or in the General Medical Council – good faith and the growing feeling that young people have a right to their own lives would protect him.

The fitting of contraceptive devices to female minors is a form of surgical operation and therefore falls to much the same analysis as does abortion. The supply of contraceptive drugs, however, raises no question of assault but, nevertheless, introduces problems of its own. Thinking sociologically, contraception is surely preferable to abortion; only a few young girls are likely to consent to their parents being told they 'are on the pill'; and refusal to supply is unlikely to deter those who want sexual intercourse. On this basis, the doctor who

1 93 S Ct 705 (1973).
2 *Bellotti v Baird* 443 US 622 (1979).
3 *HL v Matheson* 101 S Ct 1164 (1981).
4 See fn. 19, above.

secretly supplies contraceptives on request of a girl under the age of 16 is performing a duty to society. On the other hand, it is widely agreed that parents have a right to know what is happening to their children and should, ideally, give consent to medical treatment irrespective of the minor's capacity to understand the complexities. But is this so in this particular context? Parental concern is with sexual intercourse and if their lack of control is such that intercourse is occurring, it implies either that they are indifferent or that they regard the practice as inevitable or that the situation is beyond their control. They thus forfeit any absolute right to know of the steps which are being taken to limit the ill effects of their daughter's life style. Certainly, the doctor has a duty to explain to his young patient the undesirability and dangers of indiscriminate sexual intercourse, certainly he must point out that his patient's partner is committing an offence but, beyond that, he is arguably acting in the best interests of all if he respects confidentiality when it is demanded. There is official backing for such policy[5] and professional support is given in the BMA *Handbook of Medical Ethics*.[6] Nevertheless, the concept of parental responsibility does attract sympathy. A case was reported in 1971 in which a doctor informed the parents of a girl already aged 16 that she was using contraceptive medication;[7] he was held not guilty of serious professional misconduct on the grounds that he took what he believed was the best course in protecting his patient.

The longest established family relationship is that of the spouse – what are his or her rights in both the positive and negative aspects of confidentiality? If the treatment is for a medical condition, a married person has the same rights to confidentiality in respect of the spouse as in respect of anyone else and, since the Abortion Act 1967 refers only to medical certification, it can be assumed that this applies also to abortion. It can be implied also from the legal aspect that, since the husband has no right of veto either in Great Britain or in the United States,[8] he, similarly, has no right to information and it

---

5 DHSS Family Planning Service Memorandum of Guidance HN (81) 5, February 1981, admittedly vacillates more than its predecessor. There is a specific discussion in A Samuels 'Contraceptive Advice and Assistance to a Child under 16' (1982) 22 Med Sci Law 215 which, incidentally, disagrees with our view on the law and consent.

6 See p. 97, fn. 7, above.

7 *General Medical Council v Browne* (1971) Times, 6 and 8 March. See also the Editorial Comment in (1971) 121 NLJ 214 which was severely critical of the decision. Very few commentators believe that the Professional Conduct Committee would take a similar view today.

8 *Paton v British Pregnancy Advisory Service Trustees* [1979] QB 276, [1978] 2 All ER 987; *Planned Parenthood of Missouri v Danforth* 428 US 52, 69 (1976).

is not hard to think of instances where disclosure of an abortion to the spouse could be construed as being malicious.

The conditions are not quite so clear, however, when treatment of an individual is not primarily based on medical considerations but, at the same time, affects the whole family – effectively, this is a matter of sterilisation. Lord Denning was in no doubt in an early, minority, opinion already discussed in chapter 4 that the surgeon should 'approach the spouse in order to satisfy himself as to consent'.[9] This must certainly be the case when genetic considerations are involved. Either or both parties may be contributing to a multifactorial trait; genetic counselling is impossible unless both husband and wife are involved. There is, however, less certainty when sterilisation is purely a matter of convenient family planning. On the face of it, there ought to be a consensual decision but the twentieth century couple are not certainly going to be together until parted by death, religious differences may prohibit agreement and there must be times when one spouse feels compelled to act for his or her individual reasons. The doctor may rightly refuse to sterilise in the absence of consent to spouse consultation but he would, it is thought, be acting correctly both in law and in ethics were he to do so; adults have a right to privacy and it could probably be left to the Divorce Court, as in *Bravery*, to decide whether such unilateral action rendered marriage intolerable.

Other special groups

Finally, there are many special groups which can be conceived of as raising particular problems in relation to medical con-fidentiality – those which spring to mind most readily are accused persons, prisoners and members of the Armed Forces. Accused persons are legally innocent and therefore have the same rights as any member of the public. The police surgeon must state that the results of his examination will be reported to third parties and cannot proceed if, as a result, consent to examination is refused. In the interests of justice, however, he may make, and transmit the results of, observations which need not be confined to purely visual impressions.[10] The doctor/patient relationship is complicated in respect of prisoners and confidentiality is best considered as part of the whole spectrum (chapter 1). Much loose talk is often voiced as to the status of Medical Officers in the Armed Forces. In practice, their relationship to individual patients is precisely the same as in civilian practice with the proviso that the doctor's duty to society is

9 *Bravery v Bravery* [1954] 3 All ER 59 at 67, [1954] 1 WLR 1169 at 1177, CA.
10 *Forrester v HM Advocate* 1952 JC 28.

accentuated when this is formulated as a duty to a fighting unit; eventually the lives of many are dependent upon the health of individuals. There is, thus, a wider justification for disclosure than exists in civilian life and the serviceman has tacitly accepted this in enlisting; nevertheless, the principle of justification remains valid. Similar considerations apply, say, to doctors in medical charge of sports teams; the discussion has come full circle in that, basically, one's ethics depend upon one's definition of society.

For the purposes of medical research
Confidentiality is included in the general discussion of medical research in chapter 15, below.

Due legal process
Disclosure of confidential medical information as part of the legal process can be looked at in two main categories – statutory and non-statutory.

Statutory disclosure, whether by virtue of the primary or subsidiary legislation, presents no problem to the doctor but is, nevertheless, showing signs of encroachment on traditional values. Thus, the original requirements for reporting by the doctor of infectious diseases[11] or industrial poisoning[12] are clearly directed to the good of society. More recently, however, compulsory notification has become required more for statistical purposes[13] or for the protection of individuals by the state.[14] The two latter examples also show an increasing acceptance of some state control of the medical profession itself. Despite occasional protests at 'interference', there can be very little valid objection to such regulations.

It is to be noted that no immunity is granted to the doctor when a statutory duty is imposed on 'any person' to provide information. Few would complain at this in relation to the Prevention of Terrorism (Temporary Provisions) Act 1976, section 11. There is less uniformity of opinion as to the working of the Road Traffic Act 1972 when, by virtue of section 168, the doctor must provide on request any evidence which he has which may lead to the identification of a driver involved in an accident. The patient can scarcely expect the doctor to breach confidentiality; yet the doctor's liability under the law has been

11 Public Health (Infectious Diseases) Regulations 1968, SI 1968/1366, as amended.
12 Factories Act 1961, s. 82 as amended.
13 Abortion Regulations 1968, SI 1968/390; Abortion (Scotland) Regulations 1968, SI 1968/505 (s. 49).
14 Misuse of Drugs (Notification of and Supply to Addicts) Regulations 1973, SI 1973/799.

confirmed.[15] Other than by regulations, courts of law can compel the disclosure of medical material either through the production of documents or during evidence and cross examination.

Disclosure of documents
Authority for the order to produce documents is to be found in the Administration of Justice Act 1970, sections 31 and 32 and the Administration of Justice (Scotland) Act 1972, section 1. Section 31 of the 1970 Act empowered the court to order disclosure to the applicant of documents related to negligence suits before litigation was started. Section 32 extended this, once suit had been filed, to the disclosure to the applicant of any records held by a third party which might be relevant to cases involving personal injury. In so far as they indicated a further breach of medical confidentiality and, consequently, a possible restriction of information given and opinions recorded, these sections – and particularly section 32 – caused some concern in medical circles; to an extent this was unnecessary as the information sought was bound to come out at trial and the purpose of the Act was to ensure fairness to both sides and, at the same time, forestall any hopeless actions. Nevertheless, the judges also saw the danger and the Court of Appeal held that disclosure should only be made to the medical advisers of the applicant;[16] counsel could, if necessary, confer with and question the medical experts.[17] The Northern Ireland Court of Appeal, however, took the view that the Act implied no such limitation and this opinion was upheld in the House of Lords.[18] The question has now been resolved in the Supreme Court Act 1981, sections 33 and 34, by which the Court is empowered to order disclosure as it sees fit either to the applicant, the applicant's legal advisers or to his medical advisers. Reports are based on examinations and documents must be exchanged with an eye to fairness and saving of litigation time;[19] court directions may be made for the disclosure before trial of expert medical reports which it is proposed to bring in evidence.[20] There is, thus, no justification for hospitals or doctors to employ delaying tactics based on the principle

15 *Hunter v Mann* [1974] QB 767, [1974] 2 All ER 414.
16 *Dunning v United Liverpool Hospitals Board of Governors* [1973] 2 All ER 454, [1973] 1 WLR 586, CA; *Davidson v Lloyd Aircraft Services Ltd* [1974] 3 All ER 1, [1974] 1 WLR 1042, CA.
17 *Deistung v South Western Metropolitan Regional Hospital Board* [1975] 1 All ER 573, [1975] 1 WLR 213, CA.
18 *McIvor v Southern Health and Social Services Board* [1978] 2 All ER 625, [1978] 1 WLR 757, HL.
19 *McGinley v Burke* [1973] 2 All ER 1010, [1973] 1 WLR 990.
20 Civil Evidence Act 1972, s. 2.

of medical confidentiality – it will be broken in court in every case in which the ends of justice so dictate.[1]

The doctor in the witness box has absolute privilege and is protected against action for breach of confidence. The Earl of Halsbury LC, provides the highest possible authority: the immunity of the witness in court 'is settled in law and cannot be doubted'.[2]

This privilege extends to pre-trial conferences or Scottish precognitions, the exception being that a privileged communication must not be made maliciously.[3] Judges may go to great lengths to protect the witness but, when so ordered, the doctor is bound to answer any question which is put to him,[4] refusal to answer in the absence of the court's discretion to excuse a conscientious witness must expose the doctor to a charge of contempt – and the court will take precedence even when there is a statutory obligation of secrecy;[5] but, in some European countries the obligation to maintain confidentiality extends to the courtroom.

The patient's remedies

If the patient has a moral right to confidentiality, it should, ideally, follow that he has a remedy for the breach of that right. The law, however, has been slow to develop remedies for breach of confidence and the juridical basis of the remedy it does grant in these circumstances is far from clear.

There is no reason why a patient who fears a breach of confidence on the part of his doctor should not obtain an injunction to prevent confidential information being revealed.[6] This may prevent future breaches but does little for the past. But can the patient raise an action for damages in respect of a previous breach? There is little doubt that damages may now be awarded for disclosure of confidential information, even if the basis of such awards is uncertain. Previous cases, however, have been concerned with the disclosure of information which has commercial value,[7] and where the information is

1 *Higgins v Burton* 1968 SLT (Notes) 52.
2 In *Watson v McEwan* [1905] 480 at 486, HL.
3 *AB v CD* 1904 7 F (Ct of Sess) 72, per Lord Moncrief. This is the Court of Session stage of *Watson v M'Ewan*.
4 The exception to this requirement being disclosure of a source of information for which special rules apply (Contempt of Court Act 1981, s. 10).
5 *Garner v Garner* (1920) 36 TLR 196.
6 *Duchess of Argyll v Duke of Argyll* [1967] Ch 302, [1965] 1 All ER 611. H Street *The Law of Torts* (6th edn, 1976) p. 377; H J Glasbeek 'Limitations on the Action of Breach of Confidence' in D Gibson (ed) *Aspects of Privacy Law: Essays in Honour of John M Sharp* (1980) p. 217.
7 See *Seager v Copydex Ltd (No 2)* [1969] 2 All ER 718, [1969] 1 WLR 809, CA.

purely personal – as would usually be the case when a doctor
disclosed the facts about a patient's health – a plaintiff may not be
able to claim damages. To remedy this defect in the law, the Law
Commission has now recommended the introduction of a new tort of
breach of confidence which would allow for the awarding of damages
where the plaintiff has suffered an insult to his feelings as a result of
the improper disclosure of confidential information.[8]

In Scotland, the matter came before the courts in two similarly
named decisions, the *AB v CD* cases. In the earlier *AB v CD*[9] the
Court of Session considered an action for damages brought against a
doctor who had disclosed to a church minister that the pursuer's wife
had given birth to a full-term child six months after marriage. The
Court held that there was a duty on the part of the doctor not to
reveal confidential information about his patient unless he was
required to do so in court or if disclosure were 'conducive to the ends
of science' – but, in that case, identification of the patient would be
improper. In the second *AB v CD*[10] the pursuer was seeking a
separation from her husband. Having been examined by the defender
at the suggestion of her lawyers, she was later examined by the same
doctor who was, then, acting on behalf of her husband. The doctor
disclosed to the husband certain information he had obtained in the
course of his first examination and the wife argued that this
constituted a breach of confidence. Once again, the court accepted
that there was a duty on the part of a doctor not to disclose
confidential information about his patient but stressed that not every
disclosure would be actionable. As Lord Trayner pointed out (at
p. 85) some statements may be indiscreet but not actionable; there
might be, for example, an actionable breach if the disclosure revealed
that the patient was suffering from a disease which was a consequence
of misconduct on his part.[11] In fact, disclosure of the background to
the illness may be of greater importance than the disclosure of illness
itself. It would, for example, not be actionable to say of a woman that
she has a cold; but to allow it to be inferred that the only reason for
her cold was that she spent some time under the hedge with the
gamekeeper most certainly would be.

This really amounts to no more than saying that the patient is
entitled to protection against defamatory statements, a protection

8 See p. 96, fn. 5, above.
9 (1851) 14 Dunl (Ct of Sess) 177.
10 1904 7 F (Ct of Sess) 72.
11 Scots law provides a potential remedy in the form of the *actio iniurarium*. For
comments on the possible application of this delict in cases of breach of confidence,
see Scottish Law Commission, Memorandum no 40, Confidential Information
(1977) p. 28.

which is hardly adequate. In both English and Scots law, the patient is not being defamed if what the doctor says is true. Moreover, in England, the law of slander (spoken defamation) requires that the plaintiff should be able to prove special damage – which is, essentially, pecuniary damage – except in those limited cases of slander which are actionable *per se*. The protection provided by the law of defamation in cases where the doctor verbally reveals confidential information to another is, thus, unlikely to be significant.

Qualified privilege should, in the absence of malice or reckless unconcern as to the truth of the statement, be a defence against a tortious action for breach of confidence, as it already is in the law of defamation – qualified privilege in this context being but another expression of the 'need to know' principle. This is the ultimate determinant of ethical disclosure. The profession is not, or should not be, so concerned with the niceties of intraprofessional relationships or of communication in good faith with paramedical or other responsible groups; what really matters is irresponsible gossip.

Final reflections might, appositely, be concerned with death. The Declaration of Sydney says: 'I will respect the secrets which are confided in me, even after the patient has died.' In practice, this is incapable of fulfilment as a death certificate, signed by a doctor, is a public document. One's concern, however, is, firstly, with conditions discovered after death and, secondly, with the circumstances leading to death. A medical opinion says: 'The death of the patient does not absolve the doctor from the obligation to maintain secrecy',[12] but the legal position is summed up: 'As the confidence is *prima facie* a personal matter, the legal duty ends with the death of the patient.'[13] We believe that a post-mortem report merits the same degree of confidentiality as does the report of the clinical examination; insurance companies and the like have an obvious interest in its content but their right to disclosure is the same as the right to discovery of hospital records – in the absence of a court order, consent to disclosure from the next of kin of the deceased is essential.

But has the public any rights to details of the medical history of the dead?[14] While the principle remains irrespective of personalities, this is essentially a problem of public figures – and it is remarkable how rapidly professional ethics can be dissipated, say, in describing to the media the wounds of President Kennedy or the psychiatric history of Lee Oswald. It is easy to say 'History will out, let it be sooner than later' but it is less easy to decide at what point revelations become

---

12 British Medical Association *Medical Ethics* (1974) p. 13.
13 See note 18. However, any action for breach of confidence before the death of the patient could be transmitted to the executor.
14 See S E Woolman 'Defaming the Dead' 1981 SLT (NS) 29.

history. Not only is it difficult to see the logic which accords to death the status of the liberator of conscience but publicity may, in turn, question the ethics of non-disclosure. It has, for example, been seriously argued that Lord Moran invited criticism not so much for his disclosures after the death of Winston Churchill[15] as for his failure to draw attention to the physical state of his patient during life. Which brings one back to the dilemma of the doctor's relationship to his patient vis à vis society. After all, we did win the Second World War.

15 Lord Moran *Winston Churchill: The Struggle for Survival, 1944–1965* (1966).

9 Consent to treatment

The paternalist might argue that there are many examples in medical practice of situations in which treatment is justified in the teeth of the patient's objection. Arguing from such a position – that the patient may be unable to appreciate that a particular treatment is in his best interest – the decision of the doctor to impose the treatment is seen as serving the patient's interest in spite of what may turn out to be short-term objections. This, a paternalist would hold, cannot be wrong. Good health and physical comfort are preferable to ill health and physical discomfort: a patient will thus be happier treated than untreated.

From a different perspective, the case for imposed treatment is sometimes couched in social terms. Illness is costly to the community and the individual is not entitled to refuse treatment which may minimise this cost. If death is to be the consequence of refusal of medical treatment, then the community may have to bear the cost of supporting the patient's family. Involuntary treatment is justified in order to avoid this burden.

The paternalist position is, however, difficult to justify except in the most limited circumstances and these circumstances depend heavily on the existence of ignorance of some sort on the part of the person for whose alleged benefit the action is taken. There will be cases in which intervention by doctors is ethically justifiable but it is difficult to conceive of this being other than when the patient is in an irrational state because of impaired or disturbed consciousness. Restraining a delirious patient is justifiable paternalism, as is the action of clearing the air passages of one who is about to choke to death. The intervention is justified by the conviction that this is what the patient would want, were he fully rational, or that such treatment is needed to restore him to a position in which he can make up his own mind about further treatment.

The argument for non-consensual treatment on the basis of social cost is also affected by significant weaknesses. Society may, indeed, be saved certain costs if a life is preserved but it can be argued that the damage to society of permitting coercion in such circumstances convincingly outweighs the damage which it seeks to avert. A coercive society can be a most cost-effective one – but this does not mean it is more desirable.

A possible, although uncommon, exception to this rejection of the social cost argument exists when a person is found to be suffering from a highly infectious and dangerous illness; few would then argue that he should be allowed to refuse treatment if such treatment is the sole way to reduce the risk of spreading the disease. Here, the only caveat to the application of coercive treatment is that it should be as non-coercive as is compatible with containment of the threat.

Non-consensual treatment

The legal justification

The common law has long recognised the principle that every person has the right to have his bodily integrity protected against invasion by others. Only in certain narrowly defined circumstances may this integrity be compromised without the individual's consent – as where, for example, a parent or one *in loco parentis* applies justifiable corporal punishment or where physical intrusion is involved in the carrying out of a lawful arrest.

The seriousness with which the law views any invasion of physical integrity finds its basis in the strong moral conviction that everyone has the right of self-determination with regard to his body. Unless there is consent to an act of touching by another, such an act will – subject to the principle *de minimis non curat lex* – constitute a battery for which damages may be awarded. Consent can make physical invasion lawful but the reality of such consent may be closely scrutinised by the law and is, anyway, subject to certain policy limitations; consent will not normally render legitimate a serious physical injury.

In medical treatment, every touching of the patient is potentially a battery on that patient. It is the patient's consent – either implied or expressed – which makes the touching legally innocuous. The theory, then, is quite simple – the reality is somewhat different. Over the past decade, a considerable volume of litigation in common law countries has focused on the consent issue and, as a result, the doctrine of informed consent, as it has come to be called, has assumed a role of some significance in the medical negligence debate. It is a doctrine which has shown every sign of getting out of control, although recent judgments in England and Canada may help to avoid some of the problems which have arisen in the United States.

Is consent always necessary?
As a general rule, medical treatment, even of a minor nature, should not proceed unless the doctor has first obtained the patient's consent. This consent may be expressed or it may be implied, as it is when the patient presents himself to the doctor for examination and acquiesces in the suggested routine. The principle of requiring consent applies in the overwhelming majority of cases, but there are certain circumstances in which a doctor may be entitled to proceed without this consent – firstly, when the patient's balance of mind is disturbed; secondly, when the patient is incapable of giving consent by reason of unconsciousness; and, finally, when the patient is a minor. The question of the treatment of those committed involuntarily to mental hospitals is the subject of statutory regulations and is discussed in chapter 17, below.

The unconscious patient
The legal justification of treating a patient without his consent can be based on a variety of grounds. One approach is to argue that the treatment proceeds with consent, although that consent is not expressed. Thus, when an unconscious patient is admitted to hospital, the casualty officer may argue that, although the patient was clearly unable to consent to treatment, his consent could be implied or presumed on the grounds that if he were conscious he would probably consent to the saving of his life in this way. Although this may be true and although the majority of patients could be expected to endorse the decision to treat in such circumstances, it is a rather fictitious way of approaching the problem.[1]

An alternative approach, which has the attraction of greater honesty, is to apply the necessity principle. It is widely recognised in both criminal and civil law that there are certain circumstances in which acting out of necessity legitimates an otherwise wrongful act. The basis of this doctrine is that acting unlawfully is justified if the resulting good effect materially outweighs the consequences of adhering strictly to the law. In the present context, the doctor is justified and should not have criminal or civil liability imposed upon him if the value which he seeks to protect is of greater weight than the wrongful act he performs – that is, treating without consent.

A major difficulty with the principle of necessity is its general nature; the court consequently experiences dilemmas in its application. The necessity argument in relation to non-consensual medical

---

1 The use of a legal fiction of this sort was disapproved of in *Marshall v Curry* [1933] 3 DLR 260 at 275; see also, P Skegg 'Justification for Medical Procedures Performed without Consent' (1974) 90 LQR 512.

treatment would probably be limited at the outset to those cases in which the patient is not known to object to the treatment in question. It could not be applied when the patient is conscious and objects to the treatment; the value of the individual's control over his own body would be held to outweigh the value of enhancing his state of health or indeed of saving his life. Suicide is no longer a crime and, although he might be justified on other grounds, a doctor could not argue that the value he was seeking to protect was the interest which the community has in preventing the commission of criminal acts. We see this view embodied in the official policy of abstaining from force-feeding of prisoners on hunger strike.[2]

Necessity will be an adequate defence to any proceedings for non-consensual treatment when an unconscious patient is involved and there is no known objection to treatment. The treatment undertaken, however, must not be more extensive than is required by the exigencies of the situation. A doctor cannot, therefore, 'take advantage' of unconsciousness to perform procedures which are not essential for the patient's survival. This principle is laid down in two well known Canadian cases where the courts explored the distinction between procedures justified by necessity and those which are merely 'convenient', a distinction which would, in all probability, be followed by the British courts.

In the first of these, *Marshall v Curry*,[3] a decision of the Supreme Court of Nova Scotia, the plaintiff sought damages for battery against the surgeon who had, in the course of an operation for a hernia, removed a testicle. The surgeon's case was that the removal was essential to a successful operation and that, had he not done so, the health and life of the patient would have been imperilled because the testis was, itself, diseased. Taking the view that the doctor had acted 'for the protection of the plaintiff's health and possibly his life', the court held that the removal of the testicle was necessary and that it would have been unreasonable to put the procedure off until a later date. By contrast, in *Murray v McMurchy*[4] the plaintiff succeeded in an action for battery against a doctor who had sterilised her without her consent. In this case, the doctor had discovered during a Caesarian section that the condition of the plaintiff's uterus would have made it hazardous for her to go through another pregnancy and, although there was no pressing need for the Fallopian tubes to be tied, the doctor went ahead with the procedure. The court in this case took

2 For a general discussion of force-feeding see G Zellick 'The Forcible Feeding of Prisoners: An Examination of the Legality of Enforced Therapy' [1976] Public Law 153.
3 [1933] 3 DLR 260.
4 [1949] 2 DLR 422.

the view that it would not have been unreasonable in the circumstances to postpone the sterilisation until after consent had been obtained in spite of the convenience of doing it on the spot.

The principle that emerges from these two cases is that a doctor is justified by necessity in proceeding without the patient's consent if a condition is discovered in an unconscious patient for which treatment is necessary in the sense that it would be, in the circumstances, unreasonable to postpone the operation to a later date. If, however, it is possible to put off any treatment until the patient has been in a position to give consent, the postponement of treatment is to be preferred.

Proxy consent and the consent of minors
Nonetheless, it is possible that a member of the family may be at hand when a patient is unconscious. In such a case, it is wise for the doctor to obtain the consent of a close relative although the legal effect of so doing is only indirect. In the case of an unconscious adult patient, obtaining the consent of a spouse or parent is not the same as obtaining the consent of the patient himself and the proxy consent of the spouse or parent would not be of much value if the procedure in question falls into the 'convenient' rather than the 'necessary' category. If, however, the procedure was to be necessary, the fact that the spouse's or parents' consent had been obtained could be significant in demonstrating that the doctor had behaved reasonably before proceeding. It might also be of value in that it would diminish the likelihood of the patient feeling sufficiently aggrieved to take matters further.

Proxy consents are only of true value when the patient has given express authority to another person to give or withhold consent on his behalf or when the law invests a person with such power. The most common example of the latter case would be that of parent and child. When proxy consent of this sort is available, the person vested with the power must use it reasonably; the unreasonable withholding of consent may justify a third party's ignoring such withholding, although this would, generally, be a hazardous course to adopt.

A common occasion on which proxy consent may be scrutinised is when parents refuse to give consent to the medical treatment of their children on the grounds that they disapprove of such treatment for religious reasons. The provisions of the Family Law Reform Act 1969 then come into effect if the child is over 16 years old. Section 8(1) of this Act provides that a person over 16 may validly consent to medical treatment without reference to the parent or guardian. A child of 16 years or more can therefore override parental objection to a particular medical treatment and can give an independent valid consent. On the other hand, the position may prove to be difficult in the case of a child under 16 years of age. The common law does not exclude a child under 16 consenting to medical treatment but whether such consent would be valid would depend on the extent of the child's ability to understand the issues involved.[5] This would certainly be the case in Scotland, although, there, the ability of a pupil child (below the age of puberty) to give a valid consent would be doubtful.

It must be a question of fact in each case. If one takes the view that the common law does not exclude the validity of a child under 16 consenting to medical treatment, then the consent of a child under that age to necessary medical procedures may well suffice even in the face of parental objections. An illustration of this is provided by a recent unreported case in which the court agreed that a schoolgirl aged 15 should be allowed to have an abortion against the wishes of her parents. Butler-Sloss J said: 'I am satisfied she wants this abortion; she understands the implications of it.'[6]

Alternatively a doctor could take steps to administer to the child life-saving treatment against the wishes of parents and subsequently, in the event of legal action, attempt to justify his actions on the grounds of necessity. Yet another approach might be for the courts to negative the parental withholding of consent on the grounds that the parental power had been exercised unreasonably. It is also technically possible for local authorities to ask the court for a child to be taken into care when parents refuse to consent to life-saving medical treatment; they can then, as the appropriate authority, give consent to the proposed procedure. This mechanism has been used in the past but it is now officially out of favour and hospital authorities are advised in such cases to rely on clinical judgment and proceed accordingly.

Although there would be little public sympathy for parents who refuse on religious grounds to consent to blood transfusion for a perilously ill child, it would be a mistake to reject their position out of hand. The refusal of blood in such circumstances may seem to many to be irrational and pointless, but there is no doubt that it is a strongly held minority position. Ignoring it involves overriding religious convictions and this is a major step in a free society. Such action also entails a fairly significant interference with the principle that parents should have freedom to choose the religious and social upbringing of their children. These factors certainly suggest caution but are

5 The common law position in Canada is stated in *Johnston v Wellesley Hospital* (1970) 17 DLR (3d) 139.
6 *The Times*, 14 May 1982, p. 24.

undoubtedly outweighed by the counter-arguments that there has been a redefinition of the role of the parents in respect of control of their children and that it is no longer possible to regard them as having an almost absolute power. The community interest in the welfare of children is vindicated in a number of ways ranging from insistence on school attendance to the provision of devices whereby parents can be deprived of the custody of children whose welfare they are neglecting. Society is prepared to remove a child from its parents if it is in moral or physical danger; the child whose life is endangered by parental refusal of consent to medical treatment may be removed from its parents on precisely the same grounds as the battered child may be removed from its home. Any difference in the two cases perhaps lies in motives. The parent withholding consent may be doing so for what he sees as good reasons and in the interests of the child; the parent who neglects his child is unlikely to feel the same. In spite of this difference, however, there must be few who will see the parents' good faith as justifying the imperilling of a child's life; death of a child in such circumstances might result in prosecution of the parents for manslaughter.[7]

Proceeding without consent – the consequences

Non-consensual medical treatment entitles the patient to sue for damages for the battery which is committed. It is also possible in such circumstances to base a claim on the tort of negligence, the theory being that the doctor has been negligent in failing to obtain the consent of the patient. There are certain important differences between the two forms of action and these differences have given rise to much legal debate. In Britain and Canada, however, the issue is now settled and the law is reasonably clear.

An action for battery arises when the plaintiff has been touched in some way by the defendant and when there has been no consent, express or implied, to such touching. All that the plaintiff need establish in such an action is that the defendant wrongfully touched him. It is not necessary to establish loss as a result of the touching and, therefore, there is no problem of causation to be overcome. By contrast, in an action based on the tort of negligence, the plaintiff must establish that the defendant wrongfully touched him and that the negligence of the defendant in touching him without consent has led to the injury for which damages are sought. There is thus a problem of factual causation to be tackled and, for this reason, the action for battery is an easier option from the plaintiff's point of view. The measure of damages recoverable will also be different. All

7 *R v Senior* [1899] 1 QB 283.

direct damages are recoverable in battery; in an action of negligence, only those damages which are foreseeable may be recovered. Thus an unforeseen medical complication arising from the procedure in question may be something for which damages are recoverable in battery but not in negligence.

In earlier cases plaintiffs often brought their action on either count and there was some confusion as to what was the proper basis for particular claims. Clarification has been given of the circumstances in which each action is available through the decisions of the Supreme Court of Canada in *Reibl v Hughes*[8] and the Appeal Court decision in *Chatterton v Gerson*.[9]

An action for battery is appropriate where there has been no consent at all to the physical contact in question. Thus, an action for battery is the appropriate remedy if a patient refuses to submit to a procedure but the doctor, nevertheless, goes ahead even in the face of this refusal. A claim based on negligence is appropriate when the plaintiff has given his consent to an act of the general nature which is performed by the defendant but when there is a flaw in this consent which means that there is no consent to certain concomitant features of the act. The distinction between the two forms of action was sharply outlined in *Reibl v Hughes* by Laskin CJC who remarked in his judgment:

> I do not understand how it can be said that the consent was vitiated by the failure of disclosure of risks to as to make the surgery or other treatment an unprivileged, unconsented to and intentional invasion of the patient's bodily integrity. I can appreciate the temptation to say that the genuineness of consent to medical treatment depends on proper disclosure of the risks which it entails, but . . . unless there has been misrepresentation or fraud to secure consent to the treatment, a failure to disclose the attendant risks, however serious, should go to negligence rather than battery.

Similarly, it was emphasised in *Chatterton v Gerson* that an action for trespass to the person is inappropriate once the patient is informed in 'broad terms' of the nature of the procedure and consent is given; an action for negligence is the proper remedy if there is a failure to disclose risks. This is in line with the court's policy of restricting battery actions to acts of unambiguous hostility.

A number of Canadian cases illustrate the sort of circumstances in which an action for battery will be appropriate. Actions for battery were sustained in *Mulloy v Hop Sang*,[10] where the plaintiff's hand

8 (1980) 114 DLR (3d) 1; Laskin CJC at 10.
9 [1981] QB 432, [1981] 1 All ER 257.
10 [1935] 1 WWR 714.

was amputated without his consent; in *Allan v New Mount Sinai Hospital*[11] where the plaintiff had an anaesthetic injected into his left arm in spite of his objection to this procedure; and, as a final illustration, in *Schweizer v Central Hospital*[12] in which the surgeon performing an operation on the back of a plaintiff whose consent was related to an operation on his toe was held liable for damages for battery. It will be seen that, in all of these cases, what the doctor actually did was quite unconnected with the procedure to which the patient had consented: there was no consent to a procedure of the 'general nature' that was performed.

The negligence action – causation problems
The essence of the causation problem in negligence actions based on a lack of consent is that the court must be satisfied that the defendant's negligence in failing to obtain the consent of the patient was, in fact, the cause of the patient's injury. To satisfy this requirement, the patient must prove he would not have given his consent and would not, therefore, have suffered injury had he had the information of which he was allegedly deprived.

The obvious difficulty here is one of discounting the wisdom of hindsight. It will be only too easy for a plaintiff, once he has suffered damage, to allege that he would not have given his consent to the procedure when, in reality, he may well have been quite prepared to do so, even with full knowledge of the risks entailed.

A number of options might be open to the courts. At one extreme is that of giving full weight to the patient's assertion that he would not have consented had he been aware of all the facts. This entirely subjective approach has the obvious drawback of being weighted overwhelmingly in favour of the plaintiff and is, therefore, unacceptable. The opposite approach – which is entirely objective – is to postulate a standard of a reasonable patient. Would the reasonable patient have given his consent when confronted with full information of the risks and difficulties of the procedure in question. If the answer is yes, then it may be inferred that the plaintiff himself would have consented. This, like all objective tests, has the disadvantage of being potentially unfair to the plaintiff. It may well be that he genuinely would not have consented; applying the objective standard might then also be unsatisfactory.

A third possibility exists. The court may opt for an entirely objective approach but qualify it by investing the hypothetical reasonable patient with the relevant special peculiarities of the

11 (1980) 109 DLR (3d) 634.
12 (1974) 53 DLR (3d) 494.

plaintiff himself. In this way the edge is taken off the objective test while the pitfalls of the purely subjective approach are avoided. This compromise is increasingly favoured in the criminal law relating to the plea of provocation.

The courts in Canada vacillated between the alternatives of the objective and subjective approaches. Finally, in *Reibl v Hughes*,[13] the Supreme Court came down in favour of an objective test modified by certain subjective factors. The effect of this is that one's starting point is to determine the extent to which the balance of risks was medically in favour of the treatment in question. This would allow a decision to be made as to whether a reasonable patient would have consented and, that done, the court can proceed to look at the particular patient's condition. Here the judgment in *Reibl v Hughes* suggested that it is important to take into account the patient's questions to the doctor, as these will demonstrate his concerns and will better enable the court to assess what a reasonable patient in the plaintiff's position would have done.

Although the matter has not been specifically discussed, the assumption in the most recent English case, *Chatterton v Gerson*,[14] would seem to have been that the standard to be applied in England would be a subjective one. This may, indeed, be the case in theory but, in practice, the subjective standard is often a thinly disguised objective standard. A court may say that it is attempting to discern the state of mind of the particular plaintiff when, in order to reach its conclusions in this regard, it is in fact using the objective tool of judging credibility by asking whether a reasonable person would have taken a similar view. It is, then, probable that, if the matter arose as a specific issue in a British court, the approach followed would be similar to that of the Supreme Court of Canada in *Reibl v Hughes*.

Informed consent – What needs to be disclosed?

Most disputes as to consent arise in the context of an alleged non-disclosure of the risks involved in a particular treatment. Looked at from the ethical point of view, the matter is one of self-determination. A person should not be exposed to a risk of damage unless he has agreed to the risk. Although this proposition would probably meet with wide approval, there are differences of opinion as to the extent of the duty to disclose risks. The more paternalistic approach is to countenance the non-disclosure of a considerable amount of

13 (1980) 114 DLR (3d) 1.
14 [1981] QB 432, [1981] 1 All ER 257.

information if the doctor thinks it would not be in the patient's interest to be told. This view accepts that, since the treatment is likely to be to the patient's benefit, then it is legitimate to withhold information which would merely serve to distress or confuse the patient. It should be noted that this is not the same thing as deciding to withhold information which it is thought would lead the patient to refuse the treatment. The latter practice is hardly acceptable ethically.

An alternative school of thought holds that, given a rational patient, the doctor must reveal all the relevant facts as to what he intends to do. It is not for him to determine what the patient should or should not hear. Obviously there must be some medical assessment of what is or is not significant but, apart from the exclusion of irrelevant material, the patient should be as fully informed as possible so that he can make up his mind in the light of all the material circumstances.

This second approach most fully satisfies the requirements of self-determination but can be criticised on the grounds that it leaves little scope for the exercise of clinical judgment by the doctor. Is there any point in burdening a patient with knowledge of risks when the doctor in charge of the case knows, or at least strongly suspects, that this will serve to retard recovery? It seems particularly pointless when there is, in any event, a shrewd understanding on the doctor's part of what the patient's eventual decision will be. Reassurance of the patient may be an essential part of the programme of treatment and any dwelling on or even mention of risks may well harm the patient's health.

The choice between a 'patient standard' and a 'professional standard' is a difficult one. There must be respect for the patient's legitimate interest in knowing to what he is subjecting himself but, at the same time, there will clearly be cases where a paternal approach is more appropriate. In addition, the practicalities of the situation must be borne in mind. Although it might be ethically desirable for patients to be as fully informed as possible, the time spent in explaining the intricacies of procedures could be considerable, particularly if a doctor is expected to deal with remote risks. Doctors simply do not have the time to waste on unduly lengthy explanations of all the ramifications of treatment. A compromise must be to place on the doctor the duty to inform of the risks of a procedure in so far as these are 'material' provided that there is no pressing clinical reason to protect the patient from a knowledge of such risks.

The courts have been of some assistance in assessing what risks are material. These have been defined as those risks which are reasonably probable and which must be considered to be fairly serious in their effect. A very remote risk need not be disclosed unless it is a risk of a very serious consequence. Risks which are attendant upon medical procedures as a whole need not be disclosed and explained; the requirement applies only to those which are specific to the procedure in question.

The cases

Whatever standpoint one takes on this matter, a decision of some court can be found to endorse one's preferred approach. In the United States, for example, there are some jurisdictions in which the full disclosure rule applies and others in which the professional standard has been accepted. Within the Commonwealth, there are decisions ranging from the endorsement of the deliberate medical lie to the acceptance of the extreme patient-orientated approach which emphasises complete disclosure of risk. The diversity of opinion is equally evident in academic discussions; some writers have thought to give the informed consent doctrine extensive scope while others have urged caution in the face of what has been seen as an indirect and inappropriate means of widening the potential liability of doctors.

Because of the varied fate of the consent issue in the United States, we propose not to deal with the American experience in this area other than to draw from it a salutary lesson of the confusion that can result from unco-ordinated judicial developments of the law.[15] Within the Commonwealth, although there has by no means been unanimity as to the ways in which the courts should deal with the question of consent, the law appears to be fairer and rather more consistent.

The three most significant cases for British courts are *Bolam v Friern Hospital Management Committee*,[16] *Smith v Auckland Hospital Board*[17] and *Chatterton v Gerson*.[18] The first of these decisions, *Bolam*, concerned the administration of electro-convulsive therapy – without an anaesthetic as was common at the time – to a mentally ill patient to whom the risk of facture in such a procedure had not been explained. The court expressed the view that the doctor was entitled to proceed without explanation of the risks in the light of the patient's condition. As the judge said in his charge to the jury:

> You may well think that when a doctor is dealing with a mentally sick man and has a strong belief that his only hope of cure is submission to electro-

---

15 A 'middle of the road' rule was enunciated in *Canterbury v Spence* 464 F 2d 772 (1972). This measures the defendant's disclosure of information against the standard of what a prudent patient would consider material to the making of a decision about treatment.
16 [1957] 2 All ER 118, [1957] 1 WLR 582.
17 [1964] NZLR 241 SC, revsd. [1965] NZLR 191, NZ CA.
18 [1981] QB 432, [1981] 1 All ER 257.

convulsive therapy, the doctor cannot be criticised if he does not stress the dangers, which he believed to be minimal, which are involved in their treatment . . . .[19]

This note of caution has been sounded in a number of other cases. In the Canadian case of *Kenny v Lockwood*[20] for example, the court held that the duty placed upon the surgeon of 'dealing honestly' with his patient does not extend to a duty to inform the patient of details which were calculated to frighten or distress him.

Smith v Auckland Hospital Board has been a particularly influential case. Here the patient alleged that he did not give his informed consent to the performance of an aortogram in that he was not told of the risks it involved. In a dictum which has since been widely referred to, the judge outlined what should be taken into account in deciding what the patient should be told:

> As it seems to me, the paramount consideration is the welfare of the patient and, given good faith on the part of the doctor, I think the exercise of his discretion in the area of advice must depend upon the patient's overall needs. To be taken into account should be the gravity of the condition to be treated, the importance of the benefits to be expected to flow from the treatment or procedure, the need to encourage him to accept it, the relevant significance of its inherent risks, the intellectual and emotional capacity of the patient to accept the information without such distortion as to prevent any rational decision at all, and the extent to which the patient may seem to have placed himself in his doctor's hands with the invitation that the latter accept on his behalf the responsibility for intricate or technical decisions . . . .[1]

This firm endorsement of the 'professional standard' of disclosure was followed by a rejection of the proposition that there should be an automatic need to describe all possible risks involved in a procedure. This, it was thought, would distract doctors from their prime responsibility of caring for the health of their patients.

This difficulty of determining just what risks should be disclosed has been grappled with by the courts in several cases. Canadian decisions are useful here. In *Hopp v Lepp*[2] the plaintiff had suffered injury as a result of a back operation. This case had certain special features which rather strained the consent doctrine – the patient alleged that the doctor should have told him that this was the first time he would perform the operation since obtaining his Specialist Certificate, an argument which the court, not surprisingly, rejected.

19 Per McNair J [1957] 2 All ER at 124.
20 [1932] 1 DLR 507.
 1 Per Woodhouse J [1964] NZLR at 250.
 2 (1980) 112 DLR 3d 67.

Apart from dealing with this rather tenuous argument, however, the court also emphasised that the doctor need disclose only *probable* or *special or unusual* risks. A doctor need not go into every conceivable detail of a proposed operation provided he describes its general nature and, particularly, answers any questions which the patient puts to him.

The evidence of expert medical witnesses as to what is established practice in relation to disclosure plays an important part in deciding whether there has been a failure to inform adequately. The significance of this is that reliance on such evidence inevitably weights the matter in favour of the medical defendant and, thereby, contradicts the principle of self-determination by the patient. British courts have clearly favoured the expert witness approach, as can be seen in the judgment in *Chatterton v Gerson*.[3] There has been a move in the other direction in Canada, with greater weight being given to the role of the court as the trier of fact in assessing what it was that the patient wanted to know or, indeed, needed to know. This was the approach adopted in *Reibl v Hughes*[4] and followed in *White v Turner*.[5] In *White*, the patient had been submitted to breast reduction surgery which left her with large scars, the possibility of which had not been adequately explained. The court held that there had been negligence and took the opportunity to observe that the upshot of the Supreme Court's decision in *Reibl* was that

> no longer does the medical profession *alone* collectively determine, by its own practices, the amount of information a patient should have in order to decide whether to undergo an operation.[6]

This was not to be taken to mean that doctors should give complicated medical seminars on medicine to all their patients: it did mean, though, that patients should be treated as intelligent, rational people to whom matters should be explained in some detail. This, the court felt, perhaps rather optimistically, would lead to the emergence of medical practitioners who were 'even more sensitive, concerned and humane than they now are'.

The consent doctrine in the future
The progress of the consent doctrine has been described by North American writers as a 'tempest'.[7] Certainly, the history of its

3 [1981] QB 432, [1981] 1 All ER 257.
4 (1980) 114 DLR (3d) 1.
5 (1981) 120 DLR (3d) 269.
6 At 283, per Linden J.
7 See, for example, E J Pickard 'The Tempest of Informed Consent' in L Klar (ed) *'Canadian Studies in the Law of Tort'* (1977) p. 129.

development in the United States has shown remarkable inconsistency, leading in many cases to absurdities and encouraging malpractice litigation unduly.[8] It has undoubtedly resulted in greater sensitivity on the part of the American medical profession to the need to inform patients of the implications of treatment but this positive result has only been achieved at the price of heightened distrust and an increase in the practice of legalistic and defensive medicine.

It is unlikely that the consent doctrine will be as widely used in British courts as it has been in the United States. The lines have now been clearly drawn on the issue of the battery/negligence distinction and that undoubtedly restricts the scope of consent actions. In addition, reliance on expert evidence is likely to continue which means that the movement towards the patient-orientated approach which is evident in the recent Canadian decisions is unlikely to occur.

The consent issue should also be seen in the context of the overall attitude of the courts towards the question of medical liability. British courts are clearly cautious, even if not all judges are as favourable to doctors as was Lord Denning. Actions based on lack of consent are generally seen by lawyers as a last-ditch attempt to obtain damages when no more obvious medical negligence is evident. In this light, consent actions may well be regarded as back door attempts to extend the scope of medical liability and may, therefore, expect to encounter both judicial scepticism and powerfully voiced policy objections.[9]

8 In *Truman v Thomas* 611 P 2d 902 (Cal 1980) a doctor was, effectively, held liable for failing to convince a reluctant patient of the importance of a screening test for cancer.
9 See, in general, G Robertson 'Informed Consent to Medical Treatment' (1981) 97 LQR 102.

10 Medical negligence

When doctors in Britain look over their shoulders at the picture of medical litigation in North America, there is a virtually unanimous dislike for what they see. Concern is regularly expressed in medical circles over the American 'malpractice crisis' and at the possibility of its export – Britain frequently attracts social and legal phenomena which have first manifested themselves in the United States, so why should we be immune to a burgeoning of medical litigation? This fear may be unjustified but it is certainly understandable; the size and frequency of awards against American doctors has had an appreciable effect on medical practice in the United States and has also added considerably to the cost of medical treatment. Doctors elsewhere now see the situation in the United States as verging on the absurd and are anxious to prevent its repetition in their own countries. In fact, although the frequency of claims against doctors has risen markedly in the United Kingdom, they by no means approach the level prevailing in the United States and they are extremely unlikely to do so.

It is difficult to single out any one cause for what increase there has been in the volume of medical negligence actions. One possibility, difficult to prove empirically, might be the existence of a growing 'compensation awareness' in the mind of the public. It might be that a greater proportion of the population are now aware that the courts can and, on occasion, do provide substantial compensation for personal injury; extensive press coverage of issues such as the thalidomide claim has undoubtedly served to alert the general public to the possibilities. Another factor which is sometimes suggested as providing an explanation for the increase in such actions is the depersonalisation of the doctor-patient relationship. It is undoubtedly easier to sue a relatively anonymous defendant such as a hospital consultant than to sue a family doctor whom one has known for many years – and this is even more true of a Hospital Authority.

There is no doubt that actions by patients against doctors are unusually time-consuming, expensive and potentially destructive. The professional time involved in the processing of such claims is considerable and the period between injury and compensation can be long. An award which has been made against a hospital will eat into funds which were originally intended for other purposes and the quality of care given to other patients may be consequently diminished. The professional reputation of the doctor may be seriously damaged by a single alleged incident of negligence and the effect which this has may be out of all proportion to the seriousness of the fault.

Yet it is impossible for the medical profession to wish out of existence the real damage so caused. A patient who has been injured by an act of medical negligence has suffered in a way which is recognised by the law as requiring compensation. This loss may be continuing and what may seem like an unduly large award may be little more than that sum which is required to compensate him for such matters as loss of future earnings and the future cost of medical or nursing care. To deny a legitimate claim or to restrict arbitrarily the size of an award would amount to substantial injustice. After all, there is no difference in legal theory between the plaintiff injured through medical negligence and the plaintiff injured in an industrial or motor accident.

A radical alternative to negligence actions is to introduce a system of no-fault compensation which will provide for the making of awards to injured patients irrespective of the requirement of proving fault on the part of medical personnel. Such a scheme has operated in New Zealand since 1974 as part of an overall no-fault compensation scheme and has been shown to work reasonably satisfactorily.[1] In the medical context, however, the claimant must establish that the injury resulted from 'medical or surgical misadventure', a requirement which has caused difficulties in distinguishing between those conditions which result from the physiological progress of a medical condition and those which are genuinely the result of misadventure occurring in the course of treatment.

The question of compensation for medical injury in the United Kingdom was discussed as a special issue by the Royal Commission on Compensation for Personal Injury (The Pearson Commission).[2] The Commission considered the arguments in favour of and against introducing a system similar to that operated in New Zealand and concluded that there were not, at this point, sufficient grounds for introducing no-fault compensation schemes. It would seem, then, that the victims of medical negligence will have to continue to seek compensation through a fault-based tort system, a system which is lengthy and which is fraught with problems for the potential litigant.

1 G Palmer *Compensation for Incapacity* (1979) p. 255.
2 Cmnd 7054-1.

In the following sections, we analyse the operation of this system and the rules it has developed for the adjudication of such claims.

The basis of medical liability

Vicarious liability

A medical injury may have been caused to the plaintiff by any one or more of the medical personnel who have treated him. Locating negligence may be simple in some cases but, in others, the patient may have to choose the responsible party from a fairly large group which may include a general practitioner, a hospital consultant, other hospital doctors and the nursing staff. The question then arises of deciding against whom the plaintiff should proceed in any claim for damages.

If an allegation of negligence on the part of a general practitioner is made, the plaintiff may then proceed directly against the doctor in question. The general practitioner in the United Kingdom is solely responsible for the treatment of his patients and there can be no question of responsibility being imposed on a health authority unless the authority has intervened in the practitioner's treatment of his patient. Normally, of course, the general practitioner will be a member of a medical defence society, to whom he will refer any claim against him; the society then advises him and undertakes the defence or settlement of the claim.

The position is different if the alleged negligence occurs after the general practitioner has referred the patient for further treatment within the NHS. If the negligent act is committed by a health service employee, the patient then has the choice of proceeding either against the individual he feels has been negligent or against the Health Authority, or against both in a joint action. In practice, many actions are brought against the Health Authority on the grounds of convenience.

The legal principle under which a health authority is liable for the negligent acts of its employees is that of vicarious liability. This provides that an employer is liable for his employee's negligent acts, provided that the employee is acting within the scope of his employment. It should be borne in mind that the employer may still be held vicariously liable even if the employee acts in direct contradiction of his employer's instructions or prohibitions.[3]

It is only comparatively recently that hospitals have been held vicariously liable for the negligent acts of their medical staff. In a long line of cases dating from the early years of this century, the courts

---

3 J G Fleming *Law of Torts* (5th edn, 1977) p. 366.

took the view that the normal principles of vicarious liability did not apply, possibly because the judges were unwilling to see hospitals, which were often charitable institutions, bearing the cost of such awards. In one of the early cases, for example, *Hillyer v Governors of St Bartholomew's Hospital*,[4] the court made a distinction between, on the one hand, a failure of hospitals to provide staff, food, etc. and, on the other, professional negligence on the part of medical staff. Damages might be awarded against the hospital in respect of the former while they would be refused in respect of the latter.

This view changed. In *Gold v Essex County Council*,[5] the various sorts of staff were distinguished. Hospitals might be liable for the torts of those staff who had contracts *of* service, while torts committed by those who had contracts *for* services would not entail the liability of the hospital. Consultants came into the latter category.

The extent of the vicarious liability of hospital authorities was considerably extended with the important decision in *Roe v Minister of Health, Woolley v Minister of Health*.[6] In this case two patients had suffered injury as a result of the injection of a contaminated spinal anaesthetic drawn from cracked ampoules. Although it was held both in the trial court and on appeal that there was no negligence on the part of the anaesthetist, it was ruled on appeal that the hospital would have been liable on the *respondeat superior* principle if there had been negligence. Although the court left the position of consultant surgeons in some doubt, *Roe* signalled the end of the hospital authorities' immunity from vicarious liability in this area which they had previously enjoyed. Further confirmation of the ending of the distinction between consultants and other medical staff came with *Razzel v Snowball*[7] and *Higgins v North West Metropolitan Regional Hospital Board*.[8,9]

The fact that a hospital authority may be sued in respect of the negligent acts of its employees does not mean that the final bill for payment of damages should be laid at its doors. Since 1954, the position in England has been regulated by an agreement between the Minister and the medical defence societies,[10] an informal agreement similarly regulating the position in Scotland. Under the terms of this

4 [1909] 2 KB 820, CA.
5 [1942] 2 KB 293, [1942] 2 All ER 237, CA.
6 [1954] 2 QB 66, [1954] 2 All ER 131, CA.
7 [1954] 3 All ER 429, [1954] 1 WLR 1382, CA.
8 [1954] 1 All ER 414, [1954] 1 WLR 411.
9 Until *Hayward v Board of Management of the Royal Infirmary of Edinburgh* and *Macdonald v Glasgow Western Hospitals Board of Management* 1954 SC 453, Scots law was in line with *Hillyer*. With the decision in these cases, hospitals in Scotland became vicariously liable for negligence on the part of consultants.
10 Circular HM (54) 32.

agreement, in the event of a successful claim involving the negligence of a hospital employee, the cost of any damages awarded will be divided between the authority and the doctor's defence society. The proportion of the award to be borne by each side is a matter to be agreed in advance or, in the event of no agreement being reached, to be borne in equal shares by both parties. This agreement also includes rules regulating the circumstances in which a claim may be settled out of court. As far as nurses are concerned, the Royal College of Nursing holds an insurance policy which provides indemnification for every member of the College. It would be improbable, however, that a hospital authority would seek a contribution from an uninsured nurse in respect of damages caused by her negligence.

What constitutes negligence?

In determining whether there has been negligence in medical treatment, the courts pursue the same line of enquiry as they pursue in any other claim based on negligence: did the conduct of the defendant amount to a breach of the duty of care which he owed to the injured plaintiff? Expressed somewhat differently, this amounts to asking whether the standard of the treatment given by the defendant fell below the standard expected of him by the law and whether there was, therefore, any fault in the legal sense. Fault remains the theoretical underpinning of the law in this area until such time as strict liability may be imposed. Moreover, the burden of proving fault lies on the plaintiff, although this may be qualified in those cases where the doctrine of *res ipsa loquitur* is applied.

The reasonably skilful doctor
There have been many judicial pronouncements by the courts on the standard of care which is expected of the doctor. As early as 1838 we see Tindall CJ ruling that:

> Every person who enters into a learned profession undertakes to bring to the exercise of it a reasonable degree of care and skill. He does not undertake, if he is an attorney, that at all events you shall gain your case, nor does a surgeon undertake that he will perform a cure; nor does he undertake to use the highest possible degree of skill.[11]

An echo of this is to be found in *R v Bateman*,[12] where the court explained that:

---

11 *Lanphier v Phipos* (1838) 8 C&P 475 at 478.
12 (1925) 94 LJKB 791 at 794, CCA.

If a person holds himself out as possessing special skill and knowledge, by and on behalf of a patient, he owes a duty to the patient to use due caution in undertaking the treatment . . . The jury should not exact the highest, or very high standard, nor should they be content with a very low standard.

The doctor is thus not expected to be a miracle-worker guaranteeing a cure or a man of the very highest skill in his calling. What then is he expected to meet? McNair J provides us with an unambiguous answer to this question in *Bolam v Friern Hospital Management Committee:*[13]

The test is the standard of the ordinary skilled man exercising and professing to have that special skill. A man need not possess the highest expert skill at the risk of being found negligent. It is a well-established law that it is sufficient if he exercises the ordinary skill of an ordinary man exercising that particular art.

The doctor having that degree of competence expected of the ordinary skilful doctor sets the standard. He is the practitioner who follows the standard practice of his profession – or, at least, follows practices that would not be disapproved of by responsible opinion within the profession; he has a reasonably sound grasp of medical techniques and is as informed of new medical developments as the average competent doctor would expect to be.

Usual practice
The 'custom test' – the test whereby a defendant's conduct is tested against the normal usage of his profession or calling – is one that is applied in all areas of negligence law. The courts have given expression to this test in the medical context in a number of decisions. In the important Scottish case of *Hunter v Hanley*, for example, there was a clear endorsement of the custom test in Lord Clyde's dictum:

To establish liability by a doctor where deviation from normal practice is alleged, three facts require to be established. First of all it must be proved that there is a usual and normal practice; secondly it must be proved that the defender has not adopted that practice; and thirdly (and this is of crucial importance) it must be established that the course the doctor adopted is one which no professional man of ordinary skill would have taken if he had been acting with ordinary care.[14]

This attractively simple exposition of the law, however, conceals a hurdle at the outset. It may, in many cases, be possible to prove that there is a 'usual and normal practice' but there will obviously be disagreement as to what is the appropriate course to follow in a

13 [1957] 2 All ER 118 at 121, [1957] 1 WLR 582 at 586.
14 1955 SC 200 at 206.

number of medical areas. In some circumstances, the existence of two
schools of thought may result in more than one option being open to
a practitioner. If this is so, then what are the liability implications of
choosing a course of action which a responsible body of opinion
within the profession may well reject? Precisely this question arose in
Bolam,[15] where the plaintiff had suffered fractures as a result of the
administration of electro-convulsive therapy without an anaesthetic.
At the time, there were two schools of thought on the subject of
anaesthesia in such treatment, one holding the view that relaxant
drugs should be used, the other being that this only increased the risk.
In this case, the judge ruled that a doctor would not be negligent if he
acted 'in accordance with the practice accepted by a responsible body
of medical men skilled in that particular art'. Negligence would not be
inferred merely because there was a body of opinion which took a
contrary view. At the same time, however, the courts specifically
rejected the possibility of a doctor escaping liability if he 'pig-
headedly' adhered to discredited techniques.[16] The doctor has a duty
to keep himself informed of major developments in practice but this
duty obviously cannot extend to the requirement that he should
know all there is to be known in a particular area of medicine. In the
case of *Crawford v Board of Governors of Charing Cross Hospital*, the
plaintiff had developed brachial palsy as a result of his arm being kept
in a certain position during an operation. Six months prior to the
operation an article had appeared in *The Lancet* pointing out the
danger of brachial palsy when the patient's arm was kept in such a
position, but the anaesthetist against whom negligence was being
alleged had not read the article in question. The Court of Appeal
eventually found in favour of the anaesthetist, Lord Denning stating
that:

> it would, I think, be putting too high a burden on a medical man to say that
> he has to read every article appearing in the current medical press; and it
> would be quite wrong to suggest that a medical man is negligent because he
> does not at once put into operation the suggestions which some
> contributor or other might make in a medical journal. The time may come
> in a particular case when a new recommendation may be so well proved
> and so well known, and so well accepted that it should be adopted, but that
> was not so in this case.[17]

Failure to read a single article, it was said, may be excusable, while
disregard of a series of warnings in the medical press could well be
evidence of negligence.

15 [1957] 2 All ER 118, [1957] 1 WLR 582.
16 For similar expressions of this view in American law, see A Holder *Medical
   Malpractice Law* (1978) p. 447.
17 (1953) Times, 8 December, CA.

Innovative techniques Resort to an innovative technique of treatment may be appropriate in certain cases but should be adopted with caution. Whether or not the use of such a technique could amount to negligence would depend on the extent which its use was considered justified in the case in question (see also discussion on experimentation in chapter 15, below). In assessing this, a court would consider evidence of trials of the technique and would also no doubt take into consideration any dangers which it entailed. It is possible that a court would decline to endorse the use of an untried procedure if the patient was thereby exposed to considerable risk of damage. Other factors which might be taken into account would be the previous response of the patient to more conventional treatment, the seriousness of the patient's condition and the attitude of the patient himself towards the use of the novel or risky treatment.

Misdiagnosis

A doctor is expected by the law to use the same degree of care in making a diagnosis that is required of him in all his dealings with his patients. A mistake in diagnosis will not be considered negligent if this standard of care is observed but will be treated as one of the nonculpable and inevitable hazards of practice.[18] Liability may, however, be imposed when a mistake in diagnosis is made because the doctor failed to conduct tests which a competent practitioner would have considered appropriate or when the doctor fails to diagnose a condition which would have been spotted by a competent practitioner.

One of the problems in determining whether there has been a mistake in diagnosis turns on the issue of deciding what investigative techniques need to be used in a particular case. Ordinary laboratory tests must be used if symptoms suggest their use but elaborate and expensive investigative procedures would not be expected other than in complicated or puzzling cases. Failure to x-ray for example, might well be negligence, as is shown in the following case dealt with by the Medical Defence Union in 1978:

> A 48 year old woman attended a casualty department after falling down some steps at work. She was seen by a locum consultant who found a painful right arm and ankle but no clinical signs of fracture. No x-rays were taken. She attended her practitioner for regular check-ups; five weeks after the accident, shoulder movement was still restricted . . . the patient has a

18 *In Crinon v Barnet Group Hospital Management Committee* (1959) Times, 19 November, the judge said of a misdiagnosis: 'Unfortunate as it was that there was a wrong diagnosis, it was one of those misadventures, one of those chances, that life holds for people.'

severe permanent disability with disfigurement and restriction of movement. The claim, which was considered indefensible, was settled. . . .[19]

At the same time, though, it is to be appreciated that all
investigations, including x-rays, carry some risk and their use cannot
be indiscriminate.

Langley v Campbell[20] and *Tuffil v East Surrey Area Health
Authority*[1] provide instances of successful actions against doctors on
the basis of failure to diagnose correctly the nature of the patient's
complaint. In *Langley*, the patient had returned from East Africa
shortly before the development of symptoms. The general practitioner failed to diagnose malaria and negligence was found, the judge
accepting the evidence of a relative who said that the family had
suggested such a diagnosis to the doctor. In *Tuffil*, the patient had
spent many years in a tropical climate; the doctor failed to diagnose
amoebic dysentery which proved fatal. This failure to diagnose was
held to be negligence on the doctor's part.

An example of an unsuccessful claim of this sort is provided by
Whiteford v Hunter. The defendant in this case had diagnosed
carcinoma of the bladder, a diagnosis which was subsequently found
to be incorrect. An important question was whether the defendant
should have used a cystoscope: he did not have one in his possession
and it would have been difficult to obtain one. The court found that
there was no negligence in the misdiagnosis, holding that the
defendant had used methods which were in common use at the time.[2]

Negligence in treatment

The most important distinction to be made here is that between a
medical mistake which the law regards as excusable and a mistake
which would amount to negligence. In the former case, the court
accepts that ordinary human fallibility precludes liability while, in the
latter, the conduct of the defendant is considered to have gone
beyond the bounds of what is expected of the reasonably skilful or
competent doctor.

The issue recently came before the courts in the case of *Whitehouse
v Jordan*.[3] In this case negligence was alleged on the part of an
obstetrician who, it was claimed, had pulled too hard in a trial of
forceps delivery and had thereby caused the plaintiff's head to

19 Medical Defence Union, Annual Report 1978.
20 (1975) Times, 6 November.
 1 *The Times*, 15 March 1978, p. 4.
 2 (1950) 94 Sol Jo 758, HL. Note 'at the time'; such an error would be indefensible
    today.
 3 [1981] 1 All ER 267, [1981] 1 WLR 246, HL.

become wedged with consequent asphyxia and brain damage. The trial judge held that, although the decision to perform a trial of forceps was a reasonable one, the defendant had in fact pulled too hard and was therefore negligent. This initial finding of negligence was reversed in the Court of Appeal and, in a strongly worded judgment, Lord Denning emphasised that an error of judgment was not negligence.[4] Implicit in Lord Denning's remarks was a strong policy based unwillingness to find negligence against doctors, an unwillingness which is to be seen in a number of the earlier judgments of the same judge.[5]

When the matter came on appeal before the House of Lords, the views expressed by Lord Denning on the error of judgment question were rejected. An error of judgment could be negligence if it is an error which would not have been made by a reasonably competent professional man acting with ordinary care. As Lord Fraser pointed out:

> The true position is that an error of judgment may, or may not, be negligent; it depends on the nature of the error. If it is one that would not have been made by a reasonably competent professional man professing to have the standard and type of skill that the defendant holds himself out as having, and acting with ordinary care, then it is negligence. If, on the other hand, it is an error that such a man, acting with ordinary care, might have made, then it is not negligent.[6]

In the event, the House of Lords held that there had not, in any case, been sufficient evidence to justify the trial judge's finding of negligence on the part of the defendant in question.

Gross medical mistakes will usually result in a finding of negligence. Operating mistakes such as the removal of the wrong limb or the performance of an operation on the wrong patient are usually treated as indefensible and settled out of court: hence the paucity of decisions on such points. Use of the wrong drug or, often with more serious consequences, the wrong gas during the course of an anaesthetic will frequently lead to the imposition of liability, and in some of these situations the *res ipsa loquitur* principle may be applied.[7]

Many cases deal with items of operating equipment being left inside patients after surgery. In these, generally known as the 'swab

---

4 [1980] 1 All ER 650 at 658, CA.
5 For further instances, see G Robertson 'Whitehouse v Jordan – Medical Negligence Retired' [1981] 44 MLR 457.
6 [1981] 1 All ER at 281.
7 *Strangeways – Lesmere v Clayton* [1936] 2 KB 11, [1936] 1 All ER 484; *Collins v Hertfordshire County Council* [1947] KB 598, [1947] 1 All ER 633; *Gray v Mid-Herts Hospital Management Committee* (1974) 118 Sol Jo 501.

cases', the allocation of liability is made according to the principle laid down in the *locus classicus* of the law on this point, the decision in *Mahon v Osborne*.[8] In this case, as in subsequent decisions, the courts have shown themselves unlikely to dictate to doctors in a hard and fast way the exact procedure that should be used towards the end of an operation in order to ensure no foreign bodies are left in the patient. At the same time, however, it is clear that the law requires that there should be some sort of set procedures adopted in order to minimise the possibility of this occurring.[9] Overall responsibility to see that swabs and other items are not left in the patient rests on the surgeon; he is not entitled to delegate the matter altogether to a nurse.

This point was emphasised in *Mahon* by Lord Goddard who said:

> As it is the task of the surgeon to put swabs in, so it is his task to take them out and if the evidence is that he has not used a reasonable standard of care he cannot absolve himself, if a mistake has been made, by saying, 'I relied on the nurse'.[10]

In the same case, however, Scott LJ qualified the surgeon's responsibility by pointing out that there may be cases where the surgeon needs to act urgently to close the wound and, in such cases, it may be necessary to dispense with normal precautions.

In the later case of *Urry v Bierer*[11] the Court of Appeal confirmed that the patient was entitled to expect the surgeon to do all that was reasonably necessary to ensure that all packs were removed and that this duty required more than mere reliance on the nurse's count.

The problem of the novice   The degree of expertise possessed by a medical practitioner obviously depends to a considerable extent on his experience. The question of the novice's status has been raised in some cases and the argument has been put forward that the standard of competence of a newly qualified doctor will be less than that expected of an experienced practitioner. Although this may be the day to day expectation, it is not the expectation of the law. In all cases the courts expect the doctor to show that degree of skill which would be shown by the reasonably competent professional man. This is an objective standard and it is therefore irrelevant whether the doctor has qualified the day before or ten years before the alleged incident of negligence – it will make no difference to the way in which his conduct is assessed.

A great deal of treatment in hospitals is carried out by junior

8 [1939] 2 KB 14, [1939] 1 All ER 535, CA.
9 See G Martin *Law relating to Medical Practice* (1979) p. 382.
10 [1939] 1 All ER at 559.
11 (1955) Times, 15 July, CA.

doctors, or even medical students, to whom the duty has been delegated. Such a doctor or student will be answerable to the injured patient if he is negligent. The hospital will also be answerable on the normal principle of vicarious liability. As Lord Denning said in *Jones v Manchester Corpn:*

> It would be in the highest degree unjust that the hospital board, by getting inexperienced doctors to perform their duties for them, without adequate supervision, should be able to throw all the responsibility on to those doctors as if they were fully experienced practitioners.[12]

Delegation of responsibility to another may, however, amount to negligence in certain circumstances. A consultant could be negligent were he to delegate responsibility to a junior in the knowledge that the junior was incapable of perforn.ing his duties properly.

A junior to whom responsibility has been delegated must carry out his duties as instructed by his superior in order to avoid liability. If he chooses to depart from specific instructions, he will be placing himself in a risky position in the event of anything going wrong.[13] At the same time, there may be circumstances in which he is entitled to depart from instructions; obedience to manifestly wrong instructions might, in some cases, be construed as negligence.

A subjective/objective problem has arisen in the United States in the shape of the locality rule. This rule was widely applied until quite recently but currently survives in modified form in only relatively few States. The essence of the rule is that different standards of competence are expected in different areas; which means that there was no single standard of sound medical practice applicable equally in the city and in the country. With the development of the referral services and with the tightening up of standards in medical education, any real rationale for this rule has now disappeared and its total demise may reasonably be expected. The rule has no application in the United Kingdom and is unlikely to be favoured in other Commonwealth jurisdictions.

Protecting the patient from himself
In certain circumstances, it is part of the duty of doctors and nurses to predict that patients may damage themselves as a result of their medical condition. The extent of the duty to safeguard against such damage is problematical and the decisions do not all go the same way.

---

12 [1952] 2 QB 852 at 871, [1952] 2 All ER 125 at 133, CA.
13 *Junor v Inverness Hospitals Board of Management and McNicol* (1959) Times, 26 March, HL.

138   Medical negligence

In *Selfe v Ilford and District Hospital Management Committee*[14] the plaintiff had been admitted to hospital after a drug overdose. Although he had known suicidal tendencies, he was not kept under constant observation and climbed on to the hospital roof and fell, incurring injuries while the two nurses on duty were out of the ward. Damages of £19,000 were awarded against the hospital.

By contrast, in *Thorne v Northern Group Hospital Management Committee*[15] the plaintiff failed to win an award of damages for the death of his wife who had left a hospital in suicidal mood. In this case the patient had slipped out of the hospital when the nurses' backs were turned, returned home and gassed herself. The court took the view that, although the degree of supervision which a hospital should exercise in relation to patients with known suicidal tendencies is higher than that to be exercised over other patients, such patients could not be kept under constant supervision by hospital staff.

More recently, in *Hyde v Tameside Area Health Authority*[16] the Court of Appeal overturned a High Court award of substantial damages to a plaintiff who, believing he had cancer, made a suicide attempt in hospital. Not only did the court take the view that there had been no breach of duty on the part of the defendants, but Lord Denning stressed in his judgment that there were strong policy grounds why damages should not be awarded in respect of attempted suicide.[17]

Res ipsa loquitur

Because it may be difficult in many personal injury actions to establish negligence on the part of the defendant, courts occasionally have recourse to the doctrine of res ipsa loquitur. This doctrine does not shift the onus of proof to the defendant as is sometimes suggested; what it does achieve is to give rise to an inference of negligence on the defendant's part. It follows that it is considerably easier for the plaintiff to succeed in his claim when *res ipsa loquitur* applies.

The doctrine is most useful in cases where damage has occurred in an incident involving machinery or in the context of damage suffered while the plaintiff was involved in some sort of complex process. It

14 (1970) 114 Sol Jo 935.
15 (1964) 108 Sol Jo 484.
16 (1981) Times, 16 April, CA.
17 This decision must now be read in the light of the comments on policy contained in *McLoughlin v O'Brian* [1982] 2 All ER 298, [1982] 2 WLR 982 where the court indicated a reluctance to limit recovery for foreseeable damage on the grounds that policy considerations excluded such recovery. See G R Douglas 'Damages for Suicide and Failed Attempts' (1982) 126 Sol Jo 455.

applies only where the plaintiff is unable to identify the precise nature of the negligence which caused his injury and where no explanation of the way in which the injury came to be inflicted has been offered by the defendant. The injury itself must be of such a kind as 'does not normally happen' in the circumstances in question unless there is negligence.

The doctrine's application in medical cases may be particularly apt because of the difficulty that the ordinary plaintiff sometimes experiences in unravelling the cause of an injury sustained during technical procedures of which he has little understanding; indeed, he may well have been unconscious during the procedures. It may also be seen as a potential corrective to the tendency of the medical profession to 'close ranks' when one of their number is accused of negligence.

In general, however, there is a marked reluctance on the part of the courts to apply the *res ipsa loquitur* principle, and this is certainly evident in medical negligence cases. Nevertheless, there are cases where the injuries sustained by the patient are of such a nature that there is an inescapable inference of negligence. The Canadian case of *MacDonald v York County Hospital Corpn*[18] provides an example. In this case the plaintiff was admitted to hospital for treatment of a fractured ankle and left with an amputated leg. All the requirements of *res ipsa loquitur* were present: a leg is not usually lost in such circumstances unless there is negligence; the plaintiff was not able to explain what had happened, nor was the defendant; and the plaintiff had identified the doctor whose negligence must have been responsible for the injury.

Similarly, in *Cassidy v Ministry of Health* the doctrine was applied in an English case in which the plaintiff went into hospital for an operation to remedy Dupuytren's contracture of two fingers and came out with four stiff fingers. Denning LJ (as he then was) expressed the view that the plaintiff was quite entitled to say:

> I went into hospital to be cured of two stiff fingers. I have come out with four stiff fingers and my hand is useless. That should not have happened if due care had been used. Explain it if you can.[19]

Other examples of the application of the doctrine are to be found in 'Swab cases' discussed above. Although *res ipsa loquitur* will not automatically be applied, there are many cases of this sort in which it has been successfully invoked. In *Mahon v Osborne*,[20] for example, the court held that the patient could know nothing about swab

18 (1972) 28 DLR (3d) 521.
19 [1951] 2 KB 343 at 365, [1951] 1 All ER 574 at 588, CA.
20 [1939] 2 KB 14, [1939] 1 All ER 535, CA.

procedures in the operating theatre and it was therefore for the surgeon to show that he exercised due care to ensure that the swabs were not left there.

Injuries caused by drugs

The extensive use of drugs in modern medical practice, coupled with the wide variety of available products, inevitably leads to a high incidence of injuries for which they are responsible. The number of persons affected will be small in some instances due to the speedy detection of the dangers and the rapid withdrawal of the drugs concerned. In others, notably in the case of thalidomide, the damage suffered will be catastrophic and, for this reason, the question of compensation has become an intensely political issue. Drug companies, the profits of which have recently been appreciably higher than in other sectors of the manufacturing industry, are frequently cast in the role of the villains of the piece, at whose door the bill for compensation should be laid in its entirety and irrespective of any question of fault.

In theory, the current system of compensation for injury caused by the medical use of drugs does not differ in any respect from the system applied to any other injury. Effective remedies are available if a contract can be established between the supplier and the injured party. In the absence of a contract, as is normally the case in the use of prescription drugs, the plaintiff must rely on tort to achieve compensation and to be successful here there must, as with any other injury, be a finding of fault on the part of the defendant. Fault is often difficult to prove and this difficulty will be considerable when suing the manufacturer of a drug. Not only must the individual plaintiff establish that the company producing the drug foresaw, or ought to have foreseen, that his product would produce damage, but he must also establish that there was a causal link between the action of the drug and the injury of which he is complaining. The problems entailed in this may be daunting in view of the fact that the plaintiff will have been suffering from a medical condition – or a combination of medical conditions – prior to the ingestion of the drug and this, in turn, may have been only one of a number of drugs taken.

Dissatisfaction with the inadequacy of the system of compensation for the victims of drug injury has been expressed in demands for the abandoning of the existing system of fault-based compensation. Various alternatives have been suggested, including a New Zealand type system of state compensation, a system which would reverse the burden of proof in favour of the plaintiff (which the Pearson

Commission thought would make little difference) and a system of strict liability. This last alternative would apply not only when the injuries were caused by drugs but also in all other cases in which defective products were involved. Compensation for drug injury should thus be seen as part of the overall problem of compensating those injured by defective products.[1]

Opinion in favour of the system of strict liability is now overwhelming. Not only did the Pearson Commission and the Law Commission[2] recommend in its favour but, also, the Commission of the EEC has now issued a series of draft directives which embody the principle. The EEC directive, which, if eventually approved, is required to be embodied in the domestic legislation of member states in due course, provides that the person injured by a defective product will no longer have to prove that there was negligence on the part of a manufacturer provided that he can establish that the product was, in fact, defective and that his injury resulted from that defect. The radical implications of this are self-evident: a drug company, faced with a claim resulting from a defective product, will not be able to argue that it did all in its power to ensure the safety of its products. If the drug caused the damage, and there was no warning to the patient of contra-indications, then the company must bear the cost of compensation.[3]

Not unsurprisingly, the drug industry has reacted very strongly to suggestions that strict liability should be imposed. The industry's policy arguments against such a system focus on a variety of grounds: the unfairness of strict liability, the increased cost of the insurance which will be passed on to the consumer and the inhibitory effect which the system will have on the development of new drugs. The pharmaceutical industry's view is that, if strict liability is to be introduced for injuries caused by defective products, drug manufacturers should, ideally, be exempted on the grounds that they constitute a special case. Alternatively, if not treated as a special case, a 'state of the art' defence should be introduced. Under the terms of such a defence, a manufacturer could escape liability if he established that the drug was as safe as could be achieved given the state of knowledge at the time of its marketing. The EEC directive excludes such a defence, stating that:

> the producer of an article shall be liable for damage caused by a defect in the article, whether or not he knew or could have known of the defect. The

1 For a full discussion of the issue, see H Teff and C Munro *Thalidomide: The Legal Aftermath* (1976).
2 Cmnd 6831.
3 For an analysis of the implications of strict liability in this area, see R Smith 'Compensation for Drug Injury' (1981) 282 Brit Med J 1443, 1535, 1610.

producer should be liable even if the article could not have been regarded as defective in the light of the scientific and technological development at the time when he put the article into circulation.[4]

The drug companies' objections are understandable, given the financial consequences for themselves – or for the insurers – which such a scheme would entail. But not all the doubts over such a system are based on considerations of self-interest. There is, first and foremost, a philosophical question as to the morality of providing an elaborate system of compensation for those who happen to be injured by drugs when others, who may have identical injuries caused by different factors, go uncompensated. Is it fair that a person who loses the use of a limb because of the action of a drug should receive a large award, while one who is similarly affected because of the action of a virus should receive no financial compensation at all? It is undoubtedly unfair; the only difference lies in the former being able to identify a party responsible for his injury while the other is not able to do so. This 'unfairness' pervades tort law and can be tackled only by the radical reform of social welfare and compensation arrangements. For this reason, it is essentially a political rather than a legal problem.

A more pertinent criticism from the legal point of view is raised by the questions of causation and of acceptable risk-taking. The causation problem does not disappear when strict liability is introduced; the injured patient must still establish which drug it was which caused his injury. Then, as to risk taking, the question arises as to how such a scheme will deal with known risks which are voluntarily undertaken by the patient in order to seek some therapeutic benefit. Drugs are, after all, inherently dangerous yet they still serve a valuable purpose. The same cannot be said of many of the other products which people purchase.

From the point of view of the doctor or the pharmacist, the major concern over strict liability laws along the EEC lines lies in the need to ensure that the manufacturer can be adequately identified in order to avoid claims being made against himself.[5] This might entail elaborate bureaucratic procedures and the fear has been expressed it could lead to further development of the practice of defensive medicine.

---

4 Commission of the European Communities COM (79) 415 final.
5 On the problems associated with inability to identify the manufacturer of drugs, see the discussion of the series of American cases relating to DES-provoked cancer in (1981) 7 Amer J Law Med 213.

11 Health resources and dilemmas in treatment

No resources are infinite. Even if a basic material is widely available, the costs of harvesting, treating or assembling it put some restraint on its use; moreover, the manpower required for distribution and exploitation of the finished product is always going to be limited. Applying this to medicine, it is clear that it is impossible to provide every form of therapy for everyone – some sort of selective distribution is inevitable.

The logistics of medicine get no easier despite the massive technological advances of the last half century. Costs of all types are rising while the world faces persistent economic difficulties; the average span of life is increasing – at least in the developed countries; as a result, people need treatment for longer and this treatment is not of the 'easy-cure' type appropriate to infectious diseases but it is rather a matter of sophisticated care for the results of degenerative change. In addition, the public are better informed on medical matters and are better able to assimilate the information they are given; the choice of treatment is increasingly influenced by the patient's demands with proportional erosion of the doctor's discretion.

Somehow, a compromise must be achieved between demand and supply and, although there is very little law established on the subject, the distribution of scarce resources poses some of the more complex ethical problems of modern medicine. These are not confined to the higher administrative echelons nor to the more esoteric departments of major hospitals. They may, indeed, arise and be answered subconsciously – every time a doctor travels to visit a patient he is distributing his resources in favour of one priority and this is possibly at the expense of others with which he could have dealt during his non-productive driving time.

Such an example relates to the treatment of individuals. But the ethics of health service distribution can also be considered on a global scale; the problems arising on a national level occupy an intermediate position. We propose examining these as three separate issues.

143

Global distribution of resources

It is beyond question that the world's medical resources are distributed unevenly both in material and in human terms. The money to buy the expensive paraphernalia of what has been termed 'engineering medicine'[1] is simply not available in the developing countries; at the same time, there are inadequate facilities for the local training of doctors who must, therefore, travel to obtain experience. The result is a vicious circle in which doctors accustomed to the sophisticated methods of the developed nations return to their own countries only to depart again dissatisfied with what they have found. The response of the richer states is to attempt to fill the vacuum by supplying the highly complex diagnostic and therapeutic apparatus which characterises modern medicine. But does such well-intentioned aid represent either good medical morals or good medical politics? – morals and politics may, indeed, be synonymous because, as Davis[2] has pointed out, decisions on priorities of allocation can be translated as 'politics', 'management' or 'clinical judgment' depending on whether one is speaking in terms of international, national or individual needs.

Kennedy[3] is one of the most recent to criticise this policy openly but such criticism is not new, nor is it confined to those with a special interest in medical jurisprudence; it has long been realised that it is absurd to spend much effort in eradicating disease in underdeveloped areas only to allow the population to die of starvation because the necessary farming technology was not supplied at the same time. But the nature of medical aid to the developing countries cannot avoid being politically influenced and is certainly a matter beyond the control of the average doctor or lawyer.

We believe, however, that doctors could well look more closely at their attitude to the supply of medical manpower to those countries in need. Every year, large numbers of medical graduates go to the developed Commonwealth countries to obtain higher degrees. While it is true that these often mark the completion of a period of valuable higher training, it is also true that the effect is to divert such graduates away from the provision of that primary care which is so urgently needed in their countries and towards hospital based medicine which is clearly orientated to a wealthy society. It could be argued that, in so doing, we are doing our neighbours a disservice in that we should,

---

1 A term we discovered in a somewhat ironical article by A Davis and G Horobin 'the Problems of Priorities' (1977) 3 J Med Ethics 107.
2 See fn. 1, above.
3 I Kennedy *The Unmasking of Medicine* (1981) p. 35.

rather, be positively encouraging first line medical care at what would seem to some to be a relatively primitive level.[4] Again, however, it is conceded that this is mainly a matter for political decision.

The allocation of national resources

We come closer to personal reality when discussing resource allocation on a national scale and, here, a mass of relevant literature has built up in recent years – much of which admits the near impossibility of a wholly just solution.

Ideally, resource allocation should provide equal access to health care for those in equal need. Attempts have been made in recent years to achieve this by systematically correlating the financial help given to the Area Health Authorities with their needs.[5] The needs have, in general, been assessed on the basis of the standardised mortality rates as representing the underlying morbidity. This, in itself, is open to criticism as it reflects the needs at hospital level rather than those of the provision of primary care; nevertheless, it appears to be an objective formula and one which can be readily understood – as a result of its use, the major discrepancies are being ironed out slowly. Even so, it has been pointed out that RAWP, as the formula is generally known, acts to the detriment of regions with rising health care targets[6] while the difficulty of reaching a mean level of allocation is shown by the fact that the rigid application of the formula across the United Kingdom would result in a reduction of about 15 per cent in Scotland's allocation with a less dramatic, though considerable, fall in the fortunes of Northern Ireland.

It may well be that both these countries have special problems – the influence of civil disturbance on the budget for Northern Ireland is an obvious feature which cannot be ignored. But the moral danger of manipulating the principle of equitable distribution in order to buy political support is obvious and is an area which might deserve more analysis. It has been suggested that one value of an explicit, albeit imperfect, formula for distribution of health resources on a national scale is that, as a result of its use, vote maximising policies become more obvious and are, thus, more

4 A symposium held in Edinburgh at which such views were widely supported is summarised by A G Fraser 'Medical Migration and World Health' (1977) 3 J Med Ethics 179.
5 DHSS, Sharing Resources for Health in England: Report of the Resource Allocation Working Party (1976). Similar studies have been made for Scotland, Wales and Northern Ireland.
6 G P A Winyard 'RAWP – New Injustices for Old?' (1981) 283 Brit Med J 930.

difficult to carry out.[7] Such reflections are, no doubt, extreme but the fact that problems in medical ethics may arise even at high level cannot be totally ignored.

When allocation is considered at stages further down the line – at regional or area level – equity becomes a less significant factor and gives way to the dictates of demand. This inevitably involves a choice and this choice must be, to some extent, arbitrary and must also reflect the purposes of those who impose that choice.[8] The ethical control of resources then depends, firstly, upon the broad base of representation on the allocation committee and, secondly, on the willingness of the constituent members not to press their own interests too hard – the lay influence of community health councils may be important at this point.

Even so, the choice can never be easy – is it possible to decide the relative importance between, say, strict economy, the avoidance of suffering or the prolongation of life? And, having done so, by what criteria is one to measure the extent of the priority chosen? Thus, if morbidity as a whole is taken as the yardstick, the alleviation of bronchitis and asthma has been found to take precedence; if, on the other hand, one considers total hospital in-patient days, mental health may be the single most important consideration.[9] But to say that mental health and respiratory disease constitute the most serious burdens on the Health Service is not necessarily to say that they merit the greatest allocation of resources. The nature of the population concerned must be taken into account – in other words, there is an economic incentive to apply some sort of 'productivity test' in distributing the resources of society; the question is – is it ethical to do so?

It seems inevitable that, so long as there is a restriction on resources – and there must be a limit even in Utopia – some principle of maximum societal benefit must be applied;[10] the individual's right to equality must, to some extent, be sacrificed to the general need. The precise determination of a maximum benefit policy may be difficult to make – Weale[10] has suggested the test of a 'prudent man' assessing his chances in a future situation – but the decision is societal rather

7 As suggested by A Maynard and A Ludbrook 'Applying Resource Allocation Formulae to Constituent Parts of the UK' (1980) 1 Lancet 85. The same authors suggest, somewhat cynically, that the remarkable differences may be the price to pay for maintaining the Union!

8 E G Knox 'Principles of Allocation of Health Care Resources' (1978) 32 J Epidem Com Hlth 3.

9 D A K Black and D J Pole 'Priorities in Biomedical Research' (1975) 29 Brit J Prev Soc Med 222.

10 A Weale 'Statistical Lives and the Principle of Maximum Benefit' (1979) 5 J Med Ethics 185.

than medical and involves a 'cost-benefit' analysis which, in turn, means placing a value on life. The problems are that society is not homogenous and that the only objective form of valuation available is retrospective – in effect, how much *has* it cost to save a life in a given situation; such parameters vary widely and it is unreal to expect to discover a true mean value of human life by these means. Nevertheless, some sort of figure would be useful if only to indicate when a given method of treatment or prevention was wildly unproductive. It seems to us to be self-evident that some form of cost evaluation in health care is essential at the resource planning level, if only to ensure impartiality – pressure groups are bad advocates in that they take no account of the deprivation elsewhere which is the concomitant to success in their own particular sphere. We would agree with those who believe that the ethical problem does not lie in the application of economics to health resource allocation; it should, rather, be accepted that without such control there is likely to be an unethical maldistribution of resources.[11] But this, we admit, does not resolve the practical difficulties of applying such a policy.

The legal situation
Financial restraints clearly place the Secretary of State in some difficulty in discharging his statutory duty to provide, to such extent as he thinks necessary to meet all reasonable requirements of the health service, health services including, inter alia, hospital accommodation.[12]

In some ways it is surprising that there have not been more actions brought by patients who feel that he has failed in these duties but, on reflection, it is probable that the dearth of cases results from the extreme improbability of a successful outcome. In the event, there appears to be only one apposite report.[13] In this case, patients in an orthopaedic hospital complained that they had waited an unreasonable time for treatment because of a shortage of facilities arising, in part, from a decision not to build a new block to the hospital on the grounds of cost; accordingly, they sought a declaration that the Secretary of State and the health authorities were in breach of their duty. In dismissing the application, Wien J said it was not the court's function to direct Parliament what funds to make available to the health service and how to allocate them. The duty to provide services

11 G H Mooney 'Cost-benefit Analysis and Medical Ethics' (1980) 6 J Med Ethics 177. See also W I Card and G H Mooney 'What is the Monetary Value of a Human Life?' (1977) 2 Brit Med J 1627.
12 National Health Service Act 1977, s. 3.
13 *R v Secretary of State for Social Services, ex p Hincks* (1979) 123 Sol Jo 436.

'to such extent as he considers necessary' gave the Minister a discretion as to the disposition of financial resources. The court could only interfere if the Secretary of State acted so as to frustrate the policy of the Act or as no reasonable Minister could have acted; and no such breach had been shown in the particular case. Moreover, even if a breach was proved, the Act did not admit of relief by way of damages.

The case went to appeal[14] where, as might be expected, the judgment turned on the interpretation of 'reasonable requirements'. Lord Denning MR considered this to mean that a failure of duty existed only if the Minister's action was thoroughly unreasonable. It was further thought that we should be faced with the economics of a bottomless pit if no limits in respect of long term planning were to be read into public statutory duties; the further the advances of medical technology, the greater would be the financial burden placed upon the Secretary of State.[15] As Finch[16] has pointed out, this litigation, although negative if taken in isolation, will have served its purpose even if it has done no more than shed light on the overriding economic considerations which conclude arguments as to the nature of public standards of care. But the case takes one very close to the more important ethical arena – that is, restriction in treatment of the individual.

Treatment of the individual

The whole practical and moral situation changes when the allocation of scarce resources falls to be considered at the level of the individual patient. Here we are dealing not with the hypothetical patient who may become ill but with one who is actually at risk. Objectivity is no longer the main arbiter and is replaced by need – and, in the event of enforced rationing, the assessment of relative needs dictates a value judgment.

How, then, is that judgment to be made? In practice, many decisions are made instinctively and without the need for profound analysis – thus, the single-handed doctor will unhesitatingly choose the patient in greater pain for treatment despite the fact that this will simultaneously delay the treatment of those in lesser pain. There may well be moral arguments against such a policy – it does, for example, act to the detriment of the stoic – but the circumstances are acute

14 This does not seem to have been reported. The findings are extracted from J D Finch *Health Services Law* (1981) pp. 38–9.
15 Per Bridge LJ.
16 See fn. 14, above.

and, with comparable urgency, the doctor has selected a single criterion on which to base his judgment. The moral agonising is, therefore, reserved for the treatment of chronic, life-threatening diseases not only because they offer the opportunity for analysis but because they attract the use of expensive resources and they will consume these resources for a long time – at which point, the dilemma relates not only to the allocation of resources but also to their withdrawal. In practice, the treatment of chronic renal disease and of brain injury provide good examples on which to base discussion.

It is easy to say that enough dialysis machines should be made available to treat all cases of chronic renal failure but we have already seen that this is simply not practicable in existing circumstances – it merely means that some other financially dependent resource must be curtailed. Costs can be cut by, say, changing a policy of hospital dialysis to one of home treatment but the fact of financial restraint is not thereby removed – only its degree is altered. But, at the same time, the modern patient undoubtedly regards access to 'engineering medicine'[17] as his individual right and such a view is tenable when there is an urgent need. If the doctor is, perforce, to qualify those rights, his reason for so doing must be beyond reproach and therein lies the problem – which we admit to finding virtually insoluble.

There is a growing tendency to discuss the allocation of resources in terms of triage. Triage is a curiously derived expression meaning the separation of casualities into priority treatment groups. It is essentially a military concept, the current British policy being to allocate four categories of casualty ranging from those whose slight injuries can be managed by self-care to those who cannot be expected to survive even with extensive treatment and who are, therefore, treated on a humanitarian basis only;[18] the policy is closely associated with that of casualty evacuation. Triage in this sense is not only good emergency surgical practice but is also ethically acceptable because it is directed to a single discernible end – that is, to win the war or the battle and we accept that this, in itself, is a morally acceptable objective with which the medical branch of the armed services can quite properly associate itself. It may, however, have unusual applications. The story is told that, with the advent during the Second World War of the new and scarce drug penicillin, instructions were given in an allied army that top priority was to be given for its use in the treatment of venereal disease rather than of

17 See fn. 1, above.
18 Triage is well described by M S Owen-Smith *High Velocity Missile Wounds* (1981) ch 4.

battle wounds on the grounds that this represented a maximum
return by way of military efficiency. The story may well be
apochryphal but it serves to illustrate two features. Firstly, given the
fact that there is an easily definable and ethically desirable objective,
the logical means taken towards that end may still be suspect.
Secondly, it reinforces the view, which we share, that the concept of
triage, which is an emergency procedure, cannot be simply trans-
muted to civilian practice.[19] It may be possible to do so in special
circumstances – for example, in a civil disaster when the single most
pressing objective is to mitigate the effects of that disaster. It is also
acceptable practice in the context of the emergency room or of the
intensive care unit because, there, one can select those who are
untreatable whether or not full resources are available – a point to
which we return later. But the term triage, and its underlying
principles, cannot be used as a convenient substitute, or subterfuge,
for resource allocation and should be abandoned for that purpose.
What, then, does one put in its place?

Alternative models
There have been many attempts to solve the problem[20] but none are
satisfactory – all generalisations fail when applied to the particular
but we will briefly outline some proposals which have been made. It
is, perhaps, easiest to progress from those parameters which we
consider to be least appropriate at the individual patient level.

We do not believe that cost-benefit should be a major influence
here. It needs no profound philosophical analysis to make one
appreciate instinctively that it is right to deploy a helicopter to rescue
a man on a drifting pleasure raft despite the fact that his danger is of
his own making, despite the expense and despite the fact that the
helicopter is designed to carry ten persons. The immediacy of the
situation has placed a very high value on life which it would be quite
immoral to ignore. The value cannot, however, be infinite otherwise,
faced with the choice of saving one man on a raft or ten men in a
sinking dinghy, the grounds for the 'value choice' would be equal
whereas, in practice, no one would doubt the correctness of choosing
the larger number – always provided the operational circumstances

19 N K Bell 'Triage in Medical Practices: An Unacceptable Model?' (1981) 15F Soc
Sci Med 151 gives an interesting philosophical discussion.
20 See, for example, the Editorial Comment 'Who Shall Die?' (1980) 6 J Med Ethics
171. An exhaustive analysis of the alternatives is given by H J J Leenen 'The
Selection of Patients in the Event of a Scarcity of Medical Facilities – An
Unavoidable Dilemma' (1979) 1 Internat J Med Law 161. See also the results of an
Edinburgh study: K M Boyd (ed) *The Ethics of Resource Allocation in Health Care*
(1979) ch 4.

were similar. Such choices must, however, be very rare in practice. In the chronic situation, as exemplified by dialysis, we are effectively confronted with a one to one choice between two individuals; at this point it is possible to introduce a cost-benefit argument which takes the form of assessing the relative gain to society of saving one or the other. In practice, this would invoke the use of some formula such as 'earning capacity × (65 – age)'. We believe that neither age nor income group should be significant criteria of choice *per se* – it might be that the mentally sub-normal or the aged respond less well to treatment than do others but that would be a different consideration. Such an assessment would, in addition, offend 'moral' practices which have almost attained the force of common law and of which 'women and children first' is an obvious example; women would, in general, come out worst if such objective cost-benefit criteria were to be applied.

The corollary to this line of thought is that scarce resources should be distributed on the basis of the 'deserts' or basic merits of the recipients. One aspect of this is discussed further in chapter 13 where we note a United States experiment which attempts to distribute a very scarce resource – human kidneys – to those hospitals which have, themselves, provided organs; while such a system has much to commend it, any benefit accrues to the hospital rather than to the individual patient who still has to be 'chosen' by some other method. Others would look at this criterion from the opposite point of view and would exclude those who could positively endanger the treatment programme – a group who aie exemplified by those carrying the virus of hepatitis. Such reasoning is a purely technical matter and is, in a sense, a criticism of the dialysis unit itself as being unable to contain the potential hazard by, for example, segregation. Moreover, if the argument were carried a few stages further, no haematological investigations or treatment involving the spillage of blood would ever be carried out on such patients on the grounds that some hospital worker might be injured.

More often, the assessment of 'deserts' is taken to apply to the intrinsic worth of the subjects to society – and, again, we may look at this from the negative or positive aspect. Firstly, there could be patients who, by reason of some other disability, could be regarded as being unlikely to benefit from treatment in a societal sense; this group, however, is essentially included among those falling to be assessed under the 'medical benefit' test and are best discussed within that context. The alternative, positive, approach in the event of shortage of facilities for treatment is to select those who offer the greatest contribution to society now and in the future. In our view, allocation tests which attempt to distinguish between, for example, the philanthropic mafia millionaire and the contestant for an international prize in applied mathematics serve no useful purpose in that they are hopelessly subjective. Even if the physician can adduce good reasons for preserving musicians at the expense of others – which is improbable – who is to choose between Benjamin Britten and John Lennon? Choices so based are clearly beyond the capacity or function of the doctor – and a 'committee decision', which is sometimes advocated, is no more than a sum of individual subjective assessments; we reject the concept. Similarly, we are not convinced that mothers have any clear rights over single women nor, for that matter, have breadwinners over housewives; in allowing such considerations to have a dominant influence in decision making, one is starting on a slippery slope which leads to such absurdities as considering the comparative re-marriage prospects of patients or of their spouses.

A test which has considerable backing is that which takes into major account the likely capacity of the treated patients to enjoy or profit from the results of their good fortune. While agreeing that this has some merit, we also find it to be too subjective to be of great value; it is, for example, difficult for a doctor with a middle class background not to believe that his middle class patient will have a better life than will one who is less fortunate financially. We would, however, suggest that, from the opposite point of view, it would be perfectly correct to exclude a patient who was physically incapable of making or intransigently unwilling to make use of the scarce resources offered.

Clearly, the most widely acceptable criteria of selection would be those determined by medical benefit. But, once again, this is easier to believe than to put into practice. Unless one is dealing with a recoverable condition – and dialysis, which provides the main theme for discussion, is only palliative – medical benefit is a relative matter and, moreover, prognosis is unpredictable. Further, it is virtually impossible in the circumstances under discussion to dissociate the purely medical criteria from those of social worth; as Bell[1] has pointed out, salvageability necessarily takes in social and economic overtones. Once again, however, there is an alternative viewpoint – in this case, that from which to consider the patient who is already using a scarce resource but who is obtaining no benefit. The most clear example of this is one who is brain damaged and is being maintained in intensive care – a situation discussed in detail in chapter 14, below. We believe that, once treatment is clearly of no avail, it is not only permissible but positively correct to discontinue heroic measures. Of the many reasons for taking this view, the one

1 See fn. 19, above.

which is presently apposite is that a resource is thereby released for someone who is likely to benefit.

Random selection

We have effectively left ourselves with only the option of random selection – or lottery, or 'first come, first served' which come to much the same thing in slightly different circumstances.

Such a policy has the advantage of apparent objectivity and may be adopted because those concerned regard it as morally preferable to the use of any other parameters; it is equally justified on the grounds that one has simply run out of alternatives. It is, however, a bad option medically because it takes no account of the gravity of the patient's condition and no account of 'medical benefit'; moreover, the sheer length of waiting lists may prevent the most acceptable cases from the physician's point of view from ever obtaining treatment. The option is, in addition, socially suspect in that it treats human beings as 'things' and pays no attention to human values and aspirations. Nevertheless, it may be the least offensive way of allocating scarce resources particularly if it is combined with the positive rejection of those who are *un*likely to benefit from their use.

Help from the law?

It is surprising that there is no case law on which to judge the attitudes of society in respect of allocation – perhaps this is because the most likely source of litigation, the use of dialysis, has been recognised as a special case and has been treated as such in the United States. For any assistance, it is necessary, we suspect, to go back to the classic case of *US v Holmes*.[2] In this instance, a ship's officer ordered a number of passengers to be ejected from a sinking life-boat; Holmes, who helped effect the instructions, was convicted of manslaughter. A main argument for the prosecution was that the passengers, at least, should have been chosen by lot. It seems fair to assume that this decision would lend support to a policy of randomisation in the event of competition for scarce medical resources; the inferred element of an 'appeal to God' certainly adds moral weight to the argument in favour.[3] We are, of course, aware that, in both *Holmes* and *Dudley*, the major element was that the decision-maker's own life was involved and this factor is not present in the case of a decision to be

2 (1841) 26 Fed Cas 360, No 15383.
3 But in the comparable English case *R v Dudley and Stephens* (1884) 14 QBD 273, another life-boat incident, the concept of a lottery was rejected. Here, it was indicated that inactivity was the correct legal solution; English case law is, thus, unhelpful in the present situation.

made between two or more patients; the precedent is, therefore, at best only loosely applicable to the present discussion.

As to the withdrawal of resources from a patient already using them, both United Kingdom and United States law is discussed in chapters 12 and 14. It is to be noted, however, that nowhere is there any authority for such action on the grounds of competing medical benefit – that is, that a second latecomer to the scene would be likely to do better; withdrawal action is only condoned when the patient can receive no further benefit.

A solution of the insoluble?
We have thus reached a position when no single parameter seems entirely satisfactory – and a combination of tests carries with it the combination of objections to the individual tests. Gordon,[4] in a discussion of the doctrine of necessity, speaks of offending 'against the feeling that no human being has a right to decide which of his fellows should survive in any situation'; but, while most would agree with this proposition, doctors cannot opt out of such decisions. Some idea of the complexity of the dilemma is given in a recent study of dialysis decisions.[5] In this, 40 specimen patients' records were sent to 25 renal units with the request that ten patients be rejected on the grounds of inadequate treatment resources. Only 13 patients would have been accepted in all the units, but, at the same time, none were rejected by all; in the event, it was discovered that six of the ten most commonly rejected cases had already been successfully treated by the authors! It would seem that something of a lottery system operates despite the most earnest endeavours of the physicians to improve upon the system.

We have not discussed a final possible criterion of selection – that is, the ability to pay for a resource. The omission probably derives from a natural repugnance to such an idea, particularly among those accustomed to a National Health Service. But, on reflection, we wonder if a modified concept of this type does not have its attractions as a way of alleviating the scarcity while still retaining moral respectability. We suggest that it is not so much the shortage of, say, dialysis machines which lies at the root of the problem but, rather, the shortage of money to pay for them within the confines of a free medical service; the consideration which stops a factory increasing its production of machines is an inadequate market. In these circumstances, it might not be unreasonable to allow patients to contribute

4 G H Gordon *The Criminal Law of Scotland* (2nd edn, 1978) p. 422.
5 V Parsons and P Lock 'Triage and the Patient with Renal Failure' (1980) 6 J Med Ethics 173.

to the purchase of 'engineering hardware' according to their means on the principle that a machine which is bought releases another for the use of others who are unable to do so. Such a system now operates in the United States as regards dialysis where, admittedly, it was introduced for precisely the opposite reasons – that patients with chronic renal disease would be destroyed financially unless public assistance was given; but whatever the reason, it is probable that the *overall* provision of dialysis resources is better when distributed as a joint private and public enterprise.

Such a policy would be, we admit, difficult to apply with absolute equity. In particular, it could be argued that it would draw off in an unequal manner the personnel required to operate the machines and who have been trained at public expense. To which one could answer that you do not expect a University graduate in law to accept only legal aid cases; one could also point out that the greater number of cases – of dialysis cases, at least – would be treated at home and that, by and large, the efficiency of domiciliary treatment and the financial status of the patient are closely related.

But such discussion is beyond the scope of this volume – all that is implied is that, in certain circumstances, there may be a logical case for including private medicine within the public sector with possible benefit to the latter. We would, however, stress that the circumstances could not morally include payment for resources of which the supply is strictly limited – in the context of the present discussion, we would cite the provision of biological material such as donor kidneys; we return to this specific question in chapter 13.

The responsibility of the individual

No discussion of this type would be complete without a passing reference to the responsibility of the individual to avoid the need for medical resources. The argument that prevention is better than cure has been widely popularised – for example by Kennedy[6] in his Reith Lectures of 1980 who emphasised the importance of politics in directing the individual. No-one would deny the importance of the theory at all levels but, equally, it is difficult to decide when friendly persuasion ceases and restriction of liberty begins – Davis and Horobin[7] for example foresee a day when illness may be seen as a failure to keep healthy and, thus, be culpable! In the face of a reluctance to be advised, it may well be that subtle pressures – some of which are of legal origin – contribute more effectively to the saving

6 See fn. 2, above.
7 See fn. 1, above.

of resources. Thus, the reduction of life insurance premiums for non-smokers is likely to be more persuasive than is a stereotyped Government health warning on an advertising hoarding, while a regular loading for obesity may help to reduce the admissions to the coronary care unit. We would suggest that the policy of limiting awards for damages following road traffic accidents in which the failure to wear a seat belt is considered a contributory factor to injury[8] will, if it is publicised, do more to save pressure on neurosurgical units than will even statutory compulsion to wear a harness. But such musings run beyond the confines of the doctor's dilemma.

8 *Froom v Butcher* [1976] QB 286, [1975] 3 All ER 520, CA.

Death

12 The diagnosis of death

Death is defined in *Chambers's Twentieth Century Dictionary* as 'the state of being dead; extinction or cessation of life'. *Steadman's Medical Dictionary* adds to this 'in multicellular organisms, death is a gradual process at the cellular level with tissues varying in their ability to withstand deprivation of oxygen'. There is, therefore a conceptual conflict between layman and doctor, the latter being forced to accept an academic formula such as death being 'a permanent state of tissue anoxia'. Tissue anoxia arises naturally in two ways – either respiration ceases, in which case there is a failure to harvest oxygen, or the heart fails, when oxygen is no longer distributed to the tissues. In either case, the diagnostic problem rests on what is meant by permanence.

In practice, it is astonishing how often the moment of 'death' is perfectly clear. One can tell to the second when a loved one or a carefully observed patient dies; it is easy to understand the religious concept of the soul leaving the body. The patient has 'breathed his last' and his heart stops beating; this is 'somatic' death. But the individual cells of the body are not dead; they will continue to function until their residual oxygen is exhausted. How long this takes depends upon their oxygen consumption which, in turn, is correlated with their specialised activity. Theoretically, therefore, there should be evidence of cellular death before the state of permanence is accepted but, in practice, this would be absurd. The doctor can rely on his senses and on his stethoscope because death is to be expected and is accepted on the vast majority of occasions when it visits.

But what if death is unheralded and unexpected? It is common knowledge that the apparent permanence of cessation of the respiration or blood flow can, in many instances, be challenged by physical or mechanical intervention. Thus, an apparent sudden heart failure due to the common 'coronary attack' may, in suitable cases, be reversed by electrical stimulation (cardioversion) or by cardiac massage coupled, perhaps, with artificial respiration or ventilation. But, while the patient has been 'saved from the dead', the process of cellular death has been initiated by the temporary failure of oxygen distribution. The majority of organs will recover from such an insult but the cells of the brain are outstandingly the most sensitive to oxygen deprivation in the body and, moreover, they are irreplaceable. Thus, a situation may arise whereby the body as a whole is brought back to life but where it is now controlled by a brain which is damaged to an uncertain degree. The decision to restore an interrupted cardiac function is not, therefore, a simple choice between the good – life – and the bad – death. It poses serious and urgent ethical problems which provide a base from which to discuss the more measured, and in some ways more complicated, issues arising from ventilator deaths.

When death strikes unexpectedly on its second front – by way of acute respiratory failure – it may be countered by the use of artificial ventilation. This may be accomplished by a mechanical respirator which simulates the movements of the chest wall or, more commonly in the context of the present discussion, by a ventilator which forces air in and out of the lungs.

Brain function as a measure of death

The mechanisms underlying acute heart failure and respiratory failure need to be distinguished. Given an adequate oxygen supply, the heart will continue to beat independently of higher control – it did, for instance, commonly beat for some 20 minutes following the broken neck of judicial hanging; the cause of acute cardiac failure, therefore, lies within the heart itself. Respiration, on the other hand, is controlled by the respiratory centre – a nervous 'battery' situated in the brain stem. Moreover, peripheral conditions in the respiratory tract which would lead to acute failure – for example, complete blockage of the airways or extensive injury to the lungs – cannot, in general, be corrected by the ventilator. It follows that acute respiratory failure of the type which is of importance in the present context is almost invariably the result of central damage – that is, damage to the brain stem. Oxygenation of the tissues, or cellular life, is, thus, based on a servo-type mechanism: the heart depends for its own tissue oxygen on the lungs which, in turn, are useless without the heart; together they supply oxygen to the brain which, therefore, cannot function in the absence of competent heart and lungs; the lungs are, themselves, dependent upon a functioning brain stem. The only segment of this triad which cannot be substituted is the brain. There are, therefore, strong logical arguments for defining death in terms of brain death rather than in the generally accepted terms of cardio-respiratory failure; logic is imposed by practical necessity when the natural functional condition of the lungs – or, occasionally, the heart – is obscured by the intervention of a machine.

The brain itself is not uniformly sensitive to hypoxia. Simplistically, it can be divided into three main areas – the cortex, which is responsible for our human intellectual existence and is the least able to withstand oxygen deficiency; the thalamus which roughly regulates our animal existence; and the brain stem which controls our purely vegetative functions including breathing. The brain stem is least affected by hypoxia; if it is so damaged, it can be assumed, as near certainly as is possible, that the rest of the brain is damaged to a similar or greater extent. Conditions producing hypoxia of the brain may be natural – e g heart failure or internal haemorrhage – or unnatural, including violence or drug overdose. The effect in either case will be general in nature and will affect all tissues of the body but to an extent less than the brain – such a situation arises from 'shock' resulting from lowered blood pressure or from reduced oxygen intake due, say, to a poorly given anaesthetic. Other causative lesions may be localised within the skull and injure the brain in secondary fashion by occupying the confined space and, effectively, squeezing the vessels carrying the blood. Whatever the cause, the hypoxic damage is irreversible; but, once an efficient oxygen supply is restored, further damage is prevented. In such a situation, therefore one can speak in terms of degrees of brain damage, or resultant coma, but not of stages of coma because the condition is now no longer progressive. The person who is brain damaged but treated may present varying clinical appearances which were well described by French writers.[1] Four degrees of coma were recognised. *Coma vigile* which represents no more than a blurring of consciousness and intellect; *coma type* and *coma carus* which are characterised by increasing loss of relative functions followed by vegetative functions; and, finally, *coma dépassé* – something beyond coma in which all functions are lost and the patient can only be maintained by artificial means.

Thus, while all appropriate cases may properly be given intensive care for the purposes of diagnosis and assessment, it would be well-nigh impossible to justify long term treatment for a patient who was likely to end up with no cortical and minimal thalamic function remaining – and the identification of such a case presents a formidable technical dilemma.

The decorticated patient falls into the category defined by Jennett[2] as the persistent vegetative state – in layman's terms, the 'human vegetable'. Such a person has certainly lost a human personality but,

1 P Mollaret and M Goulon 'Le Coma dépassé' (1959) 101 Rev Neurol 3.
2 B Jennett and F Plum 'Persistent Vegetative State after Brain Damage' (1972) 1 Lancet 734.

in so far as he is capable of existing without mechanical support, he is equally certainly not dead – indeed, he is in some ways more 'alive' than is the fully conscious sufferer from poliomyelitis who exists only by virtue of the respirator. There have been serious suggestions that the decorticated patient should be regarded as dead – may not *homo sapiens* be weakened in its own fight for survival if it devotes strength and resources to maintaining *homo* when he is no longer *sapiens*?[3] Such attitudes may be tenable in a general discussion on euthanasia but, if related to death, they can only confuse the issue and enhance the already strong public apprehension of 'premature grave robbery'. The concept of death must be that of an absolute; there is no place for conditional phrases such as 'at death's door' or 'as good as dead'.

It follows that, if we are to adjudge death by death of the brain, it must be by virtue of death of the *whole* brain. This principle has been unintentionally confused semantically by the Harvard group who introduced the term 'irreversible coma'.[4] One's first reaction would be to equate such a condition with the persistent vegetative state but it is clear from the paper that the group were describing what other Americans and, later, the British Royal Colleges dubbed 'brain death'.[5] Even this term is capable of misinterpretation – in particular, it can be taken as including 'partial brain death'. It is, therefore, both logical and more reassuring to follow the Scottish school[6] and speak only in terms of 'brain stem death' when measuring somatic death by brain function – and it is 'brain stem death' which currently accepted tests for death are designed to measure.

In essence, there are three equally important phases in the present British standards for the diagnosis of brain stem death. Firstly, there is the exclusion of coma being due to reversible causes including drug overdose, hypothermia and metabolic disorders while, at the same time, making a positive diagnosis of the disorder which has caused the brain damage and ensuring that this, in turn, is irremediable. Secondly, there is the carrying out of a number of tests specifically designed to demonstrate destruction of the several components of the brain stem. Thirdly, there is a carefully controlled system whereby a

3 Lord Scarman 'Legal Liability in Medicine' (1981) 74 J Roy Soc Med 11. See also, for example, the discussion in P D G Skegg 'Irreversibly Comatose Individuals: Alive or Dead?' (1974) 33 Camb Law J 130.
4 H K Beecher (Chairman) 'A Definition of Irreversible Coma', Report of the ad hoc Committee of the Harvard Medical School to examine the definition of brain death (1968) 205 JAMA 337.
5 Conference of Medical Royal Colleges and their Faculties in the United Kingdom 'Diagnosis of Brain Death' (1976) 2 Brit Med J 1187.
6 A A Watson, W A Harland and A M McLean 'Brain Stem Death' (1978) J Law Soc Scot 433.

patient's inability to breath spontaneously is proved. These tests should be repeated although the recommendations are, of necessity, somewhat open on this point.

These criteria are sometimes criticised on the grounds that the patient is 'being asked to prove he is alive' rather than that the physician is proving death. Positive tests such as an electroencephalogram (EEG) or an angiogram – by which the blood flow in the brain can be visualised – are therefore sought and one or other is, indeed, mandatory in many countries of the EEC. It is almost incredible that an EEG, which measures the surface electrical activity of the cerebral cortex, should be positive in the presence of properly performed confirmatory tests for brain stem death but there is no reason why such a test should not be added if it would serve a useful psychological purpose.

There is little doubt that public misgiving would be less if the purposes of defining brain stem death were more fully understood. Certainly, it is a valuable tool in the provision of high quality organs for transplantation (see chapter 13, below) but this is only part of the story. The major purpose of the procedure is to offer a scientific basis on which patients who can no longer benefit can be removed from ventilator support. This is essential if the patient is to die with dignity, if the relatives are to be spared wholly unnecessary suffering and if resources, both mechanical and human, are to be properly apportioned. Brain stem death is not a method of 'hurrying death along'; rather, the ventilator allows the pace of investigation, assessment and prognosis to be slackened and, when it comes to the point, the diagnosis of brain stem death is, in the great majority of cases, only confirming what is clear to clinical observation – that the patient is dead. Problems associated with removal from the ventilator are technical rather than ethical. It has been advised that the diagnosis of brain stem death should be made by two doctors, one of whom should be the consultant in charge of the case and the other suitably experienced and clinically independent of the first,[7] but there is no United Kingdom law on the point.

The legal effect of applying brain stem death criteria

The application of brain stem death criteria has obvious implications as to causation in cases of unlawful killing. But these difficulties disappear once it is conceded that brain stem death means somatic death, a concept which has been codified by the British Royal

---

7 Lord Smith (Chairman of Working Party) *The Removal of Cadaveric Organs for Transplantation: A Code of Practice* (1979).

Colleges.[8] It then becomes clear that the effect of intensive treatment has been simply to delay the inevitable result of the initial insult to the brain and there is no break in the chain of causation. This was accepted, first, in America in *People v Lyons*[9] where it was found that the victim of a shooting incident was legally dead before being used as a transplant donor. The British position has been summed up in two leading cases which are discussed further in chapter 14. Thus, in Scotland, it was held:

> Once the initial reckless act causing injury has been committed, the natural consequence which the perpetrator must accept is that the victim's future depended on a number of circumstances, including whether any particular treatment was available and, if it was available, whether it was medically reasonable and justifiable to attempt it and to continue it.[10]

The later English decision was fully confirmatory:

> Where a medical practitioner, using generally acceptable methods, came to the conclusion that the patient was for all practical purposes dead and that such vital functions as remained were being maintained solely by mechanical means, and accordingly discontinued treatment, that did not break the chain of causation between the initial injury and the death.[11]

It is therefore clear that the law has no intention of regarding doctors who remove a brain stem dead patient from the ventilator as being, thereby, responsible for his death. But what constitutes the precise time of death in such circumstances has not been decided; there are several issues which depend upon that determination, some of which are likely to cause problems in the future.

Lawyers are inclined to dismiss the problem of when death occurs on the assumption that the time of death can be equated to the time the ventilator support is removed. But a moment's reflection establishes that the diagnosis of brain stem death, and the consequent ending of treatment, must be retrospective – death has already occurred but the precise time at which it occurred is unknown and unknowable. Moreover, the choice of the time at which the necessary tests are undertaken is as likely to be based on the criterion of convenience as on anything else. It is difficult to see how the doctor can conscientiously certify the 'date and time of death' but it is not difficult to think of occasions on which he might be urgently called upon to do so.

The prospect of a victim of violence being ventilated and declared

8 Conference of Royal Medical Colleges and their Faculties in the United Kingdom 'Diagnosis of Death' (1979) 1 Brit Med J 332.
9 *People v Lyons* (1974) 15 Crim L Reptr 2240.
10 *Finlayson v HM Advocate* 1978 SLT (Notes) 60 at 61, per Lord Emslie LJ-G.
11 *R v Malcherek, R v Steel* [1981] 2 All ER 422 at 428–9, CA, per Lord Lane LCJ.

alive or dead 366 days after the incident, and, thereby, affecting the possibility of a charge of murder in England, is commonly raised but the idea of such treatment is unreal and the problem must be theoretical only. Time related factors in the payment of or withholding of life or personal accident insurance policies are far nearer to hand; one example could concern the application of a suicide clause which would be lifted on a given day. Problems as to the payment of estate duty might also arise.

But the most intractable issue would seem to be that related to succession and the possibility of disputed survival. What is to be said as to the deaths of a husband and wife who are injured in the same accident, who are both ventilated and who are both declared brain stem dead? One thing is certain – survivorship cannot be judged on the basis of the technical diagnosis because the order in which death is determined could well be purely arbitrary. To remove ventilator support from both simultaneously and measure the time for the individual heart to stop beating would be pointless – the patients have already been certified as dead and, as Skegg[12] has pointed out, you cannot have double standards of death.

The rules of succession are bound by statute and, accordingly, this is one aspect of brain stem death which could be subject to legislative action. It seems to us that a positive solution to 'ventilated commorientes' is currently impossible; but a negative direction on the lines that evidence as to the time of removal of ventilator support cannot, by itself, be regarded as sufficient to rebut the statutory presumptions might, at least, be equitable and, at the same time, relieve the doctor of one moral problem.

The ethical position of the doctor

Thus, while we have said that the act of terminating treatment once brain stem death is diagnosed is a technical problem which raises no ethical issues, the time at which this is done unfortunately does so. It is facile merely to remark that the doctor's decisions should be uninfluenced by extraneous factors because, in practice, he can scarcely avoid being aware of them – and influence is inseparable from awareness. The moral problems posed, say, by insistent pressure from relatives concerned for an insurance policy could be insoluble. A further question arises in respect of how long can a corpse be kept in a state of cellular preservation while still maintaining an acceptable ethical standard. For how long, for example, would it be proper to await a suitable heart transplant recipient? A recent press report has spoken of a brain stem dead

12 See fn. 3, above.

woman being retained on support for a week for the sole purpose of bringing her fetus to viability.[13] Such are the incremental nudges which may, ultimately, push this branch of medicine into areas of doubtful morality unless they are held in check.

The case for legislation

For these, and many other reasons, the case for a modern statutory definition of death is often canvassed.[14]

The main difficulty in framing legislation is to allow for all modes of death – from the elementarily obvious to the complex ventilator case; it would be absurd to demand that criteria designed for the latter be applied to the former. As a result, most statutes, either existing or proposed have applied some form of dual criteria of proof of death.[15] Such a compromise is expressed in what is commonly known as the Capron-Kass formula:

> A person will be considered dead if, in the announced opinion of a physician, based on ordinary standards of medical practice, he has experienced an irreversible cessation of spontaneous respiratory and circulatory functions. In the event that artificial means of support preclude a determination that these functions have ceased, a person will be considered dead if, in the announced opinion of a physician based on ordinary practice, he has experienced an irreversible cessation of spontaneous brain functions. Death will have occurred at the time when the relevant functions cease.[16]

But, in essence, all this proposal does is to attempt to legalise good medical practice which many would feel to be irrelevant.[17] It advocates no positive steps and, in this, we would certainly agree with the great majority of commentators that any statutory definition of death must be limited to an enabling concept. Medical facilities and expertise alter and do so faster than can the law; it is therefore essential that the evaluation of diagnostic techniques remains in the hands of the medical profession. In fact, the ethical, philosophical and social problems inherent in the definition of death seem to have been largely solved in recent years; definitive legislation might do little more than reanimate concerns which have long been put to rest and might, consequently, be self-defeating.

13 *Daily Record*, 4 September 1982, p. 3.
14 See, for example, P D G Skegg 'The Case for a Statutory "Definition of Death"' (1976) 2 J Med Ethics 190; A Van Till-d'Aulnis 'How Dead Can You Be?' (1975) 15 Med Sci Law 133.
15 E g Kan Stat Ann 77-202 (Supp 1974); California Health and Safety Code 7180-81 (West Supp 1975); Law Reform Commission of Canada, Working Paper 23, 1979.
16 A M Capron and L Kass 'A Statutory Definition of the Standards for Determining Human Death: An Appraisal and a Proposal' (1972) 121 Univ Penn Law Rev 87.
17 E g I Kennedy 'The Definition of Death' (1977) 3 J Med Ethics 5.

13 The donation of organs and transplantation

The juxtaposition of chapters on the diagnosis of death and on transplantation of organs should not be taken to indicate that they are necessarily associated. It is again emphasised that the concept of brain stem death is more important to neurosurgeons, who can now allow their hopeless patients to die in peace, and to the relatives, who can now accept the situation with good conscience, than it is to the transplant surgeon. Nevertheless, as will be argued later, optimum transplantation – and, with it, maximum saving of lives – depends upon the acceptance of brain stem death; furthermore, the two conditions are closely linked in the public mind. This is, therefore, a not inappropriate point at which to discuss the ethics of a procedure which is now more firmly established as good medical practice than as a well understood modern development.

Technical aspects of transplantation
Heterotransplantation – that is, the transplantation of organs from one species to another – is currently a practical impossibility. Autotransplantation, or the resiting of portions of the same body, is effectively limited to skin grafting and poses only the difficulties of highly complex surgery. Our concern is with homotransplantation or the transfer of viable tissue from one human being to another. The major biological considerations in this technique are tissue immunity, normality of the donor organ and, thirdly, its viability.

The tissue immunity problem stems from the fact that, for practical purposes, no two persons other than monovular twins are genetically identical; the body can recognise, and will reject, tissues which are 'non-self'. This 'immune reaction' can be suppressed – and techniques for so doing are improving rapidly – but the general principle is that such suppression will be effective in proportion to the genetic similarity of donor and recipient. Thus, sibling donation is likely to be very satisfactory. It is axiomatic that an organ intended as a replacement for a diseased tissue must be normal itself. The practical result is that donors should be relatively young and they must either be living or have died from accident or from localised natural disease which has no effect on the donated tissue.

Viability is that essential element which combines most clearly the technical and ethical problems of transplantation surgery. As has been discussed above, the cells of the body will deteriorate when deprived of oxygen; the process of deterioration can be slowed markedly by chilling the organ, the viability, or competence, of which then depends on the 'warm anoxic time' – that is, the interval between cessation of the circulation and chilling of the specimen. In terms of practical transplantation, it becomes increasingly pointless to transplant a kidney after more than one hour's warm anoxia and the likelihood of a successful result depends to some extent upon how far that time can be reduced. Any imposed delay must, therefore, jeopardise the validity of the operation.

It will be evident that organs can be provided for transplantation by the living or by the dead. Living donation offers many technical advantages – tissue compatibility can be measured at leisure, the operation can be elective rather than done in an emergency and the warm anoxic time can approach zero. Potential cadaver donors are widely available and transplantation of their organs provides a source of satisfaction that waste material is being put to life-saving use. On the other hand, their availability is capricious, both donor and recipient operations must take on the character of emergency surgery and the total efficiency of the graft cannot be guaranteed. Recognition of brain stem death, however, introduces the possibility of a variation on cadaver donation – the 'beating heart donor' – which bridges the gap between the living and the conventional dead and carries with it many of the advantages of both types of donor. The legal and ethical limitations of these three methods therefore deserve consideration.

The living donor

The donation of tissues which can be replaced rapidly – such as blood and bone marrow – presents, in practice, no technical or ethical problems other than that of commercialism to which we refer briefly later. We are concerned here only with non-regenerative tissues.

The legal regulation of living donations is not absolutely clear. The starting-point must be the common law principle that no person is to be deemed capable of consenting to his being killed. This principle would thus preclude the altruistic donation of a liver or other organ without which the donor cannot live. This of course is the extreme case; the position as to organ donations which will not necessarily lead to the death of the donor is not so straightforward. In the case of a kidney donation the life expectancy of the donor need not be significantly reduced as, barring localised trauma, the remaining kidney is quite capable of performing the necessary functions. The only legal objection which might be voiced here is that the surgery in question is non-therapeutic and therefore there may be questions of criminal liability in respect of the infliction of what amounts to a maim. The law on this matter is far from clear, but it is reasonably certain that the infliction of a serious injury can be an assault even if there is consent on the part of the injured person. No crime will be committed, however, if the infliction of the injury is in the public interest.[1]

It is highly unlikely that any court would take the view that the removal of a kidney from a live donor would be anything but in the public interest if it was performed for the purpose of saving the life of a seriously ill patient. This presupposes that it is from an adult donor capable of giving a free and informed consent to the removal of an organ; the position of children or the mentally incompetent raises a number of thorny issues.

The minor as a donor
The living child donor is often a valuable source for the transplant surgeon and, in practice, children are used as living kidney donors not uncommonly in the United Kingdom. The legality of such operations has not been decided by British courts and the issue must thus be considered on the basis of the general legal principles applied to the medical treatment of minors. As discussed in chapter 9, consent to an operation on a minor below the age of 16 years should normally be obtained from the parents, subject to the possible common law rights of the child.[2] Valid parental consent, however, refers to treatment for the advantage of the child; troublesome questions arise in relation to procedures which are not calculated to be to his or her benefit – does parental consent in such circumstances constitute an abuse of parental power?

It has been argued that the principle that a minor cannot legally be subjected to any procedure which is not to his advantage is not an

---

1 G Williams *A Textbook of Criminal Law* (2nd edn, 1978) pp. 540ff.; see also P D G Skegg 'Medical Procedures and the Crime of Battery' [1974] Crim LR 693.
2 P D G Skegg 'English Law relating to Experimentation on Children' (1977) 2 Lancet 754 takes the view that the Family Law Reform Act 1969, s. 8 has no application to non-therapeutic procedures and that the roles of non-statutory law do not vary with different categories of persons.

absolute one. In *W v Official Solicitor*,[3] the court was prepared to hold that a minor could be subjected to a blood test in order to determine paternity on the grounds that it was in the public interest for this to be done. This decision, if it was generalised, could be applied to the situation when a kidney or other tissue is donated.

It is also possible that a court might consider that the donation of an organ is not only in the public interest but is also in the interest of the minor donor, who will, almost certainly, be a sibling of the recipient. In such circumstances, it might be argued that it is in the interests of the minor that a member of his family should be saved rather than that his relative should die. This line of argument was successfully pursued in the important American decision in *Strunk v Strunk*.[4] In this case, the donor, who, although adult, had a mental age of six, was chosen to donate a kidney to his brother who was critically ill. The court came to the conclusion it would be in the donor's best interests for his brother's life to be saved after hearing evidence of the close relationship which existed between the two boys. Consequently, the operation was allowed although the donor was not in a position to give consent. This principle has been applied in a line of decisions since *Strunk*.

Other jurisdictions have been less ready to allow the taking of organs from minors. In Canada, for instance, the Ontario Human Tissue Gift Act provides an example of statutory prohibition of donation by minors.[5] The severe limitations imposed in France are outlined below.

While the complete exclusion of minor donors would seem to many to be too extreme, there are powerful reasons why some limits should be placed on the use of children as donors of non-regenerative tissue and very great caution should be exercised in the case of young children in whom there is unlikely to be any significant understanding of what the donation entails. It is probably undesirable to set an arbitrary age at which such understanding may be said to exist as this will clearly be different from case to case. The suggestion is made in one American discussion of this question that a child aged 7 may well be able to give consent to acting as an organ donor to a member of his immediate family.[6] This suggestion has been described by a Canadian lawyer as 'incredible'.[7]

Even if the minor shows a reasonable degree of understanding of

3 *S v S, W v Official Solicitor* [1972] AC 24, [1970] 3 All ER 107, HL.
4 445 SW 2d 145 (1969).
5 B M Dickens *Medico-legal Aspects of Family Law* p. 96.
6 W J Curran and H K Beecher 'Experimentation in Children' (1969) 210 JAMA 77. The consent of the parents would, of course, be needed in addition.
7 G S Sharpe 'The Minor Transplant Donor' (1975) 7 Ottawa LR 85.

the donation and of the risks involved, a sharp distinction is to be made between instances when the recipient is a member of the immediate family and when he is not. It would probably be regarded as ethically acceptable for a minor to be used as a donor in the former case; generosity towards a brother or sister is to be encouraged ethically and may even be regarded as a social duty. The situation is less clear with relatives other than siblings. Should one apply the same rule to a situation where the prospective recipient is a cousin in the first degree? It is possible that the minor donor may be as fond of such a cousin as he is of a brother or sister and the illness of the cousin may be as distressing to him as would be the illness of a sibling. Nevertheless, a policy of limiting approved donation by minors to the immediate family has the attraction of certainty and, in practice, the clinical limitations must be taken into account – donation to an adoptive brother, for example, would be unethical simply because, other than by chance, genetic incompatibility would compromise the success of the operation.

A policy of limitation was advised by the Australian Law Reform Commission in their report on transplantation. The Commission took the view that the donation by minors of non-regenerative tissue should not be forbidden without exception but that the circumstances in which it should be allowed should be circumscribed. The enabling conditions were suggested as being: when the donor and recipient are members of the same immediate family; when there is independent medical evidence that the prospective recipient will die unless the transplant is carried out; where the parents of the donor (or those *in loco parentis*) agree to the donation; where the donor has sufficient mental capacity and agrees to the donation; and, finally, when an ad hoc committee consisting of a judge and two other persons come to the conclusion that the donation is desirable and in the interests of the donor.

This cautious attitude has the force of law in France[8] where, very similarly, a living minor may only donate to his brother or sister; consent must be given by the donor's legal representative; and the procedure must be authorised by a committee composed of at least three experts two of whom must be doctors, one of whom must have practised for 20 years. If the minor can be consulted, refusal on his part must be respected in all cases. Such stringency, derived from countries with very different legal systems, is noteworthy.

8 Law of 22 December 1976.

Cadaver donations

The deceased has very limited rights as to the disposal of his body in common law and the wishes of the next of kin would normally be supported rather than those of the dead person in the event of conflict. Statute law is, however, replacing common law and the use of cadaver organs and tissues is now regulated in Great Britain by the Human Tissue Act 1961.[9] This statute provides, in section 1(1), that removal of an organ is authorised if there has been a specific request to this effect by the deceased. This removal may be for therapeutic, educational or research purposes. In the absence of such a request, section 1(2) provides for the authorisation of organ removal if the person 'lawfully in possession of the body' has, after making such 'reasonable enquiry as may be practicable', no reason to believe that the deceased had expressed any objection to organ removal or that the surviving spouse or 'any surviving relative' of the deceased objects to the body being so dealt with.

The somewhat loose wording of the Act has caused occasional difficulty in its implementation. This was particularly so as to the definition of the person in lawful possession. For some time it was considered – and the view is still held by the English Medical Defence Union – that the term implied one with a right to possession, that is, the next of kin. The alternative view is that it refers to the person who has physical possession of the body who is, in practical terms, the hospital administrative officer. This latter interpretation is supported by the wording of other sections of the Act and is now widely accepted by the administration, the legal profession and the British Medical Association but the point has not been tested in the courts. The matter is of more than academic interest in that, were the next of kin to be in lawful possession, they could overrule any specific request made by the deceased. Even allowing for the fact that the relatives have no *locus standi* to object to the removal of organs under section 1(1), the doctor is in a difficult position in the event of their objections being voiced. On the one hand, he has legal justification to proceed and he may, rightly, be thinking of the potential recipients. On the other, it would be extremely hard to justify in ethical terms a decision to add further suffering to the bereaved. We believe that to accede to the relatives in such circumstances would be the lesser of two evils but it is fortunate that such conflicts are very rare in practice. It should be noted, in passing, that the coroner or procurator fiscal may veto any authorisation if the death comes within their jurisdiction (section 1(5) and (9)).

9 In America, the Uniform Anatomical Gift Act serves the same purpose.

The concept of 'such reasonable enquiry as may be practicable' is also vague, reasonableness being a matter of highly subjective judgment. The partial solution is to consider what is *un*reasonable – and it would clearly be unreasonable to prolong one's enquiries until the intended donor organ was non-viable. Such a pragmatic approach is, however, less tenable in the context of a beating heart donor which is discussed below. Finally, the contrast between the open-ended wording in the 1961 Act – 'any surviving relative' – and the specific reference to the 'husband or wife or nearest known relative' in the Anatomy Act 1832 is worthy of note. The 1961 Act must, again be interpreted in a practical sense – 'any surviving relative' must be taken to mean 'any relative who can reasonably be contacted within the limited time available' which, effectively, limits one to the immediate next of kin.

The unamended Human Tissue Act 1961 is unpopular on theoretical and practical grounds within both the legal and medical professions and it is, therefore, interesting to note that at least one academic commentator has questioned whether there is any offence committed in its non-observance;[10] the same authority suggests that an apparently unauthorised action to save the life of a recipient might be justified on the basis of necessity. From the civil aspect, there seems no reason in principle why an action in tort for nervous shock should not be available to relatives who believe that the conditions of reasonable enquiry have not been met; the majority opinion is that, while such actions have succeeded in the United States, they would be unlikely to do so in Great Britain.[11]

Beating heart donors

It is apparent that the major technical criticisms levelled at the Human Tissue Act 1961 relate to the prolongation of the warm anoxic time entailed in strict adherence to its terms. But such objections are valid only when death is measured by the irrevocable failure of the cardiovascular system. In practice, the overwhelming proportion of cadaver donated material will come from patients who have been maintained on ventilator support and in whom it will be appropriate to reach a diagnosis of death by means of brain stem criteria. There is no logical reason why ventilation should not be continued after death and the heart beat be maintained during an

10 P D G Skegg 'Liability for the Unauthorized Removal of Cadaveric Transplant Material' (1974) 14 Med Sci Law 53.
11 I M Kennedy 'Further Thoughts on Liability for Non-observance of the Provisions of the Human Tissue Act 1961' (1976) 16 Med Sci Law 49.

operation for organ donation. The ideal situation of the living donor is thus achieved in a cadaver.

The technical advantages of a beating heart donation are not in dispute and may, indeed, become a legal demand; we are told that successful actions for negligence have been raised in the United States in that conventional cadaver donation did not supply the best available treatment.[12] Why, then, is there such antipathy to the procedure?

Much must stem from an inherent revulsion at performing what is a maiming operation amid the conditions pertaining to a living patient but this is irrational once the concept of brain stem death has been accepted – any emotional bias should be directed towards the recipients. Perhaps the major problem lies in the fact that there are still those who, in all good conscience, cannot accept the technical criteria advocated for the diagnosis of brain stem death; such doubts are still being publicly expressed as this text goes to press.[13] While fully accepting that every doctor is entitled to his own clinical judgment, we do suggest that the subject would be, so to speak, defused were it to be made compulsory for a death certificate to be issued, and the notification handed to the next of kin, before any donation could be effected. This would serve not only to satisfy the professionals involved but would, we feel, set the minds of the relatives at rest.

The relatives must be confused and distraught unless given sympathetic counselling and, in practice, this should always be possible in modern circumstances when, as a result of ventilator support, relatives will have been aware of the impending death for some time and will, no doubt, have been attending at the hospital. Every assistance should be given. Thus, while we accept the view of the highest medical tribunal available that an electroencephalogram is not necessary to establish the fact of death, we also believe that the relatives should have the right to such evidence should they ask for it. It is only by such adaptation of the principle of informed consent that beating heart donation will become widely accepted and that, as a consequence, the best therapy will be available to those in dire need.

The availability of suitable organs

It has been calculated that there are enough suitable cadaver kidneys available in America to satisfy the demand but that the requirements are still not met because only one in eight potentially useful organs

12 'Brain death' (1975) 1 Brit Med J 356.
13 For example, D W Evans 'Questioning View of Heart Transplants', *The Times* Correspondence, 13 September 1982, p. 9.

are obtained in practice;[14] a very similar situation probably exists in the United Kingdom where anything up to 30 per cent of those suffering from kidney failure are said to be denied the benefit of modern treatment. Since the care of the living must be our main concern, it is important to consider how this situation can be improved.

There are essentially two avenues – to reform the law or to change public attitudes; the question as to which is to be preferred forms the basis of what might be called the Kennedy/Sells debate.[15] Sells, a transplant surgeon, argues that the existing law does not interfere with the supply of organs because of the intimate association between doctors and relatives which is imposed by ventilation techniques; he finds that, given good counselling, over 90 per cent of relatives will give permission for organ donation. Nevertheless, the supply on the whole is lamentably inadequate and it may well be that professional apathy is at the root of the problem. One still has to ask why the public should have to be cajoled into saving lives in this way – the same public will flock to donate their blood at the sight of a poster advertising an appropriate time and place. Ignorance may be one factor, antipathy on the part of the entertainment media another and, undoubtedly, the suggestion of ambivalence, as regards both techniques and ethics, among the medical profession plays its part. It is also probable that a greater response would be forthcoming were the well-established technique of kidney transplantation to be separated from experimental procedures such as heart transplants. Society reads of individual heart transplant operations which, currently, offer little more than a postponement of death for elderly persons on a one-to-one donor-recipient basis and fails to distinguish this from the positive salvage of young lives with an incremental health benefit ratio of two lives saved for every one lost. It is to be regretted that at least one Renal Transplantation Bill has failed because of the inability of the legislature to appreciate the present unique status of kidney donation.

Kennedy, by contrast, believes that the law should be changed. The Human Tissue Act 1961 is something of a hybrid. Section 1(1) depends on 'contracting-in' – that is, a positive commitment to take part in the programme. Section 1(2), on the other hand, represents 'contracting-out' in a modified form – the subject has not refused to join the programme but action as a result of his failure to do so is subject to controls and familial veto. It is argued that a full

14 J S Pliskin 'Cadaveric Kidneys for Transplantation: is there a Need for More?' (1976) 21 J Forens Sci 83.
15 See, inter alia, (1979) 5 J Med Ethics 13; 5:165 and (1980) 6:29.

'contracting-out' system, whereby it would be assumed that there was no objection to donation in the absence of evidence to the contrary, would materially increase the number of kidneys available – and, incidentally, improve their quality in that many young people who lacked the maturity to 'contract-in' would be included as donors.

That the numbers available would increase is simply a matter of elementary mathematics. But, despite the force of the argument, we believe that the introduction of a contracting-out system would represent a major change in legal policy. While admitting that there is no positive evidence to substantiate the impression, we doubt if the British public is, as yet, ready to accept what might be seen as a coercive measure – this nothwithstanding that such systems have been adopted in other countries including some within the European Economic Community. We are in no doubt that the 1961 Act should be amended in several ways – in particular, to remove ambiguities. But, for policy, we lean towards the approach of the published Code of Practice[16] which interprets the current law in a practical way.

Payment for tissues

Any discussion on the availability of organs must take into account the possibility of their provision on a commercial basis. Debate on the subject is normally confined to the buying and selling of organs from the living and the practice is widely condemned – 'the sale of organs, living or dead, is indefensible under any circumstances'.[17] The possibility is, however, by no means excluded. Manoeuvres to avoid ethical restrictions such as payment for a service rendered rather than for the tissue[18] or sale to kidney banks[19] have been mooted and there is no reason why the practice should not spread to cadaver tissues unless it is checked. Pliskin[19] has referred to several forms of 'payment in kind' to next of kin and to the increase in organ availability with the appointment of organ procurement physicians who are paid by results.

Legal objections to the commercialisation of human organs are many – for example, would a contract for sale be regarded as valid? what would be the effect of product liability legislation? and the like.

16 *The Removal of Cadaveric Organs for Transplantation: A Code of Practice* (1979) Part IV.

17 J P Merrill 'Statement of Committee on Morals and Ethics of the Transplantation Society' (1971) 75 Ann Int Med 631. The sale of tissues other than blood is prohibited by Statute in Canada (Ontario Human Tissue Gift Act 1971, s. 10) and in France (Law of 22 December 1976, art 3) amongst others.

18 B M Dickens 'The Control of Living Body Materials' (1977) 27 Univ Toronto LJ 142.

19 See fn. 14, above.

But the overriding objections must be those based on moral grounds. No sophistry, such as the suggestion that it is more immoral to deny a person the right to buy a kidney than to tolerate the practice, can hide the fact that a market in human organs would be repulsive to all save those rich enough to benefit from it. The intervention of commercialism in the transplantation service would have such disastrous consequences that we feel advantage should be taken of any legislation amending the 1961 Act to include a clause banning the practice absolutely. The methods of Burke and Hare are outdated; the cast of *Coma* are those we have to fear today.[20]

---

20 *Coma* by Robin Cook (1978). A science fiction novel which expresses vividly the potential abuses of having organs for sale.

14 Euthanasia

Euthanasia has already been reviewed in the special context of neonaticide. Here it is proposed to discuss the subject only in relation to the incurably or terminally ill adult patient. Fraught though the subject is from both the legal and ethical viewpoints, the complications at this time are fewer than are met at the beginning of life. The main reasons for this qualitative difference have already been discussed in chapter 7. In summary, the adult patient is likely to be able to express his wishes as to the quality of his own life or, in default of this, those responsible for the patient's management have a background of previous abilities and aspirations from which to measure the likely shortfall; clinical decisions can be based on history rather than on clairvoyance.

'Mercy killing' has never been regarded as a separate legal entity – 'the law does not leave the issue in the hands of the doctors; it treats euthanasia as murder',[1] and, theoretically, this is surely so although, in practice, the courts are sympathetic to a plea of diminished responsibility – particularly in cases that arise within the family. But since so few cases relevant to the medical profession have come to court, the great majority of statements on the doctor's position as to the termination of life are necessarily extra-judicial. Indeed, the only authority available is Devlin J who advised that, if the acts done intended to kill and did in fact kill, it did not matter if a life were cut short by weeks or months, it was just as much murder as if it were cut short by years.[2] Later in the same directive, however, the judge said this: 'The doctor is entitled to relieve pain and suffering even if the measures he takes may incidentally shorten life.'

It is, therefore, clear that, while the doctor's motive in shortening life is irrelevant, intention is all important. If a doctor intends to kill he is as liable to prosecution as is the layman; if, however, he intends to treat the patient symptomatically and, thereby, shortens his patient's life he may properly be regarded as being not guilty of murder. This test was firmly relied upon – and, indeed, extended – by

1 G Williams *Textbook of Criminal Law* (2nd edn, 1978) p. 532.
2 H Palmer 'Dr Adams' Trial for Murder' [1957] Crim LR 365.

Farquarson J in his summing up in *R v Arthur*[3] (see chapter 7, above). The scene is thus set for the implementation of the major philosophical concept of 'double effect'.

Allowing the patient to die

The principle of double effect, in simple form, is that an action which has a good objective may be performed despite the fact that the objective can only be achieved at the expense of a coincident harmful effect. It is implicit in this doctrine that the good effect must outweigh the bad and this may involve a value judgment. Thus, it might well be ethically right to administer pain-killing drugs in such dosage as simultaneously shortens the life of a terminally ill patient; it would not be justifiable to give the same dose to a young man with identical pain who stood a reasonable chance of recovery. Lord Edmund Davies[4] has put the counter argument that death is the worst of all evils and, by implication, that it cannot, therefore, be a good objective. Such a view would, however, have little support among moral and religious spokesmen – the Archbishop of Canterbury firmly approved the principle[5] as did Pope Pius XII, with certain limitations, in 1957;[6] the Sacred Congregation for the Doctrine of the Faith has recently confirmed this view.[7] Yet, once again, the lawyers give no certain lead. Thus, in the same paper which, it is to be noted, was written 20 years after the *Adams* verdict, Lord Edmund Davies comments 'Killing both pain and patient may be good morals but it is far from certain that it is good law'[4] while, by contrast, Williams (at p. 533) finds the proposition easily justified by necessity. Public opinion clearly supports this view – Dr Adams' patient was not terminally ill but he was, nevertheless, acquitted of murder. The lesson would seem to be that no British jury is likely to adjudge a doctor guilty of a serious offence when applying the principle of double effect in good faith. Prosecution is now extremely unlikely in such circumstances.

The terminally-ill patient
The principle of double effect is most clearly applicable to the terminally-ill patient – when death is inevitable. Only in the presence of persistent and unbearable pain is it equally relevant to the

3 *R v Arthur*, *The Times*, 6 November 1981.
4 Lord Edmund-Davies 'On Dying and Dying Well' (1977) 70 Proc R Soc Med 73.
5 Most Rev D Coggan 'On Dying and Dying Well' (1977) 70 Proc R Soc Med 75.
6 (1957) 49 Acta Apostolicae Sedis 1027.
7 *Declaration on Euthanasia* (1980).

management of the incurably, but not terminally, ill. The distinction between intolerable and terminal illness may, however, depend upon what therapy is available – it may, in short, be possible to keep a moribund patient alive, but this will involve the use of increasingly invasive and undignified methods with, at the same time, decreasing advantage to the patient himself. Along with this there is concurrently increasing distress to near relatives who see their loved ones in misery; outside the National Health Service there is progressive and, sometimes, crippling expense and, even when such a service operates, the problems associated with the allocation of scarce resources cannot be ignored. Pope Pius XII, who may be taken as representative of the quintessential advocacy of the preservation of human life, firmly admitted[8] that such extraneous circumstances could be taken into consideration when applying what he effectively described as the ordinary/extraordinary treatment test.[9] Our translation of his Holiness's directive is:

> Man has a right and a duty in case of severe illness to take the necessary steps to preserve life and health. That duty . . . devolves from charity as ordained by the Creator, from social justice and even from strict law. But he is obliged at all times to employ only ordinary means . . ., that is to say those means which do not impose an extraordinary burden on himself or others.

Clearly the difficulty about such a test is to distinguish ordinary treatments from extraordinary and the Pope, himself, qualified 'ordinary' as 'according to personal circumstances, the law, the times and the culture.' Thus, the ordinary/extraordinary test should not and cannot be applied as a general, all embracing rule. Some have, accordingly, suggested that the comparison should be between proportionate and disproportionate therapy; we would take this concept one stage further in preferring the contrast of productive and non-productive means. The use of these terms firmly concentrates decision making within the context of the individual patient and his unique conditions; such an interpretation is endorsed both by the Anglican Church[10] and by the Roman Catholic Sacred Congregation.[11] It then follows that the withholding of treatment is a purely clinical decision based on moral principles and, as would be expected, there have been no reports of criminal charges being laid against a doctor for withholding treatment for good reason.

There, further, appear not to have been any successful civil actions

8 See fn. 6, above.
9 See fn. 7, above.
10 See fn. 5, above.
11 See fn. 7, above.

either in the United Kingdom or the United States for this type of medical care. It is doubtful if there is any case to be made out quite apart from any ethical considerations. A doctor may have a common law authority to act positively but, as Glanville Williams has pointed out, this does not mean that he *must* do so; a doctor is not bound to save life merely by reason of his qualifications.[12] Even if such an argument appears tenuous, as it may do so particularly within the framework of a National Health Service, there can be no doubt as to the right of the patient to speak for himself as an autonomous being. So long as the patient is capable of giving or withholding informed consent, it will be tortious to continue treatment in the face of refusal. Even the unconscious patient may have previously indicated his views on terminal care; the execution of the oddly termed 'living will' is now a commonplace in America and is supported by statutory approval in many States. In the absence of both consciousness and evidence of intent, the doctor must, of necessity, take a decision as to treatment which is based upon his own judgment and on what he assumes would be the wishes of the patient. No doctor likes to lose a patient and a decision in favour of death is, therefore, not one which will be taken lightly.

The doctor may then be faced with a further moral dilemma in that he has to choose between watching his patient die slowly by omission or taking positive action which would accelerate the inevitable. But does the law allow him to do the latter? Veatch[13] has described the legislation in Idaho, Montana and Oregon – which would permit such action – as being clearly out of step with mainstream thought and against public judgment; it is doubtful if the medical profession as a whole, either in the United Kingdom or elsewhere, would wish to be given such a power. But the failure to face this issue is difficult to justify. A legalistic argument can be based on the premise that there is a rational and consequential difference between committing murder with the consent of the victim and failing to prevent him committing suicide through refusal of treatment. It is probably more honest to say, rather lamely, that there is a distinction to be made between, on the one hand, allowing nature to take its course without officious interference and, on the other, positively intervening with a lethal syringe.

The incurable patient
The relative simplicity of the euthanasia debate has, thus far,

12 G Williams 'Down's Syndrome and the Doctor's Responsibility' (1981) 131 NLJ 1040.
13 R M Veatch quoted by M Lappé (1978) 4 J Med Ethics 195.

depended upon the use of the adjective 'terminal' which defines a patient status which can only deteriorate. The problems for the doctor become less easily soluble when discussion is extended to the incurably ill whose condition may certainly get worse but which is also likely to remain static for varying, but often long, times. Many variations on such a state can be envisaged and different therapeutic solutions adduced. There are, however, two overriding considerations likely to influence one's thinking – firstly, whether the patient is sentient or non-sentient and, secondly, whether or not the distinction between incurable illness and death depends upon artificial means.

The incapacitated patient

Thus, at one extreme, we have the fully conscious, incapacitated patient able to breathe naturally who is exemplified by the paraplegic or quadriplegic whose condition results from an accident. The clinical and moral solutions here are based on the same principles as relate to the terminally ill but conscious patient – any differences are those of emphasis. In particular, great weight must be given to patient autonomy. Suicide is no longer an offence but abetting suicide remains one; the central problem then becomes to what extent can the sentient patient who prefers death to existence involve others? In practice, the dilemma arises surprisingly rarely. All doctors who have been concerned with disabled patients who are in receipt of care and love have been impressed by their tenacity for life and their ability to adapt. In theory, one thing is certain – the doctor cannot kill that patient with intent; it is probable that the greater part of the profession would resist any enabling legislation in this respect and this was a major factor in the failure of the Euthanasia Bill 1975 and for the absence of any such clause in the similarly defeated Incurable Patients Bill 1976. The prosecution and conviction of a member of EXIT[14] indicates that it is illegal to advise a sufferer on suicidal methods and, while the widespread acceptance of the profession's good faith by British juries might alter the consequences – the EXIT conviction was contemporaneous with the acquittal in *Arthur* – there is no reason to suppose that the same principle does not apply to doctors. The occasionally suggested tactic of leaving an obvious means of suicide available to the patient may solve the doctor's legal or ethical conscience but it is such an example of moral cowardice as to be beyond consideration. It is, however, perfectly proper to apply the 'double effect' doctrine – *R v Adams* has clearly demonstrated this – and the productive/non-productive treatment test is available;

14 *The Times*, 31 October 1981, p. 1.

their rationale needs to be just that much more firmly based than is so in the case of the terminally ill.

The conscious patient maintained artificially
It is fortunate that the interim state – that of mental competence while life is dependent upon a machine – is now extremely rare due to the virtual disappearance of the more serious forms of acute anterior poliomyelitis (infantile paralysis). The problem specific to this state is to discover what would be the correct action to be taken in the event of a positive request for the doctor to disconnect the mechanical respirator. Not to do so would certainly constitute non-consensual treatment but the implications of compliance are frightening. Much has been written concerning the ethics of the removal of mechanical respiratory support from those who can no longer benefit and we discuss later in the chapter the suggestion that the major difficulties arise directly from the original provision of that support – the primary decision is of greater importance than are those which follow as a consequence of that action. But the doctor has virtually no choice in the situation now being considered. He is dealing with a conscious but paralysed patient and he must provide support because he cannot know which patient is going to respond either physically or emotionally to heroic treatment[15] – and, if the doctor does not know, the patient cannot give or withhold his informed consent to the initiation of treatment. Can the doctor, then, accede to a later request to remove support?

It has been suggested that switching off a mechanical support is an act of omission. Moore[16] speaking as a moralist, has argued that there is no valid distinction in principle between withholding the means of life whether the means be nourishment, antibiotics or the electric current which operates the apparatus. Williams,[17] as a lawyer, draws a comparison between a removal of electric power and removal of manual power and finds them similarly acts of omission. Kennedy[18] described such manoeuvres as logic-chopping and we would agree – you have to act to turn off a television set and the same must apply to the respirator. But, even if there were to be a moral distinction between omission and commission, is such a distinction of practical significance? Kennedy has pointed out, in the same article, that a well-wisher disconnecting a respirator which was treating a live

15 J E Rhoads 'The Right to Die and the Chance to Live' (1980) 6 J Med Ethics 53.
16 E G Moore *Decisions about Life and Death* (1966) p. 46.
17 G Williams 'Euthanasia' (1973) 41 Med-leg J 14.
18 I M Kennedy 'Switching off Life Support Machines; the Legal Implications' [1977] Crim LR 443.

patient would be guilty of homicide and, once again, the relatively
protected position of the doctor would seem to rest on the vagaries of
the jury system – and there is less than certainty that a jury would be
so forgiving in the particular circumstances envisaged. Indeed, it
would seem that no doctor or team of doctors could resolve the
conflict posed by an informed request by a conscious patient to be
removed from respirator support; were such a situation to occur it
would be a proper case to be decided by the court. It is unlikely that
public policy would allow such a concession to self-destruction.

The unconscious patient
There remain for consideration those patients who are, again, either
capable of a free existence or who depend for survival upon
mechanical aids but who are, by contrast, unconscious by virtue of
hypoxic brain damage. There are good theoretical and practical
reasons for isolating the unconscious patient as a particular ethical
problem area. The theoretical basis is summed up in the words of Dr
William Sweet: 'The rest of the body exists in order to support the
brain. The brain is the individual.'[19] The unconscious or comatose
patient is, therefore, incapable of fulfilling his human function in a
way which transcends the loss of any other capacity. He cannot speak
for himself; he cannot consent and decisions on his behalf must be
taken by others and be justified by the doctrine of necessity – that is,
that an evil of obeying the letter of the law is socially greater in the
circumstances than is the evil of breaking it – or by the doctrine of
implied consent in that, were the patient in a position to decide, he
would, in fact consent. Moreover, as we have discussed under the
diagnosis of death, brain substance which is destroyed is destroyed
beyond repair and cannot be substituted; the doctor confronted with
such injury knows that whatever degree of humanity has been lost is
irrecoverable.

When considering euthanasia within this framework, we are
concerned only with such irreversible damage. This, as we have
indicated in chapter 12, may be of such a degree as will allow the
patient an independent existence in any condition ranging from
intellectual loss to a vegetative state. At this point it is necessary only
to reiterate that the latter cases, tragic as they may be, still represent
'persons in being'. The law as to killing is unaffected by the mental
state – dements and aments are still protected in so far as the term
'reasonable being' implies no more than 'human being' – and is the
same as has already been discussed in relation to the conscious

19 Quoted by I M Kennedy 'The Legal Definition of Death' (1973) 41 Med-leg J 36.

patient. Lord Scarman,[20] while appreciating

> that there are great social problems not only in the life support of the human vegetable but also in the survival of barely sentient people who cannot look after themselves

also added

> there are implications in the right to terminate another's existence of which it is well to be fearful in the absence of a more prolonged analysis of the problem than that which it has received.

'Irreversible loss of consciousness' may, indeed, 'one day become the mark of death' but that day is not here yet – certainly not in a legal sense. These patients present an extra therapeutic difficulty as, being unconscious, they are, one supposes, free from pain – at least, pain cannot be expressed in a manner which makes it treatable; the doctrine of 'double effect' is, therefore, scarcely applicable. On the other hand, there can be few incidences in medical practice where the productive/non-productive treatment test is as readily appropriate. It is beyond argument that patients with this degree of brain damage should not be ventilated when their respiration fails.

The patient in intensive care
Which brings us to the ultimate stage of human existence – the comatose patient who is unable to sustain his cardiorespiratory functions without the aid of mechanical ventilation – and, at the same time, to the concept, aired originally by Kennedy,[1] that the ethical dilemmas associated with ventilation apply not so much to the removal of support – that is, to euthanasia – but rather to the admission of patients to intensive treatment.

It is perfectly clear that the vast majority, perhaps all, living patients with severe brain damage must be offered such care when they present at hospital. Automatic recourse of this type is for the purpose of facilitating diagnosis and assessment. If a diagnosis of irretrievable functional brain loss is made, there is no legal or ethical objection to regarding the ventilator as no more than part of the diagnostic machinery and dispensing with it once it has served its purpose. But a decision to treat, which, in this case, is within the doctor's clinical choice, is a different matter carrying with it the inescapable consequence that, at some time and for some reason, that form of treatment must be withdrawn. The critical point for the application of the productive/non-productive ethical test is, thus, at

---

20 Lord Scarman 'Legal Liability and Medicine' (1981) 74 Proc R Soc Med 11.
1 See fn. 18, above.

the beginning. With one exception, the later decisions are based on clinical or technical considerations alone.

This exceptional ethical decision relates to the allocation of scarce resources which include machines, beds, doctors and nursing staff together with the necessary technical back-up. At some time it may be necessary for a resource based value judgment to be made. Making a choice between patients may be among the doctor's most agonising moments and the weight to be given to economic and policy considerations can only be judged by the individual physician or surgeon on such factors as are outlined in chapter 11.

Resources aside, the removal of patients from ventilation depends, primarily, on a simple alternative – either he is dead or he is not dead. It can be taken that the whole brain is dead once the criteria for brain stem death have been met and we have the authority of the Conferences of the Royal Medical Colleges and their Faculties[2] that the individual is dead when the whole brain is dead. In such circumstances, continued treatment is no more than treatment of a corpse – far from being unethical to withhold support, it would be positively immoral to continue other than to serve the limited purpose of beating heart organ donation or, conceivably, of post-mortem parturition.

However, it may still be proper to discontinue artificial ventilation even if death is not diagnosed. The closely allied considerations of productive/non-productive treatment – or medically unfeasible treatment[3] – and of 'death with dignity', untrammelled by tubes and wires, may be regarded by some as being related to the moral sphere and by others as being clinical in nature. Even so, the purely clinical consideration – that the treatment is doing, and will do, no good – will justify removal of support. One of two things may then happen – the patient will either continue to breathe of his own accord or he will die. In the former case, the patient has reverted to the persistent vegetative state, the management of which has already been discussed. Such was the situation and the outcome in the widely publicised case of Karen Quinlan in which it was established that there was 'no reasonable possibility of her ever emerging from her present comatose condition to a cognitive, sapient state', that 'there would be no criminal homicide in the circumstances' and that death would 'not be homicide but rather expiration from existing natural causes'.[4] This last statement covers the second eventuality – that the patient dies once support has been removed. There is no moral

2 'Diagnosis of Death' (1979) 1 Brit Med J 332.
3 E S MacMillan 'Birth Defective Infants: A Standard for Non-treatment Decisions' (1978) 30 Stanford L Rev 599.
4 *Re Quinlan* 70 NJ 10, 355 A 2d 664 (1976), per Hughes CJ.

problem: the outcome resulted from a clinical decision taken in good faith and after due deliberation. Looked at in this way, there is no need, as there clearly was in the case of the conscious patient, to argue as to whether removal of support is a matter of commission or omission – it is a sterile discussion in the present context.

Liability for withholding treatment

The case of *Quinlan* would seem to settle the problem of criminal liability for ventilation withdrawal in the United States. Decisions taken in the criminal courts of the United Kingdom illustrate the rapid advances made in this field recently. *R v Potter*[5] was an unusual case in that the accused was committed for trial by the coroner on a charge of manslaughter; the victim, who had been assaulted, died from head injuries but his kidneys were removed for transplantation after ventilation had been commenced for that specific purpose. The accused raised a defence of *novus actus interveniens* ascribing death to the donor operation. Neither the public nor the legal profession were, at that time, prepared for 'beating heart donation' – certainly not for 'reanimation donation' – and the prosecution was virtually forced to charge assault only, for which the accused was duly convicted. This unsatisfactory position has now been resolved, firstly through the Scottish case of *Finlayson*[6] and, later, in the English case of *Malcherek*[7] both of which have been discussed in relation to causation in chapter 12.

Although *Finlayson* was not cited in *Malcherek*, the two decisions have remarkable similarities in that they, firstly, relied on the concept of good medical practice and, secondly, in that the judges declined to define death in both cases. This latter omission might, at first glance, be interpreted as vacillation on the part of the law; in fact, it reinforces the former principle in leaving the clinical decision firmly in the hands of the clinician.

There is no reason to suppose that these decisions would not be applied in the civil courts and it would now be necessary to prove negligence – with all that entails – before a doctor could be considered culpable of a ventilator death. There are no United Kingdom authorities but a similar policy line has been adopted in the United States.[8]

5 (1963) 31 Med-leg J 195.
6 *Finlayson v HM Advocate* 1978 SLT (Notes) 60.
7 [1981] 2 All ER 422, [1981] 1 WLR 690, CA, *R v Steel* being heard simultaneously on appeal.
8 *Tucker v Lower* Law File 2831, LEC, Richmond Va (1972); *People v Lyons* (1974) 15 Crim L Reptr 2240.

A need for legislation?
It will be seen that, throughout this discussion, the general conclusion has been reached that there is little need for legislation in respect of the incurably or terminally ill adult patient; the great majority of life or death decisions can be based on good medical practice which is contained by relatively clear legal and moral guidelines. Doctors would not wish to be executioners and there is no public demand to place them above the law in this respect; moreover, techniques of hospice care are improving rapidly.[9] There are, however, some advocates of what is loosely termed 'allowing to die' legislation and we have, ourselves, advocated this in chapter 7 in the case of the neonate on the grounds that steps should be taken to limit the practice. But there is very little likelihood of comparable incremental expansion of acceptable terminal or palliative care in the adult. Doctors would only seek such legislation if the profession as a whole felt threatened by uncertainty; patients, for their part, might then feel that the constrictions of 'defensive medicine' deprived them of autonomy. These considerations may have provoked the several relevant statutes which have been enacted in the United States.

It may well be, though, that legislation fails in its objects because, by its very existence, it prejudices the right to full power over one's body which has been so much a part of case law in the United States.[10] Most 'allowing to die' statutes include some limitation of self-determination in the form of admitting the right of the physician to consider whether extraneous factors justify his not effecting the patient's expressed wishes. Lappé suggests that, in addition to eroding the patient's rights, legislation may lead to deterioration in standards of care – by covering poor treatment with the cloak of obedience to a directive – and may lead to the creation of conflict between doctor and patient in so far as both autonomy and paternalism are being simultaneously attacked.[11]

The well-known California Natural Death Act of 1976 is, in fact, restrictive. It deals only with 'medical procedures or intervention which utilises mechanical or other artificial means to sustain, restore or supplant a vital function' and can be applied only when 'death is imminent whether or not such procedures are utilised'. While US legislation, either enacted or proposed, covers a wide range – from the limited Californian conditions, through the wide acceptance of

9 See, for example, R G Twycross 'Euthanasia – A Physician's Viewpoint' (1982) 8 J Med Ethics 86.
10 *Erickson v Dilgard* 252 NYS 2d 705 (Sup Ct 1962); *Palm Springs General Hospital Inc v Martinez*, Civil No 71 – 12687, Dade Co Circ Ct.
11 M Lappé 'Dying While Living: A Critique of Allowing-to-die Legislation' (1978) 4 J Med Ethics 195.

patient autonomy, subject only to public policy, as in Alabama to the potential euthanistic permissiveness of Idaho – none seem entirely satisfactory or necessary save when settling such contentious matters as the relationship between 'the living will', suicide and insurance policies. Lappé opposed the California Natural Death Act and there is much to be said for his view that 'legislation can be a smoke screen for the real problems of the dying patient'.

This is not to say that no difficulties arise in the absence of statute. The common law is clear if the dying patient is competent. But the incompetent patient raises the basic policy question of whether there is any point in prolonging the process of dying in the absence of any previously expressed wish by the patient. The fear of American hospital authorities that failure to go to extreme measures would result in civil or criminal liability has led to the deep involvement of the courts in what is essentially a clinical and ethical judgment. The difficulties are exemplified in a recent New York case.[12] The two rather different decisions raised complex problems as to what constitutes extraordinary treatment but the main thrust was to distinguish the incompetent who had expressed a preference during life – even if only as part of a conversation – from one who had not been able to do so. Arguably, this could have the result of prohibiting therapeutic decisions which could result in death being made by anyone other than the patient, including the patient's guardian or physician. The confusion so introduced reinforces our view that terminal care is best left in the hands of the doctors.

---

12 *Re Storar* 438 NYS 2d 266 (NY 1981) (consolidating *Eichner v Dillon*). The significance of the consolidated judgment in these two cases is discussed in L J Dunn 'The Eichner/Storar Decision: A Year's Perspective' (1982) 10 Law Med Hlth Care 117.

Research and Experimentation

15 Biomedical human experimentation

Until recently, biomedical experimentation using human subjects proceeded almost without comment. The researchers justified their activities as benefiting mankind; the subjects were generally happy to 'oblige' or to be reasonably recompensed; and research was of manageable quantity. Attitudes and conditions have, however, changed. The reaction against paternalistic medicine has gained momentum pari passu with an increasing concern for the rights of the individual; the world has become obsessed with financial values – under the influence of the United States where medicine *is* a matter of sale and purchase; the potential investigations and the instrumental and other means for conducting them have greatly increased; and there has been something of an explosion not only in the production of new therapeutic agents but also in governmental control of their distribution – witness the massive British Medicines Act 1968. But the greatest single impulse to regulate experiments on human beings sprang from a realisation of the appalling depths which were plumbed in the genocidal era of the Second World War – undoubtedly much information was gathered but the way in which it was obtained was such as to make many later workers question the morality of profiting from the results. Some codification became essential.

Ethical codes in human biomedical experimentation

The first internationally accepted set of ethical guidelines in this context was known as the Nuremburg code and was a direct result of the war-crimes trials.[1] It is, perhaps, unfortunate that this should be so as it inevitably puts the researcher on the defensive. To minimise this, the tribunal itself adopted the preamble:

> The great weight of the evidence before us is to the effect that certain types

1 References to the various 'Declarations' quoted in this book relate to the text published in A S Duncan, G R Dunstan and R B Welbourn (eds) *Dictionary of Medical Ethics* (2nd edn, 1981).

of medical experiments on human beings, when kept within reasonably well defined bounds, conform to the ethics of the medical profession generally . . . All agree, however, that certain basic principles must be observed in order to satisfy moral, ethical and legal concepts.

It was, however, apparent that the medical profession itself should publicly endorse the principles expressed in the ten clauses of the Nuremburg code; this movement culminated in the Declaration of Helsinki – drawn up by the World Medical Association in 1964 and revised in 1975 – which is reproduced as appendix F. Many national authorities have attempted to explain or expand upon the basic principles established at Nuremburg and, for the British reader, the most important of these is the advisory document of the Medical Research Council.[2]

All such codes have it in common that they appreciate the need for human experimentation while accepting that this can only be accomplished at the expense of some of the subject's right to self-determination. Moreover, the doctor's ethical position must show some flexibility. The Hippocratic Oath states: 'I will follow that system of regimen which . . . I consider for the benefit of my patients and abstain from whatever is deleterious and mischievous'; the absolutist could say that this precludes all experimentation on patients yet it is clear that progress in medicine depends upon some form of trial. A balance is needed and must be sought.

Potential experimental subjects

The major contribution in the 1960s to rationalising human experimentation was to distinguish between medical research 'in which the aim is essentially diagnostic or therapeutic for a patient' – clinical research – and that of which 'the essential object is purely scientific and without direct diagnostic or therapeutic value to the person subject to the research'. It follows that the experimental subjects may be of four types: individual patients, a group of patients who are suffering from one particular condition, patients who have no association with the disease or process under review but who are readily available, and, finally, healthy volunteers – a heterogeneous group which is of importance because it may involve other 'captive' populations including the researchers themselves.

The logical implication of this division of subjects is that researchers should also be categorised. Thus, the individual patient is

2 Responsibility in Investigations on Human Subjects, Report of the Medical Research Council of 1962–63 (Cmnd 2382) pp. 21–5.

under the care of a doctor. Any experimentation is, therefore, performed on a care-associated basis and, while there may be difficulties in a hospital setting where 'care' is very much a team concept, the essential doctor/patient relationship is, and should be, maintained. But it cannot be said with reference to any of the other groups that 'the health of my patient is my first consideration' and, consequently, the researchers cannot include the patients' physicians. Even so, when human subjects are involved in medical experimentation, so must doctors be; the danger of non-medical researchers being, not so much callous, as uncomprehending of their subjects' reactions are such that a situation excluding doctors would only be acceptable in the event that the researchers were their own experimental subjects.

The risks involved

Every experiment involves some risk and it is the art of the good investigator to minimise that risk. But there are certain guidelines to be followed which are spelled out in the Declaration of Helsinki (paras 4 and 5). Firstly, the risk must be proportional to the importance of the objective; secondly, the risk must be assessed before the experiments begin and, so far as is possible, eliminated by previous animal experiments and by a carefully considered experimental protocol.

The allowable risk cannot, however, be assessed outwith the context of the subject group. Thus, the risk taken in the case of the individual patient may be considerable in certain circumstances. It being axiomatic that 'experiments' with such subjects involve patient care, they are effectively confined to the use of new drugs or treatments when established methods have failed; a foreseen risk is clearly acceptable if the patient is otherwise dying or the disease process is rapidly progressive. It is, in fact, true that an element of experimentation by individual doctors is introduced every time a new drug is prescribed. The policy of the British Commission on the Safety of Medicines[3] of seeking notification of adverse drug reactions indicates that this is reasonable. The alternative is ever increasing delay in the use of a new substance with possible suffering on the part of patients thereby deprived; a balanced governmental and professional policy has taken us a long way from the leading American case

3 Established under the Medicines (Commission on Safety of Medicines) Order 1970, SI 1970/1257.

of *Carpenter v Blake*[4] and others which have, effectively, confused negligence with experimentation.

By contrast, the risks involved in true experimentation on groups of patients – and, particularly, those whose condition is unassociated with the research project – must be reduced to minimal; the risks here include such indirect effects as interfering with the appropriate therapeutic regimen. The inconsistency in the Declaration of condoning the use of 'patients' as subjects of non-therapeutic research projects has been pointed out by many commentators.[5]

The researchers themselves represent the other extreme of risk acceptance. Here, the responsibility rests squarely on the Head of Department for the safety of his staff but the dedicated work of many physiologists may involve procedures which could not be applied to others; it is doubtful if modern air travel would be possible in the absence of frankly hazardous work. Great care is essential in the use of the healthy volunteer; it is often difficult not to regard him or her as having equivalent understanding of the procedure as does the experimenter and to proceed on that basis – in fact, the healthy volunteer is more prone to subjective inducements to participate than are others and must be treated accordingly. The problems of volunteers highlight the conditions for informed consent which is discussed further below.

The design of experiments

All experiments cost money and cause some inconvenience to both colleagues and subjects. Badly planned research loses all ethical justification if, as a result, the findings are scientifically useless. So much depends upon planning that it is now almost mandatory for hospitals to establish 'Ethical Committees' whose function it is to sanction each experimental project before it is launched. Such Committees are in great vogue and wield considerable power in the United States.[6] The situation in the United Kingdom is, however,

---

4 60 Barb 488 (NY 1871) in which it was stated: 'Before the new practice can be used to shield the surgeon from the charge of malpractice it must . . . have been successful in so many instances as to establish satisfactorily the propriety and safety of adopting it', at 514.
5 See, for example, A Belsey 'Patients, Doctors and Experimentation: Doubts about the Declaration of Helsinki' (1978) 4 J Med Ethics 182.
6 Exemplified by the case of Karen Quinlan where the Supreme Court of New Jersey referred the 'life or death' decision to the hospital Ethical Committee.

different. Ethical Committees have been advised[7] but their composition and remit is not properly established.[8]

Among the still controversial problems are whether or not lay members should be included as a routine; there can be no doubt as to the value of professionals – lawyers, religious, statisticians etc. – but the inclusion of 'average citizens' may well be a necessary political gesture rather than a practical advantage. The overall derivation of committee members is of greater significance. Most committees are institutionalised – some, particularly in the United States, being even of a departmental nature; it is possible that the resulting element of 'self-review' is self-defeating and District or Area committees would seem preferable. The main concern, however, is that such decision-making committees tend to divert the investigators' sense of responsibility for the standards of research; this very real problem can be solved only on a personal basis.

The Medical Research Council now requires that any project involving application for funds must be approved by the local ethical committee but the restriction is unsatisfactory because the composition and powers – or even intentions – of such committees are not standard. In the present medico-political climate, the public requires a 'watch dog' review of human research. There seems to be a clear case for central governmental guidance or, even, dictation.

Controlled trials

A biomedical experiment almost inevitably involves a controlled trial at some time. The principle is simple – in order to decide whether a new drug or other treatment is better than an existing one, or none at all, the treatment is given to a group of patients or healthy volunteers and not given to as similar a group as can be obtained. The subtleties of experimental design are critical to the success of the project and, as stated above, a badly conceived trial is fundamentally unethical. But even the best designed trial has its built-in moral problem – depending on how one looks at it, on the one hand, a relatively untried treatment which may do harm is being given to one group while, on the other, a treatment which may be of considerable benefit is being withheld from a similar group. The doctor is doing his best for patients but the problem is to know what is best; put another way, the ethical problem is not so much whether a patient will be

7 Royal College of Physicians of London (1967, 1973), Report of Committee on the Supervision of the Ethics of Clinical Investigations in Institutions; SHHD (1972) Memorandum on the Supervision of the Ethics of Clinical Research Investigations, 30/1972.
8 See I E Thompson et al 'Research Ethical Committees in Scotland' (1981) 282 Brit Med J 718.

completely cured by a new treatment but, rather, would he have improved faster if he had not been restrained by the experimental protocol.[9] The first essential for any controlled trial is, therefore, that it must provide its answer as rapidly as possible and it must be terminable as soon as an adverse effect becomes apparent; there is a good case to be made out for an independent observer, or the ethical committee itself, being responsible for monitoring the trial from this angle.

Two further features are of major importance in ensuring the objectivity of a trial – the 'double-blind' technique and randomisation. The former is virtually confined to drug trials. It is almost impossible for a doctor not to have some preference in a choice of treatments; the double-blind trial attempts to eliminate this subjectivity by keeping the assigned therapeutic groups secret from the physicians as well as from the patients. Not only does this dictate that the patient's doctor cannot be the researcher but it also makes it implicit that the ethical justification of the trial is agreed by the 'caring' physicians involved – and this leads to considerable difficulty in implementing the second principle – of randomisation – because it involves some form of conscious pre-selection. It has been suggested that no clinical trial can be truly random.[10] Certainly, the subjects by volunteering distinguish themselves from those who do not; or, it may be necessary to exclude patients on the grounds of the severity of their disease, in which case the trial is limited to establishing the effectiveness of a treatment for the milder forms of the disease. Whether or not such restrictions interfere with the scientific accuracy of the project, they form an integral part of the basic principles of the Declaration of Helsinki (paras 5 and 9).

Groups of subjects

There is clearly an advantage whenever possible in using healthy volunteers as experimental subjects but, by definition, their use is limited to non-therapeutic research. Somewhat strangely, the Declaration of Helsinki allows for patients being used for such purposes. We believe, however, that the temptation to use a group of persons, who are already under stress and who probably have a sense of obligation to the doctors, simply because of their accessibility must often bring such research close to unethical practice; non-therapeutic research in patients should be confined to a type which adds no extra

9 H Helmchem and B Müller-Oerlinghausen 'The Inherent Paradox of Clinical Trials in Psychiatry' (1975) 1 J Med Ethics 168.
10 W Rudowski 'World Health Organisation Biomedical Research Guidelines and the Conduct of Clinical Trials' (1980) 6 J Med Ethics 58.

burden – for example, through the use of existing blood samples as is discussed below. It has been argued that the use of volunteers is, itself, unjustifiable but we prefer the view that, since everyone in the United Kingdom is receiving free medical care, there can be nothing wrong, and probably a lot right, in fulfilling an urge to help improve that care. Nonetheless, considerable caution is needed, particularly as to the repetitive volunteer who is particularly prone to exploitation even if the researchers are unconscious of this – they may, for example, be quite unaware of marital disharmony caused by frequent absences from home. Motivation of the ever ready volunteer takes several forms, some good and others bad, and, among these, the problem of recompense looms large. The Declaration of Helsinki is silent on this aspect but it is reasonably certain that, in the conditions of present day society, very few volunteers would come forward in the absence of some inducement; large payments would, however, be clearly unethical and a reasonable balance must be set – if for no other reason than to satisfy the needs of randomisation.

The topic of inducement does, however, introduce the problems of the use of special populations because of their easy access, malleability and the like. Students, and particularly medical students, provide an example about whom there is little difficulty; they are intelligent and comprehending, they may well have an active interest in the trial and all educational establishments have very stringently controlling 'ethical committees' to protect against, say, repetitive use. Much the same could be said for the Armed Forces. But the use of prisoners exposes many ethical issues essentially based on the arguments that some advantage, even if only imagined, must accrue to the prisoner participating in a trial; that advantage may be so great as to induce the prisoner to volunteer for research which involves greater discomfort or risk than would be accepted by a free man and, in particular, it may compromise his inalienable right to withdraw from the experiment. This could be the subject of lengthy debate but we would suggest that the conditions in today's prisons are such that any process which provides some relief deserves, at least, a sympathetic evaluation and, secondly, that many prisoners might be therapeutically benefited through helping society. But it is also felt that experiments on prisoners should be particularly rigidly controlled by ethical committees which should always contain lay members with experience in criminology. Nowhere is it more important to observe the maxim: 'the aims do not justify the method – the method must be judged in it's own right'.

When comparing treatments, however, the use of patients is axiomatic. This is what the Declaration of Helsinki calls medical research combined with professional care and for which it lays down clear principles. The therapeutic controlled trial must invoke the Geneva principle 'the health of the patient will be my first consideration' and Rudowski[11] has quoted: 'a patient is assigned to undergo clinical study when, on the basis of our best judgment, an equal possibility exists that each of the compared methods of treatment will be of advantage to the patient'. This is a minimum standard – a clinical trial is rarely undertaken unless there is good reason to suppose that one therapy will show an advantage over others and particularly over those currently accepted as the best available. The advantage need not be direct; it could, for example, be collateral in that the results of the method were not better but were achieved with less disfigurement or with fewer side effects. The essential feature of anticipated advantage can, in general, only be based on laboratory or animal experimentation and, while the view is occasionally expressed that the latter is less moral than is human biomedical research, it represents the first basic principle of the Declaration of Helsinki. The corollary is that an experimental method must be immediately withdrawn if it is found to be positively deleterious and the patients involved must be transferred, whenever possible, to an alternative regime.

The difficulties of such clinical research include, firstly, that each patient is a unique set of many variables. While a statistical result may be achieved, it would be a remarkably well designed trial which simultaneously solved the problems of the individual exceptions. Secondly, the results of the experimental therapies may take a considerable time to filter through and, by then, there may be no turning back. Such considerations apply particularly to trials of treatments for cancer or, as a more recent example, the prophylaxis of neural tube defects in infants.[12] But cancer is such an important disease that trials must continue. Paradoxically, the importance of cancer rests to an extent on the fact that current treatments of many forms are far from being fully effective – provided the controlled trials are conducted with maximum expertise, it is then possible to justify them purely on the basis of societal benefit, an exception to the rule laid down in the Declaration.[13]

The use of placebos
A placebo is an inert substance without pharmacological action. The

11 See fn. 10, above.
12 See *The Times*, 9 August 1982, p. 4. The results of an experiment involving 3,000 women will not be known for three years.
13 For a useful evaluation of the dilemma see B P Bliss and A G Johnson *Aims and Methods in Clinical Medicine* (1975) ch 8.

use of placebos is occasionally remarkably successful in straightforward therapeutics but, there, the practice is even more difficult to justify morally than it is in the experimental situation where the use of placebos is sometimes essential. The mere taking of medicine may lead to subjective improvement; this is the 'placebo effect' which must be considered whenever a new drug or procedure is on trial. On the other hand, the trial drug may do more harm than inactivity; but, for psychological reasons, inactivity must involve apparently comparable activity if two regimens are to be properly compared. In either case, the controlled giving of a placebo necessarily involves the deception of patients and this raises some complex issues.

The extreme position is that placebos offend against the fundamental rightness of fidelity.[14] If, as is certainly often the case, there is patient resistance to the use of such controls, this should not be regarded as an excuse for further deception but rather as an indication that such experiments are unacceptable to society. To which one could reply that a poor experiment is a worse affront to society and that the simple expedient is to leave out those who object – little is lost, other than, perhaps, absolute numbers, and, as previously discussed, experimental volunteers are, by nature, already a selected group.

More valid objections are based on the effect of the experiment on patient care; the circumstances in which it is ethical to deprive a patient of treatment must be strictly regulated. It would, for example, be improper to use placebo controls when pain was a feature of the condition under treatment despite the fact that some patients might derive benefit; many pain killers are available and can be used as reference substances. The basic circumstances in which placebo trials are ethical and, perhaps, necessary are, firstly, when there is no alternative to the experimental treatment available or, secondly, when the effect of adding a new treatment to an established one is under study. The essential purpose of using placebos is to analyse the effect of a treatment on symptoms rather than on organic disease.

Informed consent
It is apparent that an ethical experiment depends upon free, autonomous participation by the subject and this, in turn, depends upon 'informed consent', the nature of which has been discussed in chapter 9.

The principles in relation to experimentation are similar and most philosophers would say that the patient's rights are then, if anything,

14 B Simmons 'Problems in Deceptive Medical Procedures: An Ethical and Legal Analysis of the Administration of Placebos' (1978) 4 J Med Ethics 172.

greater in this situation than they are in the sphere of pure patient management – the standard of information must be that of the 'reasonable subject' rather than that of the 'reasonable doctor'. Those involved in biomedical human research, particularly that involving selection of treatment, while being well aware of their responsibilities do, at the same time, see many of the difficulties – the essential need for some measure of ignorance in the trial, the seriousness of the condition being treated, the psychology of individual patients and the like. The complications are such that in Sweden, for example, while the law lays down that the doctrine of informed consent has to be satisfied, no attempt is made to define the extent of the information given.[15]

There are more general problems. Who would impart the information – the patient's physician or the researcher? Should the patient have the benefit of a 'friend' to interpret for him? Should there be confirmation of the consent procedure? It has been fairly widely mooted that, in fact, informed consent is a double-edged weapon – token consent may take the place of the genuine and relieve the re- searcher of responsibility. Might it not be better to burden the in- vestigator with full responsibility rather than provide such a shield?[16] In general, however, it is agreed that no information which may be useful to the patient can be withheld and that consent is based on four main lines of explanation: the purpose of the experiment, the benefits to the patient and society, the risks involved and the alternatives open to the subject. The doctor may withhold some information but, if so, he would be advised to explain his action in the patient's notes. The importance attached to patient integrity is increasing and the principle of 'professional privilege' is unlikely to find great favour with the courts. It was stated in a Canadian case:[17] 'There can be no exceptions to the ordinary requirements of disclosure in the case of research as there may well be in ordinary medical practice.' Many of the states of the United States have enacted 'informed consent statutes'; while some of them may be, in fact, protective of the physician, others go so far as to lay down specific disclosure patterns for particular procedures.

These problems are highlighted in 'care associated' research when, effectively, the doctrine of informed consent implies that the patient has to choose for himself or herself whether to accept an experimental treatment or to be randomised in a comparative therapeutic trial. The philosophical basis of patient autonomy is perfectly clear but is the

15 G Giertz 'Ethics and Randomised Clinical Trials' (1980) 6 J Med Ethics 55.
16 See fn. 9, above.
17 *Halushka v University of Saskatchewan* (1965) 52 WWR 608.

ideal end attainable in practice? Ought a patient to be told of a 'last choice' effort? Is the medically naïve patient capable of giving consent as required? Can he be expected to understand the risks when the medical profession itself is divided? Such issues are crystallised in the treatment of cancer, so much so that at least two American States have statutes laying down the information to be given to patients suffering from breast cancer.[18] In California, physicians are provided with a summary of medically viable alternative treatments which can be used to comply with the Act. Whether such devices are valuable to the *patient* is doubtful; we would be inclined to agree with those who believe that the ideal informed consent in these circumstances can only be given by those who are actually employed in the caring professions. At the end of the day, perhaps the most objective test of the ethics of a therapeutic trial would be the number of doctors' wives who were enrolled.

Compensation for personal injury in research

As things stand at present, the only remedy for personal injury received as a result of research or experimentation rests in tort. The governing rules are those outlined in chapter 10 and may be very difficult to apply. This is, firstly, on the grounds that, in general, the researchers will have taken every precaution including obtaining the approval of an ethical committee and, secondly, as a corollary, on the grounds of foreseeability – almost by definition, an accident occurring will not have been reasonably likely. An action based on lack of consent would be unlikely to succeed in the absence of deliberate deception; *Bolam*[19] would apply to experimentation as much as to treatment. Such a situation is unfair to the research subject. Quite apart from problems of expense or uncertainty, he is morally entitled to believe he will be looked after in the event of something going wrong – and charity is unpredictable and often ungenerous as a remedy.

There is clearly a need for some defined method of compensation as of right, the Pearson Commission again favouring strict liability.[20] This is also unsatisfactory from the point of view of the aggrieved subject as it also involves recourse to the courts where the burden of proving causation would fall upon the plaintiff or pursuer. An

18 S Taub 'Cancer and the Law of Informed Consent' (1982) 10 Law Med Health Care 61.
19 *Bolam v Friern Hospital Management Committee* [1957] 2 All ER 118, [1957] 1 WLR 582 in which failure to disclose a minimal risk was not considered negligent.
20 Report of Royal Commission on Civil Liability and Compensation for Personal Injury (Cmnd 7054) at para 1341.

alternative is the establishment of a no-fault principle of compensation similar to that operating on a national basis in New Zealand[1] but such a scheme requires funding and administration. No-fault compensation for the research subject has powerful support[2] but only tort law remains until legislation is passed. The main ethical consideration is that the subject should be fully informed of his rights, or lack of them, before enrolment.

Random sample testing

One aspect of research which has received little consideration concerns the use of samples which have been removed for defined, usually therapeutic, reasons. The use of such samples for other investigations subjects the patient to no further discomfort and, while a patient could undoubtedly make directions as to the disposal of any biological specimen he has provided, this would be by virtue of no more than an inchoate right.[3] It would be reasonable to assume from silence that the patient intended to abandon the material, yet there is an element of invasion of the patient's privacy in 'finding out things' about him without his consent no matter how much it is felt that the geographic distribution of genes or any cultural alterations in body chemistry, for example, might provide useful research projects. But a balance has, again, to be struck since most patients, even if asked, would be disinterested in consent.

The justification of such projects would seem to rest on the consequences of a positive finding. At one extreme, a survey of random bloods for the presence of syphilis would dictate that patients were informed of positive results; such a survey would, therefore, be unethical in the absence of consent. On the other hand, a search for a particular blood group gene in a specific population could make no possible difference to the subjects and would accordingly be permissible. But one would have to think carefully before embarking on, say, a survey of abnormal haemoglobins with its consequent possible influences on marriage and having a family.

Other surveys could be of no immediate consequence to the patient but could be of significance were the results to be published. An example would be the routine estimation of blood alcohol as a

---

1 Accident Compensation Act 1972. The difficulty of defining an accident which has been experienced under this legislation would be unlikely to arise in a narrow field such as medical research.

2 Ciba Foundation Study Group 'Medical Research: Civil Liability and Compensation for Personal Injury – A Discussion Paper' (1980) 1 Brit Med J 1172.

3 B M Dickens 'The Control of Living Body Materials' (1977) 27 Univ Toronto LJ 142.

community study. In the event of the samples deriving from accidents, the results could be of particular interest to the police or insurance companies and would be normally available only by consent of the subjects. Serious consequences might arise if the result of a research project were entered in the notes and these were later subject to disclosure;[4] it is apparent that no research of potentially damaging type would be ethical if there was a chance that the subject and the result could later be associated. Practical problems in this field have, in fact, arisen in the United States in relation to drug screening surveys; preservation of the patient's anonymity must be the determining condition under which specimens are used without express consent for purposes alternative to those originally stated.

4 The evidence could be used in the United Kingdom (*R v Sang* [1980] AC 402, [1979] 2 All ER 1222, HL) or in Canada (*Wray v R* (1973) 10 CCC (2d) 215) but not in the United States in that it violates the constitutional right to resist self-incrimination.

16 Research on children and fetal experimentation

A child is by no means a miniature version of an adult. Children respond differently to drugs, as they do to a number of other treatments, and it is impossible to say that the effect of a particular therapy on an adult will be mirrored when applied to a child. Medical research on children is, therefore, necessary before a treatment can be approved for paediatric use. As in adults, such research may entail not only therapeutic research on sick children but also essential non-therapeutic research on normal control groups; it is this non-therapeutic research which poses the ethical and legal problems.

Non-therapeutic research on children

The essential difficulty with non-therapeutic research on children lies, again, in the question of consent. An adult may be able to give an informed and therefore valid consent to participation in research, but can the same be said of a child? The Nuremberg Code says nothing on the matter although one of the principal authors of the Code expressed the view after it had been drawn up that the consent of guardians would be adequate where the subject was a child or a mentally ill person.[1] The later Declaration of Helsinki specifically mentions the 'legally incompetent' participant in research, stating that the consent of the guardian should be procured; this approach is also adopted in the American Medical Association guidelines. These guidelines advise that, when a child is used as a research subject, consent should be obtained from a legally authorised representative under circumstances in which an informed and prudent adult would reasonably be expected to volunteer himself or his child as a subject.

The philosophy underlying these rules is one which assumes that a parent will have the best interest of his child at heart and can, therefore, be trusted not to make any decisions which would seriously compromise the child's welfare. Society makes this assumption about parents because, by and large, that is the way parents behave. It is

1 A C Ivy 'The History and Ethics of the Use of Human Subjects in Medical Experiments' (1948) 108 Science 1.

also an essential working assumption; the child is incompetent to decide many day-to-day matters for himself and, for practical reasons, discretion must be exercised on his behalf by parents.

We have seen in several contexts, however, that parental power is not absolute. Society reserves the right to overrule parents and, although this right is exercised sparingly, it may be used if parents are not acting in the best interests of the child over whom they have authority. Implicit, then, in the doctrine of parental power is the assumption that it ought not to be used to harm the child.[2]

It is here that we reach the nub of the issue – it may well be argued that participation in non-therapeutic research is *not* in the child's best interests. The child does not benefit from it since it is directed towards the relief of a condition from which he does not suffer. And, rather than simply not benefiting, he will almost certainly be affected adversely by it because every procedure, even the extraction of a drop of blood, contains some risk, no matter how minute. If we accept this argument, there can be no justification for the proxy consent of a parent in that there is no entitlement to a harmful consent.

The logic of this argument may be clear, but it still may be possible to refute it. One may argue that participation in research *is* in fact to the benefit of the child, in that it is a pro-social and altruistic activity which may help to develop a child's sense of duty to the community. This may be the case with older children but the argument would obviously be inapplicable to those who are very young. This need not defeat the proposition of benefit entirely. A child is a member of a class within the community – the class of children – and the individual can be said to be a potential beneficiary if research will benefit the class as a whole. It is also possible to extrapolate the reasoning used to justify organ donation (see chapter 13) and to argue that participation in research related to a disease from which a sibling is suffering will benefit the normal child in that it is in his interests that his sibling should recover. Finally, it might be said of this particular exercise of proxy consent that it is proper for parents to choose what their child *ought* to choose itself were it in a position to exercise its own will.[3]

While all these arguments have certain claims, none of them is, of itself, sufficiently convincing to establish the legitimacy of proxy parental consent in the circumstances envisaged.

2 But see the discussion of parental rights in the neonatal period in ch. 7, above.
3 This argument is advanced in R A McCormick 'Proxy Consent in the Experimentation Situation' (1974) 18 Perspect Biol Med 2. For a strong refutation of the proxy consent doctrine see P Ramsey *The Patient as a Person* (1970) pp. 44–7. Ramsey argues that proxy consent is valid only when the research involved is of a therapeutic nature.

To do so, it may be necessary to alter one's perspective and, here, it is useful to consider the recent evolution of legal and philosophical attitudes to the parent-child relationship. The direction of the law over the last few decades has unquestionably been in favour of the dismantling of the concept of parental rights over children and substituting in its place a doctrine of the rights of the child. The prime test in any matter touching upon children has become one of determining the 'best interests of the child'. This has been the yardstick against which decisions are measured and parental wishes have become of secondary significance. But the societal mood which produced this child-centred philosophy is currently changing. The integrity of the family and the primacy of the parents within the family unit are no longer unfashionable notions and there is a considerable body of opinion which argues in a reasoned fashion for the granting of greater autonomy to the family and for less state intervention in the exercise of parental decision-making.[4] This changing attitude is articulated mainly by social philosophers and psychologists and, while it by no means yet represents legal orthodoxy, the law, itself, is becoming less set in its direction. Thus, while the autonomy of children is being increasingly emphasised by the courts in some areas, as in the cases of contraception and abortion in minors, parental rights of decision have been strongly emphasised in others. It is possible, then, to justify the parental right of proxy consent by looking at the problem not so much from the point of view of the child but, rather, from the point of view of the family as a whole – and the family is a miniature reflection of society.

The societal, or familial, dilemma which must be faced in the present context then becomes that of determining the extent of any parental right to involve children in altruistic endeavour. The case in favour of recognising this right may be based on the idea that a social duty is expected of parents. A parent's interest in discharging such a duty can then be held in the scales against a child's right not to be used as a means rather than as an end in himself. It might well be seen, for example, that the parental social duty would outweigh any interests of the child if the risks of the research and the discomfort it involved were negligible. Even if this were not accepted and the child's interest in non-participation were to be seen as being more significant than any parental social duty, the non-interventionists could still hold that this is an area of the family's activities in which the law has no right to interfere. State intervention may be justified if a child's life is threatened through neglect or through a parental decision which is

4 B M Dickens 'The Modern Function and Limits of Parental Rights' (1981) 97 LQR
462.

going to lead to great danger – but these are not the stakes involved in comparatively harmless research. The protaganist of individual self-determination is unlikely to approve of a justification based on relative values but the inevitable consequence of the extreme individualistic position would be the suspension of all non-therapeutic medical research on children – which would benefit nobody, least of all the children themselves.

It is possible that doubts over the legitimacy of proxy parental consent will not need to be debated in some cases because the child himself may be judged to be capable of giving or withholding consent. The age at which a child can appreciate the implications of what he is doing will vary, but some generalisations may be made.[5] Children under the age of seven are usually considered to be incapable of that degree of morally sophisticated thought required to make consistent altruistic decisions but, above that age, a child may be perfectly able to understand that he is helping doctors to cure others by taking part in the research programme. His understanding of the full implications of the research will obviously be less than complete, but the essential consent may well be present. A child who was not able to grasp the general idea of medical research by the age of 15 would probably be an exception today.

The ethical issues might be clarified to an extent if the law could give a clear answer to this question. Unfortunately, the law itself is uncertain in this area and this uncertainty has not eased the difficulties of those involved in paediatric research. In 1962, the Medical Research Council stated that: 'in the strict view of the law, parents and guardians of minors cannot give consent on their behalf to any procedures which are of no particular benefit to them and which may carry some risk of harm'.[6] This was followed by a Department of Health circular which confirmed that interpretation in a negative way.

> Health authorities are advised that they ought not to infer [from a Royal College of Physicians recommendation that children can be used in certain forms of research provided the consent of the guardian has been obtained] that the fact that consent has been given by the parent or guardian and that the risk involved is considered negligible will be sufficient to bring such clinical research investigation within the law as it stands.[7]

5 See J Berryman 'Discussing the Ethics of Research on Children' in J van Eys (ed) *Research on Children* (1978) p. 85.
6 Report of the Medical Research Council for 1962–3 (Cmnd 2382) pp. 21–5.
7 'Supervision of the Ethics of Clinical Research Investigations and Fetal Research' HSC (5) 153.

The advice of the Department of Health was roundly attacked by doctors. It was noted by critics that this statement of the law was based on the legal view of one person only.[8] Others complained of hindrances being placed in the way of research by worried ethical committees and by warnings from the defence societies.

Lawyers have also criticised the 'strict view of the law', pointing out that there are no statutes on the matter and no court decisions in point – the rules of non-statutory law do not vary with different categories of person.[9] There are not even any judicial remarks obiter which would justify the conclusion that parental consent will not legitimise the participation of children in research of this nature. In these circumstances, the proper way of approaching the issue is to look at general legal principles governing the parent/child relationship and to infer from these what a court might decide if the matter were to come before it.

We have already seen that the consent of a minor to medical treatment may be adequate even without parental ratification provided that the child is capable of understanding what is involved. This, however, does not necessarily apply to non-therapeutic measures which constitute a separate issue and merit discussion in their own right.

It seems clear that the Family Law Reform Act 1969, s. 8 refers only to treatment – the statutory age of 16 years has, therefore, no relevance in relation to consent to experimentation. To infer from this that consent to non-therapeutic investigations was impossible below the age of majority would be to accept a total embargo on experimentation in children which would be not only absurd but which would also be thoroughly disadvantageous to children as a whole. It would be better to assume with Skegg[10] that the current interpretation should rather be that anyone who is capable of so doing may give consent – and this is because, rather than in spite of, there is no statutory prohibition. The problem then becomes that of deciding whether there is any age below which a person is deemed incapable of consent and, while there is no law on the point, it would seem reasonable, and, indeed, advisable, to place this no lower than 14 years (possibly, for the sake of consistency in argument, 12 years for girls in Scotland). It follows that consent could be considered

---

8 W J Curran and H K Beecher 'Experimentation in Children: A Re-examination of Legal and Clinical Principles' (1969) 210 JAMA 77.

9 P D G Skegg 'English Law relating to Experimentation on Children' (1977) 2 Lancet 754. An excellent comparative survey of the law is to be found in J M Burchell 'Non-therapeutic Medical Research on Children' (1978) 95 South Afr LJ 193.

10 See fn. 9, above.

valid above that age and this, in fact, seems to have been the actual interpretation of the law taken by the British Medical Research Council who advised that, above the age of 12 years, the reality of a purported consent would be a matter of fact to be determined on the evidence as to understanding. The Council, further, drew a distinction between the child who could consent and the mentally subnormal person – procedures which carry no direct benefit to the subject should not be undertaken in the latter group if they were incapable of consenting as judged by the criteria commonly used to assess testamentary capacity and the like. It therefore seems to us that the currently accepted 'strict view of the law' is founded largely on a misreading of the advice of the highly authoritative Medical Research Council.

But to say that there is no legal sanction of a procedure is not to say that it is necessarily morally acceptable; furthermore, there is no reason to assume that the court, if asked, would approve an action which was unethical. The position is, therefore, still delicately balanced. Anticipating a judicial reaction is a matter for ethical committees who may assume that the court would act as a wise parent would act – giving first consideration to the child but being, at the same time, hospitable to good research.[11] Thus, the essential measure is the 'risk-benefit ratio' of the investigation – but, within this, the 'risk' factor must, without doubt, retain primary control. We would also suggest that, notwithstanding what the true legal position may be, it would be, in practice, improper to proceed with an experiment involving a child against the wishes of its parents. The only exception might be when that refusal was clearly unreasonable and was jeopardising an otherwise essential trial; even then, a decision to go ahead should be taken only after very careful consideration. As the British Medical Journal has put it 'at a time when there is so much public questioning of medical traditions and especially of medical authoritarianism, research workers need to be especially careful not to offend these heightened susceptibilities'.[12] The courts will not be called upon to take the alternative decision – that is, to overrule parental consent – if such good advice is heeded.

It must not be thought that an ethical assessment of a project is always clear cut. A most apposite example was an experiment in preventive medicine which entailed the deliberate infection with the virus of hepatitis of children in a home for the subnormal. Although

11 G Dworkin 'Legality of Consent to Nontherapeutic Medical Research on Infants and Young Children' (1978) 53 Arch Dis Childh 443. The author notes the transition in legal thinking from paramount interests to first consideration of the child – the latter indicating that other interests are admissible.
12 Editorial Comment 'Research on Children' (1978) 2 Brit Med J 1043.

the chances of the children being infected naturally were as high as 60 per cent within six months of admission, the project was castigated by some writers.[13] Others disagreed with such an analysis – one of Britain's most respected paediatricians described the experiment as: 'a small, carefully controlled trial for which the director also deserves a great deal of credit for his scrupulous care in securing the truly informed consent of the children's parents'.[14] It is clear that there can be no generalised approach to a subject such as childhood experimentation which is governed, in the end, by humane pragmatism.

Fetal experimentation

Several of the legal and moral attitudes to fetal life have already been discussed. The possibilities of fetal research and experiment, which are repugnant to many, extend the area of debate and merit further discussion.

It must be accepted that fetal research is valuable. The Peel Report[15] listed 53 ways in which it could be of real assistance and there is no doubt that the catalogue will have increased in the last decade. Just as children are, medically, more than little adults so, or rather more so, are fetuses not just immature children; the environment in which they exist is wholly different and, as has already been discussed, it is within that environment that something in the region of half the morbidity and mortality of infancy is fashioned. Major areas of disease will never be properly understood in the absence of fetal research. Nor will the outstanding dilemma of drug therapy during pregnancy be fully resolved.

Sources of fetal material and the problems of consent

Other than those which are born alive prematurely and with which we are not currently concerned, fetuses become available either through spontaneous miscarriage or as a result of therapeutic abortion. It is axiomatic that any necessary consent to research can only be given by the mother and both her attitude and that of her physicians must be different in the two cases.

The position seems clear in the case of miscarriage. The mother is distressed and, normally, wants everything possible done for her

13 See, for a good review, L Golman 'The Willowbrook Debate' (1973) 9 World Med (1) 79.

14 A W Franklin 'Research Investigation in Children' (1973) 1 Brit Med J 402 at 405.

15 J Peel (Chairman) (1972) Report of the Committee on the Use of Fetuses and Fetal Material for Research (London: HMSO).

offspring. It seems unlikely in the circumstances that a research project will be contemplated but, were it so, the informed consent of the mother would be required. The therapeutic abortion situation is rather different. In the majority of cases, the mother will have requested termination and, in so doing, she has effectively abandoned her fetus. In either case, the recommendation of the Peel Report is acceptable:

> there is no legal requirement to obtain the patient's consent for research but equally there is no statutory right to ignore the parents wishes – the parent must be offered the opportunity to declare any special directions about the fetus.[16]

In so doing, there would seem to be three requirements to be satisfied. Firstly, the consent should be obtained before the operation in the relatively calm conditions prevailing. Secondly, and as a corollary, the mother should be able to withdraw her consent after delivery of the fetus. And, finally, the research worker requesting consent should be independent of the caring gynaecologist – every moral and public policy principle dictates that it be made absolutely clear that abortions are not being performed in order to provide research material for those recommending the treatment. Such matters must be rigidly controlled by ethical committees; in our opinion, which was not shared by the Peel Committee, the control of fetal research is so much a matter of public concern that non-professional lay representation on committees formed for this purpose should be obligatory.

But even so, conditions are not uniform. The fetus may be alive in utero or it may be killed in the process of abortion; it may be pre-viable or viable. The validity of consent and the ethical limitations on research will, therefore, differ.

The status of the fetus
Research in utero on the living fetus which may be either normal and expected to survive or abnormal and expected to die before parturition, is of immense value but, obviously, also involves an element of risk. Some useful research is non-invasive and may be coupled with patient care but even then there is no simple answer. Thus, the experimental use of x-rays, at least in the first trimester, would be unethical; ultrasonic investigations seem, by contrast, to be wholly safe – but we cannot yet know, for example, whether fetal ultrasonic investigations affect one at retiring age. Our more immediate concern is with invasive investigations and these, once

16 At para 42.

again, focus attention on the uncertainties surrounding the legal status of the unborn child (see chapter 5, above).

The fetus itself has limited rights[17] and it has been argued that no action exists in the United Kingdom in respect of 'wrongful death' of the fetus; the stillbirth has no right of action of itself and the only action available is to the parents in negligence on the grounds of distress, inconvenience and the like.[18] If, however, the fetus were born deformed, it would clearly have right of action against a research worker whose defence, assuming causation to have been proved, would rest on the standard of reasonable care having been maintained. The matter of consent then becomes paramount and must be judged in the same light as has been discussed in relation to children.

Assuming that the mother has a right of proxy consent to research procedures, the risk/benefit test would have to be very stringently applied for, whereas the child has at least minimal understanding, the fetus can certainly have none. A negligence action based on a lack of informed consent would be more likely to succeed in these conditions than in many others; if, by contrast, parental consent is impossible, the damaged infant has a cause of action for trespass which will be virtually indefensible other than on issues of causation. In practice, the nature of an invasive experiment of this type is strictly limited on clinical grounds.

But what if the fetus should die? An experiment is not a legal abortion and the fact that a later abortion was intended would not negate any offence; the question is – what offence? The Peel Committee spoke of reckless injury to the fetus but the only possible offences now existing lie under the Offences Against the Person Act 1861, section 58 or under the Infant Life (Preservation) Act 1929, section 1 if the fetus were capable of being born alive. Both these sections, however, include a requirement of intent, in the former to procure a miscarriage and in the second to destroy life. To prove an offence, it would then be necessary to show that the action amounted to constructive intent – that is, something was done when it was known that fetal death was a very high probability – and this seems a very doubtful proposition. It would seem that there ought to be a clear legal position on the point, if only to satisfy the public conscience, and we return to the subject later.

We see no difficulty as to the criminal law if the fetus is either legally viable and lives or proves its viability by living despite its prematurity. There must be general agreement with the Peel Report

---

17 See *Dehler v Ottawa Civic Hospital* (1979) 101 DLR (3d) 686.
18 By contrast, actions for wrongful death have been successful in the United States (e g *Hale v Manion* 189 Kan 143, 368 P 2d 1 (1962)).

(at para 28) that the ethical obligation is to sustain its life as far as possible. We would go further and suggest that non-therapeutic research or experiment which causes the death of such an infant must, by analogy with our discussion on abortion (chapter 5), technically be manslaughter or murder depending upon the degree of recklessness involved. It is to be noted that the Peel Report (at para 31) suggested that, as an added precaution, evidence of 20 weeks gestation (a weight of 400–500g) should be prima facie proof of viability; repeated attempts to bring such a concept into law have failed along with Abortion Amendment Bills.

The pre-viable fetus
Perhaps it is the pre-viable fetus which attracts most emotion in the general issue of fetal research. Pre-viability implies that the fetus as a whole is incapable of a separate existence but that, nevertheless, there are signs of life in some organs. There can be no doubt that this is the fetal state which offers the greatest research potential; it is also true that the time available for such research is limited and so, therefore, is the opportunity for abuse. But, again, one must ask – is this an ensouled human being with the rights of a human being? And, moreover, do we know that it has no feeling and is incapable of pain and suffering? These questions relate both to the criminal law and to our moral code.

We suggest that the criminal law is inadequate in this area. Since a stillbirth is defined, inter alia, as 'not having breathed or shown other signs of life' it may well be that, say, a visibly beating heart is sufficient 'other signs' to qualify for legal 'live birth'.[19] That being so, to destroy that fetus outside the terms of the Abortion Act is to destroy life. But in doing so, what offence is being committed? By no stretch of the imagination could a fetus which is incapable of an independent existence be described as a 'reasonable creature in being' – it cannot be murdered. The discussion may seem sterile in present conditions but, in the event of extension of techniques being coupled with a deterioration in professional standards, it might, as has already been suggested in chapter 3, be necessary to invent an offence of feticide. The moral dilemma is clear from the questions posed above and, equally, turns on the definition of 'life'.

We suggest that the problem may be resolved by considering, first, whether or not a placenta is present and whether there is or is not a competent fetal/maternal connection. If there is, the fetus is, subject

19 We are, of course, aware that the definition of a stillbirth includes gestation of 28 weeks; but this is immaterial in the present context.

to normality, clearly alive and destructive research or experimentation would be morally unacceptable; it should be disallowed on these grounds alone. In view of the difficulties associated with innominate offences discussed above, this would also seem to be the simplest solution to the issues proposed by the criminal law.

If, however, the pre-viable fetus is separated from its mother, it is no longer capable of an existence; it is, therefore, possible to argue that it's state is one of somatic death. Experiments or research conducted on the body are, by this reasoning, conducted during the interval between somatic and ultimate cellular death which has been described in chapter 12. Accordingly, we suggest that the processes involve neither moral nor legal culpability. This is not to say, however, that public anxieties do not need to be allayed and we would overwhelmingly endorse the stringent administrative controls of pre-viable fetal research recommended in the Peel Report at para 35 including the 'safety factor' of a maximum permissible weight limit of 300g for fetuses subjected to such research.

The dead fetus and fetal parts
Much useful research can be done on fetuses which are clearly dead or are incomplete and this would seem to raise neither legal or ethical problems. The tissues can be regarded as abandoned biological specimens and treated accordingly. This is subject only to the mother's ultimate discretion – whether this is actively sought will depend, as discussed previously, on the conditions in which the tissues are voided.

The Peel Committee was deeply concerned at public revulsion at the thought of such material being sold for commercial purposes. We would agree that the concept of sale of human biological materials is foreign not only to the ideals of a National Health Service but to public opinion in general. There are no rules governing the disposal of fetuses other than those related to offences against public decency; at the present time, the sale of fetal tissues clearly comes into the latter category.

Fetal materials
Fetal materials are those parts of the products of conception which are discarded by both the mother and the fetus and comprise the placenta and its membranes and the umbilical cord. The placental membranes and the cord are both valuable in therapy and their use in that way is not subject to the Human Tissue Act 1961.

As a consequence, their disposal seems to present no difficulty. Fetal materials, once discharged from the mother, represent a classic example of *res nullius* and, thus, can become the property of the first person into whose hands they rightly fall. It is proper, and desirable, that such a person should harvest the material for the benefit of the community. The only proviso we would suggest is that, again, there should be no direct sale of biological materials. On the other hand, an adequate supply is unlikely to be obtained if left to pure altruism. Collection and disposal require time and effort; there should be no ethical objection to reasonable recompense for such services rendered.

The results of fetal research

Dickens, in a consideration of fetal research, posed the question:

> is moral repugnance against the method whereby a source of information is available a sufficient and ethical ground for declining to use it to help the innocent?[20]

He thought that the argument should be put but that it should not be allowed to prevail without challenge. This chapter has been, essentially, a consideration of this attitude and we hope that we have differentiated the minority of possible research patterns which appear unethical from the majority which can, logically, be regarded as both ethical and legal. If further justification of carefully controlled fetal research is called for, we would revert again to the contention that public and professional acceptance of the Abortion Act 1967 fundamentally changed our moral attitudes in medicine. That being agreed, there is good reason to follow the logical process one stage further and strive to extract some good from what many see as a measure of doubtful morality. We submit that the law should allow for this and that, where it is in doubt, it should be adjusted with that end in view.

20 B M Dickens 'The Control of Living Body Material' (1977) 27 Univ Toronto LJ 142.

Psychiatry and the Law

17 Human rights, psychiatry and the law

The story of the 'Rosenhan experiment' is a much used weapon in the arsenal of the so-called 'anti-psychiatry movement'. In this study, eight normal people complained of hearing voices and secured admission to different psychiatric hospitals; all were, in due course, diagnosed as being schizophrenic. Once in hospital, the subjects in the experiment professed their normality; they were, however, still considered ill and were described as suffering from schizophrenia in remission when they were discharged.[1]

The story illustrates some of the problems surrounding psychiatric diagnosis which is more subjective – and, therefore, potentially less reliable – than are many other forms of medical diagnosis. Indeed, psychiatrists are accused by their opponents of diagnosing mental illness too frequently and of using a psychiatric label to describe behaviour which may be anti-social but which is not the product of illness; it is not too difficult for psychiatric hospitals to be used as dumping grounds for awkward or embarrassing members of society. Once labelled as mentally ill, it may be very difficult for a patient to establish his or her sanity. The psychiatric institution may become a prison, confining people who have no wish or, indeed, in some cases, no need to be detained.

An extreme example of this involves the authentically documented use of psychiatry to control the activities of political dissidents in the Soviet Union.[2] Opposition to the political system is seen as an indication of mental illness, justifying the label of schizophrenia or some other condition and warranting incarceration. Once in an institution, the dissident may be administered drugs which subdue, confuse or nauseate. Such abuses have, of course, met with consistent and vociferous criticism from the psychiatric profession in the West.

Even so, complacency should not obscure the fact that the psychiatric patients in Western hospitals are a vulnerable community

---

1 D L Rosenhan 'On being Sane in Insane Places' (1973) 139 Science 250; L Gostin *A Human Condition* (1975) vol 1, p. 39.
2 Amnesty International *Prisoners of Conscience in the USSR: Their Treatment and Conditions* (1976).

for whom the protection of the law may, in some cases, be unobtainable or illusory. The days of punitive psychiatry and the 'bin' approach to the mentally ill may have passed but the patient in a psychiatric hospital is still largely controlled by those who are treating him. The involuntary in-patient is deprived of his freedom and, possibly, of the right to refuse treatment. His lines of communication with the outside world may be tenuous and his access to external legal advice may be, in practice, non-existent. Such a system carries with it the possibility of suffering and injustice no matter how therapeutic are the ideals of the doctors. The task of the law then becomes one of balancing, on the one hand, the requirements of the reasonably paternalistic treatment of the patient who needs it with, on the other, the duty to protect human rights.

The basis of involuntary treatment

Few people will seriously dispute the need to detain compulsorily certain categories of the mentally ill. Those who present a danger to others constitute the most obvious group. But, while there is agreement that dangerous mentally ill people should be detained, there is argument over the identification of dangerousness. It has been suggested that psychiatrists have no greater expertise than do laymen in predicting dangerousness and that such decisions should, therefore, be taken by laymen.[3] Indeed, in one view, detention against the patient's will can only be justified when a criminal offence has been committed; this is the position taken by Kennedy, as expounded in his 1981 Reith lectures.[4] Although there is a strong libertarian appeal in such a stance, there are, also, potent counter-arguments. If a mentally disturbed person begins to develop feelings of intense hostility towards another and confesses to a psychiatrist that he has a strong urge to kill the object of his hostility, is nothing to be done until the murder is committed? This problem arose in quite dramatic form in the celebrated American case of *Tarasoff v Regents of the University of California*,[5] where the family of a young woman who had been murdered by a rejected lover sued the psychotherapists who had failed to warn her of the danger presented by their patient. It is worth noting that a psychologist who had dealt with the murderer

---

3 See, for example, J Cocozza and H Steadman 'The Failure of Psychiatric Predictions of Dangerousness: Clear and Convincing Evidence' (1976) 29 Rutgers LR 1084.
4 I Kennedy *The Unmasking of Medicine* (1981) p. 111.
5 551 P 2d 334 (1976).

had formed the opinion that he was dangerous and had informed the police that he should be committed under the Civil Commitment Statute. The tragedy would not have occurred if the advice had been followed.[6]

Kennedy, in his book, develops a critique of compulsory detention which calls into question almost all of the existing philosophy of psychiatric practice. He is deeply distrustful of the category of mental illness, regarding it as being based on challengeable suppositions and being indicative of a desire to 'medicalise' the awkward and the embarrassingly different. There is a certain element of truth in this – it *is* easy to label the eccentric or the odd as mentally ill and thereby to deprive them of dignity and responsibility; this is a disturbing modern phenomenon which must be scrutinised carefully.[7] Yet one cannot theorise psychoses out of existence. People do suffer from schizophrenia and other mental conditions which are clearly illnesses in a perfectly acceptable sense of the word to anyone who encounters them. Describing such people as ill may be seen by some as forcing them into the 'embrace of mental illness' and as depriving them of their responsibility – but what are the alternatives? Are they to be treated in the same way as 'sane' members of the community, expected to pay their taxes, hold down jobs, refrain from disturbing neighbours excessively and all the rest? The label of illness relieves as well as deprives. 'Demedicalisation' is not always a concomitant of sympathy for the mentally ill; it can indicate impatience with and antagonism towards such unfortunates as is seen in some parts of the movement in the United States to limit or abolish the insanity defence.

Kennedy also takes objection to the forcing of treatment on those who have not asked for it, an objection which he shares with many other critics of psychiatry.[8] The basis of this objection if that to do so offends the principle of responsibility and demonstrates an unacceptable assumption of paternalism. The obvious reply to this is to point out that there are many cases in which the mentally ill cannot request

---

6 For an apt discussion of this case, see A A Stone 'The Tarasoff Decisions: Suing Psychotherapists to Safeguard Society' (1976) 90 Harvard LR 358. The author of this article points out that society must accept the risk of greater violence from the mentally ill if more safeguards are introduced to the provisions relating to compulsory admission to mental hospitals.

7 There is no doubt that society has become progressively less tolerant of mental abnormality within the community. See M Foucault *Madness and Civilisation* (1971).

8 For further discussion see N Kittrie *The Right to be Different: Deviance and Enforced Therapy* (1971); J Jacob 'The Right of the Mental Patient to his Psychosis' (1976) 39 MLR 17.

help because the nature of their illness prevents them from doing so. It is a feature of severe depression, for example, that very few decisions can be made because of the effect of the illness. A doctor who 'imposes' treatment in these circumstances may justify his paternalism on the basis of implied consent and by his knowledge of what are normal human aspirations. Mental illness, after all, entails suffering and the relief of suffering is normally welcomed. A suffering person may not, by virtue of his illness, be in a position to choose whether or not to continue suffering and, in such circumstances, not to impose treatment could be little other than neglect. The analogy of unconsciousness or of childhood is not entirely inappropriate here. The patient whose consciousness is clouded due, say, to concussion may be treated paternalistically, as may the child who does not understand what is happening to him. The justification in these cases is that there can be no rational decision in view of the patient's condition; there is no reason why the same justification should not be used in the case of the mentally ill.

The basis on which a decision is made on behalf of a child is that the child may, by virtue of ignorance and an inadequately developed sense of judgment, be unable to determine which course of action is right for him in the circumstances. It is, of course, adults who judge what is right for him and, in this judgment, the child's present feelings may be little more than a marginal consideration. The focal point, however, of the paternalistic decision is not, or should not be, the wishes of the adults but, rather, their view of what the child may be expected to want in the future. A child may prefer to avoid a painful course of treatment now, even if such abstinence may entail a risk to his health. At some future time, however, he would probably regret his objections and would decide differently if he were faced with the same circumstances. The state of childhood is, after all, a temporary one during which current preferences should be, to some extent, subordinated to future goals.

In the case of the mentally ill person, the onset of mental illness heralds a period of abnormality during which the potential of the personality is diminished. A psychotic's view of the world may represent his reality, but it is a fallacy to argue that such reality is something which should be sacrosanct. The personality of the mentally ill patient is not necessarily diminished or violated if an attempt is made to change it. What is being done is to try to restore the *status quo ante* or, as in the case of the paternalistic treatment of a child, to try to give effect to what the patient may be presumed to want at some future time. The most eloquent justification for involuntary treatment comes from those who have been cured of mental illness and are restored to a happy and productive life.

The limits of paternalism

The imposition of involuntary treatment will not, however, be appropriate in all cases. It is important to recognise that there will be circumstances in which, although the patient is mentally ill, the illness need not have rendered him totally incompetent to make decisions. Our argument in favour of paternalistic intervention is predicated upon judged incompetence; it should not apply in cases where the illness does not affect the cognitive or judgmental ability of the patient. This means that a presumption that the patient is incapable of making decisions should not derive from the mere fact of involuntary admission.[9]

Assessment of a patient's competence to make decisions about treatment may be a difficult task and caution should be shown in borderline cases. The mentally ill have feelings which should be respected in the same way as are those of other patients and they should be overridden only when the nature of the therapeutic goal is clear and incompetence is established. Even then, the extent of the coercion should be strictly controlled. At the same time, it should be born in mind that respect for the patient's autonomy might well prove to be at the expense of his welfare.

The patient's rights

Certainly, there must be limits to therapeutic zeal if abuses are to be avoided and unwarranted invasions of the human personality are not to be sanctioned. The development of a theoretical basis for a system of limitation is, however, exceptionally difficult and, in the face of such difficulty, some critics of psychiatry have, we feel, been forced into a position which, if adopted, would restrict psychiatric medicine unreasonably. This is perhaps inevitable when concepts of legal rights are introduced. The law is reasonably comfortable with absolutes, but can be a remarkably blunt instrument when applied to circumstances that demand subtleties.[10] It is because they have a deep distrust of the expert that many critics of psychiatry place great faith in the virtue of lay opinion or of legal judgment – which is, in this context, merely a regulated form of lay opinion. Are lay people the best equipped people to determine the issues of involuntary

---

9 This point is made by L Gostin 'Observations on Consent to Treatment and Review of Clinical Judgement in Psychiatry: A Discussion Paper' (1981) 74 J Roy Soc Med 742.

10 There is a masterly analysis of this question in Sir John Wood's Maudsley Lecture, 'The Impact of Legal Modes of Thought upon the Practice of Psychiatry' (1982) 140 Brit J Psychiat 551.

committal to hospital as Kennedy suggests? Are lawyers better suited than psychiatrists to judge the issue of whether a particular patient's condition is likely to be alleviated by a regime of drug therapy within a mental hospital?

The solution to the apparent conflict between therapeutic objectives and the non-interventionist position might be found in the evolution of a form of psychiatric practice which is both sensitive to human rights and which is, at the same time, subject to an element of lay and legal control. This control should not bind the hands of the psychiatrist so firmly as to make it virtually impossible to treat without consent, but it should provide for the adequate policing of involuntary therapy. It is against this overall objective that the law relating to admission to mental hospitals should be considered.

In England and Wales, involuntary admission is provided for in the Mental Health Act 1959 (as amended) which allows for detention in a mental hospital either, in an emergency, for a period of seventy two hours on the recommendation of one doctor (section 29) or, on the recommendation of two doctors, for admission for assessment for a period of up to twenty eight days (section 25), or for admission for treatment, also on the recommendation of two doctors, one of whom has special expertise in the treatment of mental illness (section 26). This last form of admission can result in detention for a period of up to six months, after which further extensions are possible.

A feature of these arrangements is the comparatively minor involvement of external non-medical opinion in the admission of the patient. This is understandable in respect of emergency admission or admission for assessment and is relatively unimportant in such circumstances. But admission under section 26 is a different matter and it is certainly arguable that something more than two medical opinions should be required here. In Scotland, admissions under the comparable Mental Health (Scotland) Act 1960, section 23 are authorised by the sheriff after submission of a medical recommendation. Although it is unlikely that the sheriff will disagree with medical reports, the fact of judicial scrutiny nevertheless provides a potential check on the abuse of medical power.

The apparent severity of the conditions for admission and detention under the 1959 Act were mitigated by the existence of appeal procedures. Once admitted under section 26, a patient could go to a Mental Health Review Tribunal to appeal against his continued detention in hospital. The operation of these tribunals was, however, the subject of some criticism. It was argued that patients were frequently unaware of their right of appeal, that they were discouraged from approaching the tribunals, and that they were seldom represented in their appearances before tribunals. Such criticism is now answered by the introduction in the Mental Health (Amendment) Act 1982 of the obligatory referral to a tribunal of patients' cases. In particular, the making available of legal aid to patients who wish to appeal will serve to answer one of the more trenchant criticisms of the system.

The 1982 Act also introduces a Mental Health Commission, the membership of which is to include doctors, lawyers, social workers and lay people. This Commission resembles the Scottish Mental Welfare Commission, which was established under the Mental Health (Scotland) Act 1960, and which is empowered to investigate cases of alleged ill-treatment, deficiencies in care or treatment and of improper detention. The Scottish Commission is required to visit psychiatric hospitals and to make itself available for private interview with patients wishing to complain and is, thus, a medium by which grievances can be aired.

The debate over compulsory admission to psychiatric hospitals does not end with the issue of the involuntary detention of the patient. The fact that a patient, once admitted to hospital, may be subjected to treatment without his consent has attracted some attention. Before the passing into law of the 1982 Act, which recognises the legitimacy in certain circumstances of the non-consensual treatment of involuntarily-detained patients, there was some doubt as to the legality of such treatment.[11] These doubts are now removed and, at the same time, some of the critical objections have been met by the provision for second, external, medical opinions when certain forms of involuntary treatment are to be carried out.

The legislative reforms of 1982 attempt a compromise between concern over the patient's right to refuse treatment and the need to treat the mentally ill non-consensually. When a patient does not consent, certain forms of treatment – specified in regulations to be made by the Secretary of State or noted in a Code of Practice – may be given only with the agreement of an independent psychiatrist. This independent psychiatrist must consult a nurse and one other person (other than a doctor) who has been professionally concerned with the patient's treatment. This innovation met with opposition from some psychiatrists when first proposed, on the grounds that it would tie unduly the hands of the doctors in charge of the case and would prove unnecessarily cumbersome. Other psychiatrists, however, saw it as entirely reasonable that they would consult with colleagues in such cases. Treatments which do not fall into this category and which are not subject to the separate, more stringent controls devised for a third

11 See M Hurwitt 'Mental Health and Civil Liberty' (1975) 125 NLJ 775; D W Miller 'The Mentally Disordered Patient in Hospital – I' (1975) 125 NLJ 884.

category of hazardous and irreversible treatments such as psychosurgery, will still be able to be given without the consent of the patient. Subject to certain restrictions, emergency treatments are allowable under section 48 even if the patient does not consent. This enables a single doctor to resort in such circumstances to treatments which would otherwise require second opinions.

Behaviour control
On a more general level, there has been considerable discussion of the extent to which psychiatric medicine's pursuit of behaviour modification should be subjected to legal control. The critics argue that there should be strict control of the use of behaviour modifying drugs and of psychosurgery. Their argument relies on philosophical objections to excessive interference in human behaviour; such interference is seen as an unwarranted intrusion into the mental integrity of others and may result in manipulation of behaviour in such a way as to compromise human freedom. Thus the spectre of the mind-controlled society, dulled by drugs and manipulated by the weapons of psychiatry, is raised.

The degree of behaviour control envisaged in such an hypothesis is currently far beyond the technical reach of psychiatry but the warning is not entirely fanciful. The possibility of using chemical means to subdue aggressive behaviour has been created with the development of psychotropic drugs which are, indeed, used for this purpose. These so-called 'chemical manacles' may have a legitimate use – as when they are, for example, employed to prevent a patient harming himself or others. Yet the possibility of abuse exists and a temptation is presented to control behaviour in institutions in such a way as to minimise inconvenience for those in charge of the institution. Such use is ethically questionable when it cannot properly be considered therapeutic and it should be strictly supervised.[12]

The treatment of children suffering from 'minimal brain dysfunction' provides a case in point. This term has been used as an umbrella description of a number of loosely connected conditions, including hyperactivity and learning disorders. Children of this sort are very common; in ordinary language terms, they are fidgety, slow or uncoordinated children who do not do well in school and who are 'difficult' in other ways. The proportion of all children which falls into this category has been variously estimated at between 5 and 10 per cent. The aetiology of the condition is unclear and has been attributed, amongst other conditions, to genetic factors, subnutrition and even sub-oxic episodes. The behaviour of such children

12 We have referred briefly to a recent press report in ch 1 (p. 14, fn. 17).

can be fairly dramatically changed by the administration of drugs which have the effect of quietening the hyperactivity and of improving the child's ability to 'fit in'. This may be viewed as a positive achievement, in that it enables children in this group to compete with their peers and to lead a less tiresome life. The negative side, however, has to be recognised; such treatment involves an element of drugging into compliance and of changing behaviour for social as well as therapeutic reasons.[13]

The use of surgery in an attempt to modify behaviour poses even more dramatic problems. Psychosurgery is not now used extensively in Britain but, in the past, it has been employed in a way which can, with hindsight, be criticised. The outcome of the period of great enthusiasm for leucotomy during the immediate post-war years indicates the circumspection with which those arguments favouring psychosurgery should be viewed.

The essential claim of psychosurgery is that behaviour patterns may thereby be modified in a reasonably predictable fashion. Modern techniques, avoiding the crudities of leucotomy, involve interference with parts of the brain which influence aggressive feelings and sexual urges. A successful operation can eliminate or satisfactorily control aggressive behaviour or can diminish the sexual impulses. The comparative rarity of these operations makes it difficult to assess their overall value. Some reports suggest a high rate of success in dealing with stubborn problems. Homosexual paedophilia, for example, which often reveals itself to be incorrigible, is claimed to have responded remarkably well to surgery of the hypothalmus. Similarly, aggressive behaviour associated with epilepsy has been relieved and the patients concerned have been able to enjoy a far higher degree of social integration and acceptance as a result.

The use of psychosurgery for the alleviation of anti-social behaviour has been received enthusiastically by some. The British Medical Journal welcomed the prospect of brain surgery for sexual disorders in 1969,[14] as did *The Times* in a leading article published in 1973;[15] both of these responsible journals suggested that such therapy should be available for those convicted of sex crimes. In the United States, the National Commission for the Protection of Human Subjects of Biomedical Behavioural Research, which considered the subject of psychosurgery in detail, concluded that such surgery should no longer be considered experimental and, although

13 For a discussion of the ethical issues, see P H Wennder 'The Case of MBD' (1974) 2 Hastings Center Studies 94.
14 Editorial, 'Brain Surgery for Sexual Disorders' (1969) 2 Brit Med J 250.
15 *The Times*, 2 October 1973.

it suggested safeguards in the form of review boards, the Commission recommended that psychosurgery should be available to those institutionalised.[16] The Commission explicitly rejected the *Kaimowitz* decision[17] in which it was held that an institutionalised person could not give a free consent to psychosurgery by virtue of the fact of being detained there involuntarily.

Objections to psychosurgery tend to focus on its drastic and irreversible nature. The consequences of drug therapy, while possibly unpleasant, are usually reversible and a mistake, or a change of mind, can be rectified. Any alteration in behaviour following psychosurgery is likely to be permanent and it is this which gives rise to misgivings. By what right do doctors take it upon themselves to change others in this way? Is the consent of the patient in these circumstances at all real, in view of the fact that he may be offered, implicitly if not explicitly, the choice between continued incarceration without surgery – or hormonal treatment or aversion therapy – and surgery leading to freedom?

To make out a case for psychosurgery, the central issue of the aim of treatment must be confronted. If it is seen principally as a means of *controlling* behaviour, then there are sound reasons for objecting to it as representing a draconian and ethically unacceptable method of control. A different conclusion may result if, on the other hand, the therapeutic intention is predominant. There is no reason why patients should be denied a potentially effective treatment purely because it is open to abuse or is hazardous. Such treatments should, of course, be subjected to control – preferably control which embodies an element of outside, lay opinion – but they should not be excluded from the range of those available by virtue only of their nature. Moreover, the fact that the treatment is administered to control behaviour does not necessarily mean that it may not also have a therapeutic goal. The sex offender whose hypersexuality is diminished through surgery is not only being controlled for the protection of others but is being treated in the truly medical sense. It can be argued that he will be happier if he is enabled to live safely in society after the operation than he would be if living in constant conflict with the criminal law. In this sense, control and therapy are both achieved.

It remains to establish a satisfactory control regime if psychosurgery is accepted as a legitimate therapeutic device. It will not be enough to rely on the consent of the patient whose condition often definitely precludes real consent, and there will always be a residual

---

16 United States, National Commission for the Protection of Human Subjects of Biomedical and Behavioural Research Report 1976.

17 *Kaimowitz v Michigan Department of Mental Health* 42 US LW 2063.

question mark over the reality of consent given in prison or in other circumstances of detention. The option chosen in the Mental Health (Amendment) Act 1982 provides a statutory system of control of irreversible treatments. Under section 43 of the Act, three people, of whom only one may be a doctor, will have to confirm that the patient understands what the treatment entails and that he has consented in order for it to be sanctioned.[18] This involvement of lay opinion will be welcomed by those arguing for greater control of psychosurgery but there will still be those who claim that judicial involvement is necessary in such cases for patients to be afforded adequate protection against radical behaviour-modifying operations. The publicity entailed in a legal hearing is not the least of the factors claimed to be in favour of the involvement of the courts in these decisions.[19]

18 The medical practitioner concerned with the case is also required under s. 43(3) of the same Act to consult with two other persons who have been involved in the patients' treatment, one of these to be a nurse and another to be a person other than a nurse or doctor.
19 As this chapter went to press, changes in the Scottish legislation were before Parliament.

18 Psychiatry and the criminal law

The psychiatrist may become involved with criminal law at a number of points in the process of trial. Most dramatically, he may be called upon to provide evidence to the court of the accused person's mental state. This evidence goes to the heart of the issue of responsibility and intimately involves the psychiatrist in the essential function of any criminal trial – the determination of guilt or innocence. In addition to fulfilling this need, psychiatric evidence may be invoked to assist the court in the exercise of its sentencing power. Psychiatric reports on an offender may help the court to impose a more lenient custodial sentence or may point to what would be a more appropriate means of dealing with the offender; moreover, the court may ensure, as a result, that an offender gets further psychiatric or other medical treatment. The psychiatrist may be called upon to assist the court in other ways. Even when the sanity of the accused is not in question, evidence may be called as to the mental state of a witness, if that is relevant to the issue of the reliability of his or her evidence.[1] Attempts have been made to introduce psychiatric evidence which is aimed at demonstrating that an accused person's disposition was such that he could not have formed the necessary intention to commit the offence with which he is charged, but the courts have generally been reluctant to allow what they see as the usurpation of their exclusive power to decide such issues of mens rea.[2]

The psychiatrist gives evidence to the court as an expert. He does not provide an irrebutable conclusion as to the state of mind of the accused but, rather, tenders an expression of opinion which will ultimately be decided upon by the judge or jury as the case may be. As a Scottish judge said of expert witnesses:

their duty is to furnish the judge or the jury with the necessary

---

1 This was accepted in *Toohey v Metropolitan Police Comr* [1965] AC 595, [1965] 1 All ER 506, HL. See also *R v MacKenney* (1981) 72 Cr App Rep 78.
2 An exception to this general rule is the Canadian case of *R v Lupien* (1970) 9 DLR (3d) 1 when psychiatric evidence of the accused's strong antipathy to homosexuality was held admissible in a charge of a homosexual offence. See also F Bates 'Admissibility – Psychiatric Evidence –Towards a Coherent Policy' (1977) Can Bar Rev 178; A Samuels 'Psychiatric Evidence' (1981) Crim LR 762.

scientific criteria for testing the accuracy of their conclusions, so as to enable the judge or jury to form their own independent judgment by the application of these criteria to the facts proved in evidence.[3]

While a jury does not have to accept psychiatric evidence, it is not justified in discounting such evidence when it is not contradicted in any way. This has been clearly laid down in a number of cases[4] but forensic psychiatric evidence is sometimes ignored in spite of this legal acknowledgment. In the trial of Peter Sutcliffe, the so-called 'Yorkshire Ripper', the jury, in returning a verdict of guilty of murder, rejected the evidence which had been presented by four psychiatrists to the effect that Sutcliffe was mentally disordered in a way which affected his responsibility.[5] This decision emphasises that the weight given to psychiatric evidence by a court may depend in large measure on the circumstances surrounding the case. Psychiatric evidence favourable to the accused is more likely to be accepted in a case where the accused attracts sympathy – where, for example, a woman is charged with the killing of a tormenting and violent husband – rather than in those where such sympathy is likely to be absent – a brutal murder committed for purposes of sexual gratification.[6]

The insanity plea

The plea of not guilty on the grounds of insanity is the most 'extreme' plea available to the mentally disordered offender. Such pleas were quite common in the days of capital punishment for murder, as a verdict of 'not guilty by reason of insanity' provided an escape route from possible execution. In the decade prior to the passing of the Homicide Act in 1957, and the consequent availability of the plea of diminished responsibility, the proportion of those committed to trial for murder in England who were found to be guilty but insane[7] or

3 *Davis v Edinburgh Magistrates* 1953 SC 34 at 40, per Lord Cooper.
4 *R v Matheson* [1958] 2 All ER 87, [1958] 1 WLR 474, CCA; *Taylor v R* (1978) 22 ALR 599.
5 For a criticism of this outcome, see G Silverman 'Psychiatry after Sutcliffe' (1981) 125 Sol Jo 518.
6 G Williams *Textbook of Criminal Law* (2nd edn, 1978) p. 599.
7 The nomenclature of the insanity verdict in English law has undergone a number of changes. Prior to the Criminal Procedure (Insanity) Act 1964, the verdict was 'guilty but insane'. This wording was introduced by the Trial of Lunatics Act 1883 at the instance of Queen Victoria, who had been shot at by a man named McLean. The Queen was surprised to find that McLean had been declared not guilty when, in her view, he was clearly 'guilty but insane'. After 1964, the verdict became that of 'not guilty by reason of insanity'. See R Cross and P A Jones *Introduction to Criminal Law* (9th edn, 1980) p. 83.

insane on arraignment averaged over 40 per cent of the total. Between 1971 and 1973, by contrast, this fell to 2.9 per cent despite the fact that slightly over 40 per cent of those committed for trial were found to be either of diminished responsibility or insane on arraignment or guilty but insane.[8] The insanity plea has thus become comparatively rare, although it is still the catalyst of fierce controversy.

The belief that the insane should not be punished because they are not responsible for punishable acts lies at the root of the insanity defence in criminal law. In simple language, the insane are not 'to blame' for what they do. At a more theoretical level a variety of grounds can be postulated as the justification for acquittal in such cases. By measuring the behaviour of the insane offender against the behaviour of the sane person who commits the same offence, it will become apparent that the state of mind of the insane person is likely to be different in many significant respects and, therefore, mens rea may be absent. The insane offender may be ignorant of the fact that what he is doing is wrong, in either moral or legal terms, or he may be unaware of the consequences of his actions. His intentions or his motives in acting might likewise differ from those of the sane offender. The mental state of the man suffering from the delusion that he is about to be poisoned by his wife colours the nature of his actions; an attack on her then becomes, from the subjective viewpoint, an act of self-defence.

The acts of the insane may also be analysed in terms of involuntariness. That an act should be voluntary is a pre-requisite for the attribution of responsibility: if it is not willed by the actor, the law takes the view that there is no actus reus and that there can, then, be no criminal liability. The insane offender can therefore be exculpated either on the grounds of lack of mens rea – in that he did not act with the requisite criminal intent – or because there was no actus reus.

Involuntariness is, however, a difficult concept in the criminal law and is generally used to describe only those acts over which the actor has no muscular control. A nervous spasm is classically an involuntary act in the criminal law, as is an act performed while asleep. The status of acts falling into the category of irresistible impulses is, however, different. A mental disorder may well have prompted an accused to steal or set fire to property but, although this may be something over which he really has no control, it would not be accepted as an involuntary act in terms of the criminal law if it were shown that the act was performed consciously. It is only in those states where somebody is so disturbed as to be 'out of control' that their actions might fit into the usual criminal law category of involuntary acts.

In many cases, a mentally abnormal offender may act in a way which would not exculpate him prima facie in terms of the mens rea and actus reus requirements. The accused may know exactly what he is doing and intend to achieve a very specific and logical objective in acting as he does. He may, for example, assault somebody because he dislikes him and his assault may make perfect sense to the outside observer. And yet, in the background, there may be a grossly disturbed personality or a long-standing mental illness. As the Royal Commission on Capital Punishment pointed out, there are many offenders who know what they are doing and who know that it is wrong but who are nonetheless clearly insane and should not therefore be held responsible for their actions.[9] In considering such cases, there may be an inclination to treat the accused in a way which is different from the way in which we treat sane offenders. The reason for this difference in treatment might lie not so much in the absence of the constitutent elements of mens rea but, rather, in the assumption that there is a causative link between the mental disorder and the act. The act may be seen as the product of a mental disorder and, since blame would not be attributable for mental illness, it should neither be so attributed in respect of the concomitants of the illness. The illness may be a *sine qua non* of the criminal behaviour; it is arguable that the accused would not have acted as he did if he had not been suffering from the mental condition.[10] This is the theory of the matter; practice, as will be seen, can be different.

The place of deterrence is also an important consideration. If it be accepted that one of the principle purposes of the criminal law is to impose sanctions aimed at deterring offenders, then there is no point in convicting the insane because the deterrent effect is unlikely to have much personal impact. As Barry J put it:

> It is useless for the law to seek to deter persons from committing crimes if they cannot be influenced by the possibility or probability of subsequent punishment because of their psychotic condition. The kind of mental awareness which justly exposes the person to punishment for a criminal act is thus sane awareness, not the distorted or confused or unreal awareness of a diseased mind.[11]

The M'Naghten Rules

Merely being insane does not, in itself, qualify as a defence to a

9 (Cmnd 8932) para 295.
10 For a full discussion on the theoretical basis of the insanity defence, see H Fingarette and A Hasse *Mental Disabilities and Criminal Responsibility* (1979).
11 *R v Weise* (1969) V R 953 at 964.

criminal charge in English law. In order to benefit from the special verdict, an accused person must satisfy the test laid down in the M'Naghten Rules, the controversial text which has dominated English law on the subject since the mid-nineteenth century. The rules originate in the pronouncement of the House of Lords in 1843 in the case of *Daniel M'Naghten*,[12] who had been charged with the shooting of the Prime Minister's secretary in the belief that the secretary was the Prime Minister himself. The House of Lords laid down the basic test that acquittal on the grounds of insanity was appropriate if, firstly, the accused 'was labouring under such a defect of reason, from disease of the mind, as not to know (1) the nature and quality of the act he was doing, or, if he did know it, (2) that he did not know he was doing what was wrong'. This test, variously formulated and interpreted, has since been applied throughout the Commonwealth as well as in the United States.

Criticism of the M'Naghten Rules has been forceful and continuous. At the root of the problem is the very antiquity of the rules; nineteenth century psychiatry differed from modern psychiatric notions in terminology and in substance, and it seems remarkable that Victorian concepts should still dominate the modern test of insanity. At the outset, the rules place too great an emphasis on reason as the controlling element in human behaviour. Secondly, the concept of disease of the mind, which forms a vital part of the Rules, is one which is no longer in favour amongst psychiatrists.[13] Nor is there an accepted legal definition of what constitutes such a disease, and this raises the question as to the status of a host of conditions including psychopathy and other personality disorders. The judges, however, have not necessarily been deterred by this uncertainty. In *R v Kemp*,[14] for instance, the court held that arteriosclerosis was a disease of the mind and could, therefore, provide a defence to a criminal charge. *Bratty v A-G for Northern Ireland*[15] provided another example of a judge determining what is a disease of the mind; Lord Denning, emphasising that this question was one for judicial resolution, expressed the view that any mental disorder which has manifested itself in violence and is prone to recur is a disease of the mind.[16]

More important than the objections on the point of reason are

12 (1843) 10 Cl and Fin 200, HL. M'Naghten experienced delusions of persecution and would probably be diagnosed today as suffering from paranoid schizophrenia.
13 G Williams *Textbook of Criminal Law* (2nd edn, 1978) p. 592.
14 [1957] 1 QB 399, [1956] 3 All ER 249.
15 [1963] AC 386, [1961] 3 All ER 523.
16 See H Fingarette 'The Concept of Mental Disease in Criminal Law Insanity Tests' (1965–6) 33 Univ Chicago LR 229.

those which refer to the emphasis in the Rules on the knowledge of the accused. The controversy here has focused on the interpretation of the word 'know'. Narrowly interpreted – and the majority of the critics of *M'Naghten* have assumed that it is the narrow interpretation which will be favoured by the courts – the word 'know' implies cognitive awareness rather than broader emotional understanding. As a result of this, many insane offenders might be held to fail the M'Naghten test on the grounds that, in this sense, they would probably know what they were doing. In fact, courts have tended to take a broader view of the knowledge requirement and have often required something more than an intellectual knowledge of the nature and quality of the act in question.[17]

In Canada, section 16 of the Criminal Code essentially embodies the M'Naghten test of insanity but states that the defence may be established if it is shown that the accused failed either to know or to *appreciate* the nature and quality of his act.[18] In interpreting this provision, the Canadian courts have ruled that, in order to be said to appreciate the nature and quality of his act, an accused person must not only know what he is doing but also must be able to understand the consequences of his act. As the Supreme Court of Canada held in *Cooper v R*[19] appreciation involves emotional as well as intellectual awareness and, thus, is not the same as knowledge as conceived in the M'Naghten test.

There has been some judicial debate over the significance of the term 'wrong' as it is used in the context of the M'Naghten Rules. Does the accused have to know that his act is morally wrong or does he have to know that it is legally wrong? English courts have come down in favour of the latter; a successful defence must show that the accused did not know that the act was legally wrong.[20] In theory, at least, this might lead to the absurd result of the denial of the insanity defence to an accused who heard voices commanding him to commit murder and, although he knew murder to be illegal, thought that the voices came from God and acted accordingly.

The Canadian courts have followed the English rule on this point, not without severe criticism,[1] but, in Australia, the non-code States have abandoned the English approach in favour of a test based on the

17 See A Goldstein *The Insanity Defence* (1967) p. 49.
18 For the background to the Canadian test of insanity, see S N Verdun-Jones 'The Evolution of the Defences of Insanity and Automatism in Canada from 1843 to 1979: A Saga of Judicial Reluctance to Sever the Umbilical Cord to the Mother Country' (1979) 14 UBC Law Rev 1.
19 (1980) 110 DLR 3d 46.
20 *R v Windle* [1952] 2 QB 826, [1952] 2 All ER 1, CCA.
 1 *Schwartz v R* (1976) 67 DLR (3d) 716; A Mewett 'Section 16 and Wrong' (1975–6) 18 Crim LQ 413.

knowledge of moral wrong since the decision in *Stapleton v R*.[2] As the court there pointed out, cases would not often arise where the accused would know of the illegality of his acts and yet still feel that he was acting morally. Where there is an inability to see that an act is wrong 'according to the ordinary standards adopted by reasonable men' there may still be a 'back of the mind awareness' that the act is punishable by law but, in such circumstances, acquittal will still be appropriate.

In whatever way one interprets the M'Naghten Rules, it is only by stretching them almost beyond recognition that one will be able to encompass within them many cases in which an offender deserves to be treated as insane and yet is shown to have a knowledge of right and wrong. One avenue which has been seen as providing an escape from the strictness of *M'Naghten* is the test which emphasises control over action. This test, of which the irresistible impulse theory is a prominent example, concentrates not on the cognitive aspects of the matter but on volitional features – an accused is not to be held responsible if he is shown to be incapable by reason of mental disorder of conforming his conduct to the requirements of law. Irresistible impulse theories tended to suggest that this lack of control occurs in moments of impulsive action, but this approach has been criticised on the grounds that anti-social acts by those suffering from mental disorders are more likely to be the result of long-term states of mind rather than from momentary lapses. Control theories need not, however, always be tied to the irresistible impulse concept; this is demonstrated by some American decisions in which the suddenness of the prompting to act has not been regarded as being a significant matter.

A final, and wider ranging, difficulty associated with these tests of responsibility which focus on ability to control behaviour lies in the fact that such theories view the cognitive and volitional functions of the mind as being quite separate and isolated. Modern psychiatry rejects this and regards the human personality as an integrated whole – one cannot distinguish these functions and view them in isolation from other mental processes.

Alternative attitudes

The American experience of the insanity defence has been particularly interesting. Criticism of the M'Naghten Rules in the United States has been particularly intense and vocal and the courts have

2 (1952) 86 CLR 358; Comment by N Morris '"Wrong" in the M'Naghten Rules' (1953) 16 MLR 435. A similar approach has been favoured in New Zealand: *R v MacMillan* [1966] NZLR 616.

responded by experimenting with a variety of alternative approaches. One test which, although not widely applied, occasioned much discussion was the test in *Durham v United States*,[3] in which the Court of Appeals of the District of Columbia abandoned the M'Naghten approach in favour of what appeared to be the more scientific test of linking the crime with a diagnosed 'mental disease or mental defect'. The problem with this test is twofold: how has a mental disease to be defined – the test takes us no further in this direction – and how can one ascertain a firm causal link between the criminal act and the disease? The mere fact of mental illness need not exculpate; the criminal act must be *explained* in some way by the illness and this may be a difficult, if not impossible, task.[4] A more helpful solution was suggested by the American Law Institute in its Model Penal Code.[5] The test outlined in the Code is a conventional one, involving a combination of the cognitive and control criteria: an insanity defence will be available if, in the presence of mental disorder, there is a failure to appreciate the criminality of the act or, even in the event of an appreciation of this sort, there is an inability to conform conduct to the requirements of the law.

The courts in Scotland now seem to have developed a fairly simple test of insanity. The M'Naghten Rules have never been part of Scots criminal law and the courts have therefore not been tied to their specific formula. In *HM Advocate v Kidd*,[6] the judge's instruction to the jury, although couched in terms of reason and of alienation – which are not terms which would necessarily be accepted by psychiatrists today – stated quite simply that the defence would be available if the accused was considered to be of unsound mind at the time of the offence. That is language which anybody can understand and, although a psychiatrist might argue that it begs a lot of questions, at least the psychiatrist himself should find it quite possible to give an opinion to a court in terms of mental soundness or unsoundness. In adopting such an approach, Scots law is, in fact, in harmony with the French Penal Code; this does not define what constitutes insanity but merely provides that the defence will be available if the accused person was, at the time of committing the offence, in a state of démence.[7]

3 214 F 2d 862 (1954).
4 In those jurisdictions where the *Durham* rule was applied, the courts became disenchanted with its effect and the rule was abandoned; see G Fletcher 'Rethinking Criminal Law' (1978) p. 840.
5 Model Penal Code, 4.01. See also *US v Brawner* 471 F 2d 969 (1972).
6 1960 JC 61. For an analysis of the development of the Scottish cases, see G H Gordon *The Criminal Law of Scotland* (2nd edn, 1978) pp. 364ff.
7 Translatable as 'mental disorder'.

The reform of English law was considered at length by the Butler Committee, which reported in 1975.[8] The Committee accepted the fact that there were major flaws in the M'Naghten Rules and proposed that there should be introduced a verdict of 'not guilty on evidence of mental disorder'; this would be appropriate if there was adequate psychiatric evidence of the existence in the accused of a sufficiently severe degree of mental disorder at the time of the commission of the offence charged. The existence of such disorder would be determined by establishing in the accused the presence of any of a number of characteristics such as delusional belief, impairment of intellectual function and seriously disordered thinking. The attractiveness of the Butler suggestions is that they do not rely on diagnostic labels and the terms used are capable of lay understanding. Causal difficulties are likewise avoided by accepting the inference that a causal link between the offence and the mental condition can safely be presumed if such characteristics are manifested in the offender's behaviour. Unfortunately, no action has been taken on this recommendation and the M'Naghten Rules remain the governing test of insanity in English criminal law.

Diminished responsibility

The plea of diminished responsibility was devised as a means of allowing the court to avoid a conviction for murder where the mental condition of the accused made the attribution of full responsibility inappropriate. The doctrine was first used in Scotland in the case of *HM Advocate v Dingwall* in 1867[9] and was eventually introduced into English law in the Homicide Act 1957, section 2(1). This provides that, in cases of homicide, there should be no conviction for murder if the accused is found to be suffering from 'such abnormality of mind (whether arising from a condition of arrested or retarded development of mind or any inherent causes or induced by disease or injury) as substantially impaired his mental responsibility for his acts and omissions in doing or being a party to the killing'.

The doctrine is really required only because of the existence of the fixed penalty of life imprisonment for murder. By reducing the offence to one of manslaughter, the court can exercise discretion in sentencing and can choose a sentence ranging from the leniency of a probation order on the one hand to life imprisonment on the other. Sentencing discretion already exists in respect of most other offences

8 Report of the Commitee on Mentally Abnormal Offenders (Cmnd 6244).
9 1867 5 Irv 466.

and, as a result, the case for extending the application of the plea is hardly strong.

Some have criticised the whole concept of a diminished responsibility plea, arguing that we are either responsible or irresponsible for our actions and that there should be no half-way house. Such iconoclasm discounts the fact that we do regularly make allowances which influence the extent to which we hold people to account for their acts. More usually, such allowances are described as mitigating circumstances rather than as factors influencing responsibility, but the ultimate effect will be the same. The usefulness of the concept of diminished responsibility lies in its flexibility: through its operation, those who are accused and for whom sympathy is felt can be treated in a lenient fashion on conviction without there being any condoning of their offence. A plea of diminished responsibility will, for example, enable the courts to look with equal mercy on cases of 'mercy-killing'.[10] Inferring diminished responsibility in such circumstances does not involve any diminution of the seriousness with which the taking of life is viewed; what it does say is that something other than a long prison sentence may be appropriate by virtue of the accused's mental condition.

The conditions which may give rise to a successful plea of diminished responsibility vary considerably. Conditions such as reactive depression or hysterical disassociation, which are unlikely to qualify as mental disorders requiring prolonged psychiatric treatment, have been so accepted on occasion and, at the other end of the scale, psychopathy has also succeeded as the basis of a plea.[11] General guidance as to what constitutes abnormality of mind for the purposes of the Homicide Act 1957, section 2(1) was given by Lord Parker CJ in *R v Byrne*[12] where he stated that such abnormality existed when there was a state of mind 'so different from that of ordinary human beings that the reasonable man would term it abnormal'. This concept, it was stressed, was wide enough to cover 'the mind's activities in all its aspects', including both the ability to form a rational judgment as to right and wrong and the ability to control behaviour in accordance with that judgment.

The psychopath
In spite of such a broad test of diminished responsibility, there remain

10 For examples of the successful pleas of diminished responsibility in such cases and of the lenient sentences imposed, see G Williams *Textbook of Criminal Law* (2nd edn, 1978) p. 269.
11 Ibid, p. 627.
12 [1960] 2 QB 396, [1960] 3 All ER 1, CCA.

certain categories of abnormal offender who will pose problems both for the courts and for psychiatrists. The main group of such offenders is that of psychopaths, with whom nobody feels entirely comfortable. The concept of psychopathy is itself a contentious one and there is by no means medical consensus on the nature of the condition. Broadly stated, the psychopath is one who persistently shows a tendency to deviant behaviour together with an incapacity to show remorse and who is usually resistant to treatment. Such a broad description has, inevitably, been criticised. In one Scottish case[13] the judge, on having the features of psychopathy described to him, commented that it sounded remarkably like a description of the behaviour of a recalcitrant common criminal and, although this approach is unduly dismissive, one can appreciate the reasoning behind it – the main badge of the psychopath who comes into contact with the criminal law is deviant behaviour and legal scepticism can be understood in the absence of more specific clinical features; while a judge or jury may be prepared to accept the presence of insanity when the condition of the accused is described in terms of delusions, hallucinations or blunting of affect, they may be less swayed by a general term such as personality disorder.

The fate of the psychopath in the British criminal process has varied. In some cases, courts are sympathetic to the argument that the accused should be given psychiatric treatment rather than sent to prison; in others, the psychopathic offender is dealt with in the same way as is any other criminal. In 1980, it was estimated that 143 out of the 577 mentally disordered persons in prison establishments in England and Wales were classified as psychopaths.[14] The Butler Committee concluded that 'the psychopath is, in general, untreatable, at least in medical terms'. In these circumstances, he can expect to find little haven in the psychiatric hospital and it is significant that the Butler Committee also endorsed the practice of dealing with psychopathic offenders through the medium of imprisonment. The Committee recomended that psychopaths should not be admitted to hospital unless there was some other mental disorder which was susceptible to treatment, although it was also thought that the possibility of transfer to a psychiatric hospital should be kept open in appropriate cases.

There is an alternative view which holds that the expedient of imprisoning a psychopath is unacceptable. Such persons, it is argued, are suffering from a personality disorder and are therefore not fully

13 *Carraher v HM Advocate* 1946 JC 108.
14 A Ashworth and J Shapland 'Psychopaths in the Criminal Process' [1980] Crim LR 628.

responsible for their actions. Conviction and imprisonment are quite different qualitatively from acquittal and admission to a psychiatric institution and it is inadmissible to impose the former on those who offend by reason of a personality disorder. The refutation of this argument takes one to the heart of the issue of responsibility. There is no obvious reason why a personality disorder of this nature should be treated as being any different from what one might loosely term a 'criminal or anti-social disposition'. The aetiology of psychopathy is certainly controversial but the psychopath will probably always have been what he is at the time of the offence –that is his 'nature'. By contrast, the person who is mentally ill is not anti-social 'by nature' – his anti-social behaviour is likely to be the product of the illness. And this leads one to the question as to whether it is wrong to punish somebody for what their nature dictates. If one argues that it *is* wrong, then the entire basis of the system of criminal justice must be seen as being immoral. People are regularly punished because they are bad. The reasons why they are bad may be of some criminological interest but do not affect the basic issue of accountability in the courts; only the determinist will argue otherwise.

This view may seem unsympathetic but its critics will have to contend with the realities of the penal and hospital systems. If psychiatrists can do little or nothing to the psychopath and, at the same time, the psychopath will be a highly disruptive element within the hospital, then the viable alternatives are those of prison or freedom – by excluding the latter on grounds of public safety, one is left with prison. All that can then be attempted is the practice of what psychotherapy is possible within the framework of the prison (and here, certainly, more might be attempted, as Butler recommended) and to await any improvement in the condition which might come with time.

Automatism

The difficulty of reconciling legal requirements with medical insight into the nature of human action is also illustrated by the development of the automatism defence in criminal law. This comparatively new defence is now well established although its precise boundaries require a certain amount of tidying up. Like the insanity plea, it is a controversial concept which raises some tricky problems in balancing justice to the individual against the protection of society.

The basic principle of the criminal law that only voluntary acts will result in criminal liability clearly suggests that acquittal is appropriate if the accused has acted automatically. Automatic behaviour consists of acts of which an actor is not conscious or over which he has not control. Somnambulistic acts provide a classic illustration of this sort of behaviour.[15]

Automatic behaviour can result from a variety of causes which may be organic or non-organic. Organic automatism is the product of a bodily condition such as hypoglycaemia,[16] epilepsy or concussion and other cerebrally significant conditions such as arteriosclerosis.[17] Organic automatism may also be caused by the ingestion of alcohol or other drugs but offences committed while intoxicated are usually considered by the law to be a discrete problem and are dealt with in a different context from other types of automatism. The non-organic automatisms, which are more legally controversial, are usually the product of acute emotional stress which has, essentially, resulted in a state of disassociation.

The main problem with the defence of automatism lies in the difficulty of establishing with certainty that a given physical condition actually produced automatic behaviour. Epilepsy, the predisposition to which can usually be established through the use of the electroencephalogram, can be taken as an example. It is beyond question that complicated actions, of which the subject may later have no recollection, may be performed either during a seizure or in the post-ictal period. These actions are clearly unconscious and are therefore involuntary from the point of view of the law.

That, unfortunately, is as far as certainty can go. If an epileptic performs an act of violence which is out of character, the question may be raised as to whether the act was involuntary. There is very little concrete evidence of the occurrence of violent behaviour in such states but automatism at least provides an explanation of otherwise inexplicable behaviour and its rejection in such circumstances would be substantially unfair to the accused. Whether an acquittal is appropriate in such cases or whether some other form of disposal is to be preferred involves complicated policy issues.

Logically, a finding that the criminal offence was committed automatically should result in an acquittal. This will, in fact, be the result in some cases but, in others, the reluctance of the courts to release potentially dangerous offenders has led to the development of two conceptual categories of automatism – insane and non-insane automatism. If the automatic behaviour is classified as insane, the court will then be able to deal with the offender in the same way as it deals with other insane offenders and so ensure that society is

---

15 See N Morris 'Somnambulistic Homicide: Ghosts, Spiders and North Koreans' (1951) 5 Res Judicatae 29.

16 *R v Quick, R v Paddison* [1973] QB 910, [1973] 3 All ER 347, CA.

17 *R v Charlson* [1955] 1 All ER 859, [1955] 1 WLR 317; *R v Kemp* [1957] 1 QB 399, [1956] 3 All ER 249.

protected from potential danger. The question which the courts have thus set for themselves is: in what circumstances will automatism count as insanity?

The problem was addressed by Lord Denning in *Bratty v A-G for Northern Ireland*.[18] The accused in this case, for whom evidence was given of a history of epilepsy, was charged with the murder of a girl whom he strangled when a 'terrible feeling of blackness' came over him. According to Lord Denning, the basis for deciding whether automatic behaviour should be classified as insane depended upon the question of whether or not it resulted from a disease of the mind and a disease of the mind was described as any mental order which had manifested itself in violence and which was prone to recur. These criteria are useful in that they point to the main policy objective behind the distinction – the protection of the public – but the decision is open to criticism in that it suggests that a non-recurrent disorder cannot be a disease of the mind; the reasoning is also somewhat circular in that the definition of mental disease depends upon the inference of the mental disorder which is, itself, not defined.[19] The courts have grappled over the years with the concept of mental disease in this context and have tended to adopt an increasingly narrow interpretation of the term; this has led to the exclusion of a number of transitory conditions. Where the offence was alleged to have been committed when the accused, a diabetic, was in a state of hypoglycaemia, the court spoke of the distinction between insane and non-insane automatism as being based on the application, in the latter, of some external factor causing a temporary disturbance of the mind.[20] Such reasoning may justify the labelling of hypoglycaemic automatism as non-insane automatism but it will also result in the epileptic being treated as insane.[1] The grounds for this may be stated by courts to be that epilepsy is a disease of the mind rather than a disease of the brain, but the policy reality behind the matter is undoubtedly a reluctance to set at liberty a person in whom the condition causing the automatism is seen as something inherent which will continue to be present and which may lead to a recurrence of anti-social behaviour.

Non-organic automatism, or psychogenic automatism, has been received very much more sceptically by the courts. Such automatism

18 [1963] AC 386, [1961] 3 All ER 523, HL.
19 P A Fairall 'Irresistible Impulse, Automatism and Mental Disease' (1980) 5 Crim LJ 136, 149.
20 *R v Quick, R v Paddison* [1973] QB 910 at 922, [1973] 3 All ER 347 at 356, per Lawton LJ.
1 See *R v Meddings* [1966] VR 306; *R v Foy* [1960] Qd R 225; *R v O'Brien* (1965) 55 DLR (2d) 65.

may occur when there is subjection either to prolonged stress or to a sudden shock. In each case, a state of disassociation may result in which actions are performed without the exercise by the subject of conscious control.

In a series of decisions, the Canadian courts recognised what became known as 'psychological blow automatism' as being grounds for acquittal as non-insane automatism; more prolonged states of disassociation were treated as insanity.[2] In *R v K*,[3] for example, the accused, who had been undergoing treatment for a severe neurotic condition, killed his wife after the shock of hearing that she planned to leave him. Psychiatric evidence to the effect that the killing took place while he was in a state of automatism was accepted by the jury and the accused was acquitted. Similarly, in *R v Gottschalk*[4] the accused was acquitted of assault after psychiatric evidence was led of his state of depersonalisation which was productive of automatism. A reverse in the trend of the Canadian decisions occurred, however, with the decision of the Supreme Court of Canada in *Rabey v R*[5] in which it was held that disassociation resulting from a psychological shock should be treated as insanity rather than as non-insane automatism. It is significant in this case that the accused, who assaulted a woman after she had rejected him, did not have the sort of psychiatric record which was produced by the defendants in *K* and *Gottschalk*. It may be suspected, too, that the court wished to restrict defences of psychogenic automatism for policy reasons, as the whole concept is an obvious candidate for abuse and non-meritorious defences.[6]

In England, the possibility of a non-insane automatism defence based on disassociation was rejected in the Court of Appeal decision in *R v Isitt*.[7] The accused in this case failed to stop after an accident and had attempted to evade the police. In considering his claim to have been in a state of shock, the court took the view that, although the accused's mind might have been 'shut to the moral inhibitions which control the lives of most of us', there was no suggestion that his mind was not working at all and the defence of non-insane automatism was, therefore, not available.

2 See M E Schiffer *Mental Disorder and the Criminal Process* (1978) p. 101.
3 (1971) 3 CCC (2d) 84.
4 (1974) 22 CCC (2d) 415.
5 (1981) 114 DLR (3d) 193.
6 For a criticism of *Rabey*, see R D Mackay 'Non-organic Automatism – Some Recent Developments' [1980] Crim LR 350.
7 (1977) 67 Cr App Rep 44, CA.

A delicate balance?

The dilemma which automatism poses for the criminal law is much the same as the dilemma to which other forms of 'mental defence' give rise. While the non-punishment of the mentally disordered is seen as an attractive goal, the need both for a certain degree of scepticism and a measure of social defence have constantly to be borne in mind. A broad, sympathetic view of excusing conditions of this sort may prevent the unjust punishment of those who are truly not responsible for their actions, but it may also have the effect of blunting our conceptions of responsibility and of imposing upon psychiatric institutions a group of people who should not be there. At the same time, too fine a net will deny a defence to meritorious cases and that, too, is socially damaging.

The inescapable task of the criminal law then becomes one of charting a course between Scylla and Charybdis. To achieve this, the criminal law should adhere to a broad definition of insanity (such as in the French or Scottish formulae) which allows maximum leeway for a court to take into account expert evidence while at the same time avoiding necessarily being bound to an acceptance of psychiatric notions of responsibility. The matter is thus ultimately left in lay hands which, although fettered to an extent by theoretical guidelines, may nonetheless exercise such discretion as the situation demands. In the final analysis, the question 'Is he responsible for his acts' is answered not in terms of a M'Naghten-style dissection of mental states but in terms of our reaction to the question 'Should he be punished?' The answer to that question, of course, will, in many cases, be as perversely difficult and unsettling as ever.

Appendices

Appendix A
The Hippocratic Oath

'I swear by Apollo the physician, and Aesculapius and Health, and All-heal, and all the gods and goddesses, that, according to my ability and judgement, I will keep this Oath and this stipulation:

'To reckon him who taught me this Art equally dear to me as my parents, to share my substance with him, and relieve his necessities if required; to look upon his offspring in the same footing as my own brothers, and to teach them this Art, if they shall wish to learn it, without fee or stipulation; and that by precept, lecture and every other mode of instruction, I will impart a knowledge of the Art to my own sons, and those of my teachers, and to disciples bound by a stipulation and oath according to the law of medicine, but to none other. I will follow that system of regimen which, according to my ability and judgement, I consider for the benefit of my patients, and abstain from whatever is deleterious and mischievous. I will give no deadly medicine to anyone if asked, nor suggest any such counsel; and in like manner I will not give to a woman a pessary to produce abortion. With purity and with holiness I will pass my life and practise my Art. I will not cut persons labouring under the stone, but will leave this to be done by men who are practitioners of this work. Into whatever houses I enter, I will go into them for the benefit of the sick, and will abstain from every voluntary act of mischief and corruption; and, further, from the seduction of females, or males, of freemen or slaves. Whatever, in connection with my professional practice, or not in connection with it, I see or hear, in the life of men, which ought not to be spoken of abroad, I will not divulge, as reckoning that all such should be kept secret. While I continue to keep this Oath unviolated, may it be granted to me to enjoy life and the practice of the Art, respected by all men, in all times. But should I trespass and violate this Oath, may the reverse be my lot.'

(This translation is that which is favoured by the British Medical Association.)

Appendix B
Declaration of Geneva
(As amended at Sydney, 1968)

At the time of being admitted as a member of the medical profession:

I will solemnly pledge myself to consecrate my life to the service of humanity;

I will give to my teachers the respect and gratitude which is their due;

I will practise my profession with conscience and dignity;

The health of my patient will be my first consideration;

I will respect the secrets which are confided in me, even after the patient has died;

I will maintain by all the means in my power the honour and the noble traditions of the medical profession;

My colleagues will be my brothers;

I will not permit considerations of religion, nationality, race, party politics or social standing to intervene between my duty and my patient;

I will maintain the utmost respect for human life from the time of conception; even under threat, I will not use my medical knowledge contrary to the laws of humanity.

I make these promises solemnly, freely and upon my honour.

Appendix C

International Code of Medical Ethics

English text

Duties of Doctors in General

A DOCTOR MUST always maintain the highest standards of professional conduct.

A DOCTOR MUST practise his profession uninfluenced by motives of profit.

THE FOLLOWING PRACTICES are deemed unethical:

(a) Any self advertisement except such as is expressly authorised by the national code of medical ethics.

(b) Collaboration in any form of medical service in which the doctor does not have professional independence.

(c) Receiving any money in connection with services rendered to a patient other than a proper professional fee, even with the knowledge of the patient.

ANY ACT OR ADVICE which could weaken physical or mental resistance of a human being may be used only in his interest.

A DOCTOR IS ADVISED to use great caution in divulging discoveries or new techniques of treatment.

A DOCTOR SHOULD certify or testify only to that which he has personally verified.

Duties of Doctors to the Sick

A DOCTOR MUST always bear in mind the obligation of preserving human life.

A DOCTOR OWES to his patient complete loyalty and all the resources of his science. Whenever an examination or treatment is beyond his capacity he should summon another doctor who has the necessary ability.

A DOCTOR SHALL preserve absolute secrecy on all he knows about his patients because of the confidence entrusted in him.

A DOCTOR MUST give emergency care as a humanitarian duty unless he is assured that others are willing and able to give such care.

Duties of Doctors to Each Other

A DOCTOR OUGHT to behave to his colleagues as he would have them behave to him.

A DOCTOR MUST NOT entice patients from his colleagues.

A DOCTOR MUST OBSERVE the principles of the 'The Declaration of Geneva' approved by the World Medical Association.

Appendix D
Declaration of Tokyo, 1975

Statement on torture and other cruel, inhuman or degrading treatment or punishment

Preamble

It is the privilege of the medical doctor to practise medicine in the service of humanity, to preserve and restore bodily and mental health without distinction as to persons, to comfort and to ease the suffering of his or her patients. The utmost respect for human life is to be maintained even under threat, and no use made of any medical knowledge contrary to the laws of humanity.

For the purpose of this Declaration, torture is defined as the deliberate, systematic or wanton infliction of physical or mental suffering by one or more persons acting alone or on the orders of any authority, to force another person to yield information, to make a confession, or for any other reason.

Declaration

1. The doctor shall not countenance, condone or participate in the practice of torture or other forms of cruel, inhuman or degrading procedures, whatever the offence of which the victim of such procedures is suspected, accused or guilty, and whatever the victim's beliefs or motives, and in all situations, including armed conflict and civil strife.

2. The doctor shall not provide any premises, instruments, substances or knowledge to facilitate the practice of torture or other forms of cruel, inhuman or degrading treatment or to diminish the ability of the victim to resist such treatment.

3. The doctor shall not be present during any procedure during which torture or other forms of cruel, inhuman or degrading treatment is used or threatened.

4. A doctor must have complete clinical independence in deciding upon the care of a person for whom he or she is medically responsible. The doctor's fundamental role is to alleviate the distress of his or her fellow men, and no motive whether personal, collective or political shall prevail against this higher purpose.

5. Where a prisoner refuses nourishment and is considered by the doctor as capable of forming an unimpaired and rational judgement concerning the consequences of such a voluntary refusal of nourishment, he or she shall not be fed artificially. The decision as to the capacity of the prisoner to form such a judgement should be confirmed by at least one other independent doctor. The consequences of the refusal of nourishment shall be explained by the doctor to the prisoner.

6. The World Medical Association will support, and should encourage the international community, the national medical associations and fellow doctors to support, the doctor and his or her family in the face of threats or reprisals resulting from a refusal to condone the use of torture or other forms of cruel, inhuman or degrading treatment.

Appendix E
Declaration of Oslo, 1970

Statement on therapeutic abortion

1. The first moral principle imposed upon the doctor is respect for human life as expressed in a clause of the Declaration of Geneva: I will maintain the utmost respect for human life from the time of conception.

2. Circumstances which bring the vital interests of a mother into conflict with the vital interests of her unborn child create a dilemma and raise the question whether or not the pregnancy should be deliberately terminated.

3. Diversity of response to this situation results from the diversity of attitudes towards the life of the unborn child. This is a matter of individual conviction and conscience which must be respected.

4. It is not the role of the medical profession to determine the attitudes and rules of any particular state or community in this matter, but it is our duty to attempt both to ensure the protection of our patients and to safeguard the rights of the doctor within society.

5. Therefore, where the law allows therapeutic abortion to be performed, or legislation to that effect is contemplated, and this is not against the policy of the national medical association, and where the legislature desires or will accept the guidance of the medical profession, the following principles are approved:

(a) Abortion should be performed only as a therapeutic measure.

(b) A decision to terminate pregnancy should normally be approved in writing by at least two doctors chosen for their professional competence.

(c) The procedure should be performed by a doctor competent to do so in premises approved by the appropriate authority.

6. If the doctor considers that his convictions do not allow him to advise or perform an abortion, he may withdraw while ensuring the continuity of (medical) care by a qualified colleague.

7. This statement, while it is endorsed by the General Assembly of the World Medical Association, is not to be regarded as binding on any individual member association unless it is adopted by that member association.

Appendix F

Declaration of Helsinki

(Revised 1975)

Recommendations guiding medical doctors in biomedical research involving human subjects

Introduction

It is the mission of the medical doctor to safeguard the health of the people. His or her knowledge and conscience are dedicated to the fulfilment of this mission.

The Declaration of Geneva of the World Medical Association binds the doctor with the words: 'The health of my patient will be my first consideration,' and the International Code of Medical Ethics declares that, 'Any act or advice which could weaken physical or mental resistance of a human being may be used only in his interest.'

The purpose of biomedical research involving human subjects must be to improve diagnostic, therapeutic and prophylactic procedures and the understanding of the aetiology and pathogenesis of disease.

In current medical practice most diagnostic, therapeutic or prophylactic procedures involve hazards. This applies *a fortiori* to biomedical research.

Medical progress is based on research which ultimately must rest in part on experimentation involving human subjects. In the field of biomedical research a fundamental distinction must be recognized between medical research in which the aim is essentially diagnostic or therapeutic for a patient, and medical research the essential object of which is purely scientific and without direct diagnostic or therapeutic value to the person subjected to the research.

Special caution must be exercised in the conduct of research which may affect the environment, and the welfare of animals used for research must be respected.

Because it is essential that the results of laboratory experiments be applied to human beings to further scientific knowledge and to help suffering humanity, the World Medical Association has prepared the following recommendations as a guide to every doctor in biomedical research involving human subjects. They should be kept under review in the future. It must be stressed that the standards as drafted are only a guide to physicians all over the world. Doctors are not relieved from criminal, civil and ethical responsibilities under the laws of their own countries.

I. Basic Principles

1. Biomedical research involving human subjects must conform to generally accepted scientific principles and should be based on adequately performed laboratory and animal experimentation and on a thorough knowledge of the scientific tradition.

2. The design and performance of each experimental procedure involving human subjects should be clearly formulated in an experiment protocol which should be transmitted to a specially appointed independent committee for consideration, comment and guidance.

3. Biomedical research involving human subjects should be conducted only by scientifically qualified persons and under the supervision of a clinically competent medical person. The responsibility for the human subject must always rest with a medically qualified person and never rest on the subject of the research, even though the subject has given his or her consent.

4. Biomedical research involving human subjects cannot legitimately be carried out unless the importance of the objective is in proportion to the inherent risk to the subject.

5. Every biomedical research project involving human subjects should be preceded by careful assessment of predictable risks in comparison with forseeable benefits to the subject or to others. Concern for the interests of the subject must always prevail over the interest of science and society.

6. The right of the research subject to safeguard his or her integrity must always be respected. Every precaution should be taken to respect the privacy of the subject and to minimize the impact of the study on the subject's physical and mental integrity and on the personality of the subject.

7. Doctors should abstain from engaging in research projects involving human subjects unless they are satisfied that the hazards involved are believed to be predictable. Doctors should cease any investigation if the hazards are found to outweigh the potential benefits.

8. In publication of the results of his or her research, the doctor is obliged to preserve the accuracy of the results. Reports of experimentation not in accordance with the principles laid down in this Declaration should not be accepted for publication.

9. In any research on human beings, each potential subject must be adequately informed of the aims, methods, anticipated benefits and

potential hazards of the study and the discomfort it may entail. He or she should be informed that he or she is at liberty to abstain from participation in the study and that he or she is free to withdraw his or her consent to participation at any time. The doctor should then obtain the subject's freely-given informed consent, preferably in writing.

10. When obtaining informed consent for the research project the doctor should be particularly cautious if the subject is in a dependent relationship to him or her or may consent under duress. In that case the informed consent should be obtained by a doctor who is not engaged in the investigation and who is completely independent of this official relationship.

11. In case of legal incompetence, informed consent should be obtained from the legal guardian in accordance with national legislation. Where physical or mental incapacity makes it impossible to obtain informed consent, or when the subject is a minor, permission from the responsible relative replaces that of the subject in accordance with national legislation.

12. The research protocol should always contain a statement of the ethical considerations involved and should indicate that the principles enunciated in the present Declaration are complied with.

II. Medical Research Combined with Professional Care
(Clinical research)

1. In the treatment of the sick person, the doctor must be free to use a new diagnostic and therapeutic measure, if in his or her judgment it offers hope of saving life, re-establishing health or alleviating suffering.

2. The potential benefits, hazards and discomfort of a new method should be weighed against the advantages of the best current diagnostic and therapeutic methods.

3. In any medical study, every patient – including those of a control group, if any – should be assured of the best proven diagnostic and therapeutic method.

4. The refusal of the patient to participate in a study must never interfere with the doctor-patient relationship.

5. If the doctor considers it essential not to obtain informed consent, the specific reasons for this proposal should be stated in the experimental protocol for transmission to the independent committee.

6. The doctor can combine medical research with professional care, the objective being the acquisition of new medical knowledge, only to the extent that medical research is justified by its potential diagnostic or therapeutic value for the patient.

III. Non-therapeutic Biomedical Research Involving Human Subjects
(*Non-clinical biomedical research*)

1. In the purely scientific application of medical research carried out on a human being, it is the duty of the doctor to remain the protector of the life and health of that person on whom biomedical research is being carried out.

2. The subjects should be volunteers – either healthy persons or patients – for whom the experimental design is not related to the patient's illness.

3. The investigator or the investigating team should discontinue the research if in his/her or their judgment it may, if continued, be harmful to the individual.

4. In research on man, the interest of science and society should never take precedence over considerations related to the wellbeing of the subject.

Index